P9-BHU-105

MODERN HUMANITIES RESEARCH ASSOCIATION

DISSERTATION SERIES

VOLUME 9

Editor

C. P. BRAND

(*Italian*)

The Early Poetry of Guittone D'Arezzo

FOR BARTOLO BARNAO
AND HIS FAMILY

THE EARLY POETRY OF
GUITTONE D'AREZZO

VINCENT MOLETA

Senior Lecturer in Italian
University of Western Australia

LONDON
THE MODERN HUMANITIES RESEARCH ASSOCIATION
1976

Published by

The Modern Humanities Research Association

Honorary Treasurer, MHRA

KING'S COLLEGE, STRAND
LONDON WC2R 2LS
ENGLAND

ISBN 0 900547 41 3

Printed in England by
W. S. MANEY & SON LIMITED
HUDSON ROAD LEEDS

CONTENTS

PREFACE

This study of Guittone's early poetry is, in substance, the first half of a doctoral thesis accepted at Cambridge in 1973. The second half was devoted to the *laude* of Iacopone da Todi, and the two authors were placed side by side as the principal Italian exponents of secular and religious verse before Dante. Both speak with a distinctive voice and their poetry records events in their lives. This led me to attempt a reading based on a distinction between the voice of the poet and that of his personae, and it was the interpretative emphasis common to both parts which gave the thesis its unity. However, Guittone's *rime* and Iacopone's *laude* stem from separate traditions, and I made no attempt to forge a simple definition that might cover both vocal ranges and thus allow a comparative study. Guittone and Iacopone were not compared, and for this reason the thesis could be split without damage to either part. To the text of the thesis a new Introduction and English translations of the Italian poems cited have been added for the present volume in the MHRA Dissertation Series.

I had the good fortune to work under the direction of Dr Patrick Boyde. He helped me to clarify the thesis proper and I wish to thank him for the pains he took over the first draft and the translations. The many detailed improvements he suggested have been worked into the present study. I owe much to Professor U. Limentani for his encouragement and support, and my debt extends beyond the Italianists at Cambridge to earlier teachers at Victoria University of Wellington. At Corpus Christi College, Cambridge, my family and I found a home and friends and it was largely thanks to the Donaldson Scholarship, which the College awarded me in 1971, that we were able to keep the wolf from the door during the period of research. I wish to thank Nancy Woodward for preparing the typescript, and Dr John Hill for reading the proofs. I am grateful to the editor, Professor C. P. Brand, for his advice and attention in seeing the work through to print.

The fine scholarship which early Italian texts have inspired is an example and a spur to those who enter this rich field of study. It has been a stimulus to discuss my authors with several scholars whose work I most respect, and in this regard I wish to acknowledge my debt to Professor Cl. Margueron, who has continued to give me the benefit of his deep knowledge of Guittone. His notes and glosses have enabled me to attempt a translation of some of Guittone's most difficult lines, and his comments on the first draft have been incorporated into the version presented here. I acknowledge with thanks the permission of the Presses Universitaires de France to quote passages from Professor Margueron's book cited in the Bibliography.

The text used is *Le rime di Guittone d'Arezzo*, edited by F. Egidi, Bari, 1940, except for the following poems taken from *Poeti del Duecento*, edited by G. Contini, volume I, Milan–Naples, 1960: sonnets 24, 25, 72, 81; *canzoni* vii, xi, xv, xx, xxv, xxviii, xxxiii.

CHAPTER I

Introduction

Guittone d'Arezzo's critical fortunes have risen over the past fifty years to the point where he now commands grudging respect from serious readers of Duecento literature. The abuse levelled at him by the emerging *stilnovisti* and later by Dante is now seen as a negative proof of his pre-eminence in the generation that followed the death of Frederick II, while his use of the vernacular for political and moral poems is now recognized as an innovation that had vast repercussions in Italian literature. Within the *canzoniere* itself it is no longer necessary to accept the rigid separation, imposed by the order of poems in the earliest MSS, of Fra Guittone from Guittone, and of the secular from the religious works. His conversion in middle life belies a steadiness of temper, an original grasp of his craft, and an unashamed didacticism which are everywhere present in his writing and confer a certain unity on the whole corpus.[1]

Unfortunately none of this makes Guittone any easier to read. His poetry remains lapidary, often wilfully obscure; and it is too sparing of fancy and verbal beauty to hold for long any but the most dogged reader. In spite of the reappraisal which recent studies have brought about, large areas of his work are still neglected, and the same few poems, reprinted in anthologies, continue to be read in isolation. The consistency of Guittone's work is taken on trust and the poet's development, if it is considered at all, is considered only at its height in the great poems written after the Battle of Montaperti (1260). Yet Guittone wrote half his poetry during the decade before the early 1260s and it is no exaggeration to say that most of this is virtually unknown except to a few specialists. The palinodes are more widely known but they cannot be understood properly unless we know what Guittone disowned when he turned his back on 'Amore'. Within ten years he had taken stock of the entire Provençal and Sicilian lyric tradition and had established himself as the first mainland *capo-scuola*. His reputation was based on the 120 sonnets and 20 *canzoni* which comprise his *rime d'amore*, and which, along with several moral and political *canzoni*, brought him into the newly founded *Milites Beatae Virginis Mariae* to become their spokesman and continue his literary apostolate.[2] This study offers an interpretation of that imposing body of work which the poet claims to have rejected.

Guittone's place in the early Italian lyric has been re-established largely by an assessment of his impact on the major poets who followed him. Theirs was a process of selection, rejection, and refinement. But deeper than questions of taste and style, which determined the new direction given to the lyric by the *stilnovisti*, there persisted Guittone's concept of the poet's mission as *cantor rectitudinis*, and none of Dante's criticism can hide his debt to the Aretino, in the late *rime* and in the *Commedia*.[3] Yet Guittone's place in Duecento literature becomes even clearer when he is seen against the poets who preceded him. Alongside the slender collections of sonnets and *canzoni* written by individual Sicilians, all of them devoted to a simple and elegant celebration of *fin' amors*, the 300 poems by Guittone d'Arezzo, on all the main themes of the medieval verse tradition, in a tense and often difficult style and in all the variations of the sonnet, the *ballata* and the *canzone*, seem a massive achievement. A closer look confirms this impression.

Although the chronology for the poems is only approximate, they range themselves on either side of a critical period from 1260 to 1266: *rime d'amore* before 1263; *rime ascetiche e morali* and most of the prose letters after his entry into the Gaudenti (1265?); and between these two bodies a small number of transitional poems culminating in the palinodes. Guittone's vigour is evident from the start. For the courtly poems he uses only the sonnet and the *canzone* but goes beyond the Sicilian development of these metres. The Sicilian sonnet had been a self-contained utterance, not coupled with other sonnets except in correspondence or *tenzoni*. Of Guittone's 120 sonnets 109 are linked together in five cycles, three of them narratives, one a low-style debate and the last an *ars amandi*. At strategic points within these cycles Guittone introduces rare or internal rhymes; there are exchanges with living correspondents; clusters of poems that draw on well-defined lyric genres; and here and there he inserts the proper name Guittone as if the lover's experience were his own. The purpose of these and other experiments will become clear in the pages that follow where I shall argue that through the courtly sonnets Guittone steadily moved away from the sheltered intimacies of *fin' amors* towards a public, moral poetic. Yet his courtly sonnets remain a tribute to the vitality of the Sicilian form and they were to lead him to a notable innovation after his conversion, that of the double sonnet.

The 20 courtly *canzoni*[4] are not linked in any discernible narrative or cyclic way, but they exhibit a wide variety of stanza and rhyme patterns. There are *canzoni* entirely in seven-syllable lines (ii, x, xi, xviii) or eleven-syllable lines (xii, xiii). There are combinations of the two in which the shorter line predominates (iii, iv, viii, ix, xv, xvii, xxi, xxii) or the longer (v, vi, xiv, xvi, xix, xx); and there are *canzoni* in which the two line-lengths are evenly distributed throughout the stanza (vii, xxiii). Added to this the rhyme patterns and rhyme words of several *canzoni* give dazzling proof of Guittone's mastery of the *trobar clus* (x, xi, xii, xiii). The rhythm is never the same from *canzone* to *canzone* and often it is enriched by the internal rhyme which can split longer lines (iii, ix, xxi, xxii) and even the short line (iv). The interlacing of rhyme and the strong pause given by the *rimalmezzo* appealed to Guittone from the start and once he had learnt it from the Sicilian[5] and Provençal poets he made it his own.

The dark colour of many of the *canzoni* is particularly evident in the poems of 'lontananza' (viii, ix, xi, xv, xxi, xxii) where Arezzo is the *terminus ad quem* of the poet's sentiments. It is unlikely that, apart from c. xv, these poems were written after his exile in the early 1260s, but the genre does reflect the foreboding that hung over the city in the late 1250s and it found in him this response in keeping with the courtly canon. It is the sustained and ample articulation of these love poems which marks them off from most Sicilian *canzoni* and points the way to the extended love poems of the *stilnovisti,* 'Al cor gentil', 'Donne ch'avete' and 'Donna me prega'.

Although they remain fixed in the sentimental polarity of joy and sorrow, which is the staple of the first eighty sonnets, Guittone's longer poems provide an instructive and brilliant sampler of the rhythmic possibilities latent in the received *canzone* stanza, enriched by the techniques of the *trobar clus*. The familiar cadences of self-encouragement and tremulous praise, set free from the confines of the sonnet, expand and contract within a flexible and extended form until they are condensed in the final stanza or sealed and despatched in the *congedo*. The *congedo* is the poet's point of entry into his poem, and in the final chapter we shall see that Guittone's handling of it allows us to reconstruct an ideal order of composition for the early *canzoni*. If we recall the stormy political climate in Arezzo and the rest of Tuscany during the 1250s,[6] Guittone's persistence with the rarified and enclosed poetic of *fin' amors* during that period has all the appearance of a last-ditch stand against the harsh invading realities which as yet could find in him no suitable poetic response; and this study will show how his defence was broken down from within, and how he began to enlarge his repertoire before turning head-on to meet the moral and political issues that dominate his later work.

The change becomes apparent in the poems written soon after the Battle of Montaperti. Guittone's voluntary exile not merely coincides with his discovery and use of the Provençal genres of the lament and the *sirventese*; it is its necessary prerequisite. Though few in number these *canzoni* mark the entry into Italian literature of a *cantor rectitudinis* whose sympathies will soon extend beyond his native Arezzo to embrace Florence, Pisa and Bologna. 'Ahi lasso, or è stagion de doler tanto', c. xix, the famous lament for the defeat of Guelph Florence, should be read with its companion letter 'Infatuati miseri Fiorentini', l. xiv, and these in turn find their post-conversion counterparts in 'O dolce terra aretina', c. xxxiii, and the admonition to the Pisan lords, 'Magni baroni certo e regi quasi', c. xlvii. 'Gente noiosa e villana', c. xv, documents his exile from the city and signs the courtly sentiments of 'lontananza' with the seal of a genuine departure. 'Ahi lasso, che li boni e li malvagi', c. xx, a defence of womankind with a post-conversion sequel, c. xlix, crystallizes that concern over the abuse of women within the courtly fictions, which runs fitfully throughout Guittone's *rime d'amore*. This *canzone*, with c. xv, looks like a final attempt to justify the ennobling power of courtly values, and like c. xix it wields its tense and elevated rhetoric in weighty stanzas prolonged for a hundred lines.

These are transitional poems. They resume key motifs in the courtly poetry without as yet declaring the religious vocation which will soon oblige him to leave his family and enter the newly-founded Gaudenti. These poems will have remained a source not of regret but of satisfaction; witness the echo of c. xx at the opening of c. xlix, and the lament for Arezzo, c. xxxiii, which renews in more sombre tones the attack launched on the city in c. xv. It was his entry into religious life, and not these poems, which brought him criticism from his contemporaries. His answer was a retraction which struck directly at the verses written in the service of 'Amore'.

The prime manuscript, Laurenziano Rediano 9, opens with a series of *canzoni* under the rubric 'Frate Guitton Daresso'. Even if their order in that manuscript does not reflect the precise order of composition, his first task on entering the Gaudenti will have been to celebrate a new source of life and literature and retract his courtly verse. The poems that have been assigned to the year 1265/6[7] number seven *canzoni* and a dozen sonnets and they add up to a comprehensive claim to a new *directio voluntatis* that defines itself according to the old. The conversion sonnets are occasional pieces written for a varied audience. There are penitential prayers which merge into general admonitions (ss. 163, 164, 165, 218); spirited defences of his conversion (ss. 174, 210), and several sonnets to named correspondents (ss. 205, 211, 220, 234). Two of these latter display *rimas caras*, the one to his pupil Guinizzelli (s. 205) a daunting reply 'per le rime'; the other to Bandino (s. 220) now asserting technical mastery where he had once deferred to him as a disciple (ss. 28, 30). Whatever his public might think of him they would have to admit that he had lost none of his old touch.

Each of these sonnets fixes on a separate aspect of his conversion and it could well be that they were his first post-conversion poems, written in response to puzzled admirers or grappling one by one with early moments of remorse, rancour and relief. The *canzoni*, on the other hand, seem the fruit of a meditative pause and a gathering of forces. In the manuscript they line up behind the opening manifesto, 'Ora parrà s'eo saverò cantare', c. xxv, in a solid phalanx, ready to match their courtly rivals.

Each of these *canzoni* is so massive (the shortest, c. xxv, has 86 lines, the longest, *c.* xxix, 219) that they tend to be read separately if they are read at all. However, as manifold expressions of a strong personality at a moment of extreme literary self-awareness, they need to be read together, and they seem to fall into pairs. 'Degno è che che dice omo el defenda', c. xxx, glosses a line from the *congedo* of 'Ora parrà s'eo saverò cantare', c. xxv,[8] for the benefit of confrères who are explaining his manifesto in Pisa. Self-recrimination in 'Vergogna ho, lasso, ed ho me stesso ad ira', c. xxvi, is balanced by joy in 'Ahi, quant'ho che vergogni e che doglia aggio', c. xxvii, where he considers not so much where he was, as where he is now. 'O tu, de nome Amor, guerra de fatto', c. xxviii, and 'O vera vertú, vero amore', c. xxix, present two faces of 'Amore', the former an attack on profane love, the latter in praise of Christian love. In the courtly *canzoni* a certain uniformity of sentiment was offset by a variation of stanza pattern. Now Guittone shifts his ground of attack with each *canzone* leaving no flank unmarked, and he surpasses those earlier *canzoni* with a sequence of rhythmic structures that show his powers to be not only unimpaired but even enhanced.

The double internal rhyme in the predominantly hendecasyllabic stanza of 'Ora parrà s'eo saverò cantare', c. xxv, sets it apart from the five courtly *canzoni* with simple *rimalmezzo*.[9] The weighty stanzas of 'O tu, de nome Amor, guerra de fatto', c. xxviii, allow him to keep up an unfaltering rhetorical assault on Love. In the matching poem, 'O vera vertú, vero amore', c. xxix, the stanza is longer but is divided evenly between short and long lines and has a serrated texture that makes no concession to fluid syntax. The insistent cryptic *sententiae* and antitheses stand on their own merits, and they demand that patient reading which alone discerns the true meaning of an abused vocabulary. Yet the conversion *canzoni* do have flashes of poetry, nowhere more evident than in 'O cari frati miei, con malamente', c. xxxii, which is a vigorous defence of his entry into the Gaudenti at the cost of deserting his wife and three young children. The Court of Love evoked in the marian prayer at the end of c. xxvii is here recalled in the opening image of blind Cupid. The sin that has bandaged the eyes of the mind is defined in this iconography as 'lussuria' and colours his view of the legitimate domestic comforts referred to later in the poem. Nor do we easily forget the blinded oarsmen rowing frantically to their doom (lines 27–9) and the ship torn from its anchor, plunging towards the reef (lines 66–9). The nebulous yet sensitive band of the 'fedeli d'Amore' is here replaced by a plain and sensible Christian company with whom Guittone will maintain a tight bond of correspondence for the rest of his life.[10] If we keep in mind the wide sphere of Guittone's courtly influence and the dispersed civic apostolate of the Gaudenti these repeated palinodes can be seen as an exhaustive statement of his final choice, reaching out to his literary disciples in all parts of Tuscany and beyond.

Guittone's vigorous and inventive handling of the two standard metres in the first half of his work intensifies and broadens throughout the second. He now devises longer forms of the sonnet, experiments with the *ballata* and begins corresponding in prose.[11] Letters, in verse and prose, make up the bulk of Guittone's post-conversion writing. The isolated letters among the courtly sonnets, introduced to give biographical colour to narrative cycles, give way to an extended correspondence in which the poet, now 'peccator frate' and 'vilissimo religioso', gives his own literary currency to the ideals of the Gaudenti. The choice of prose reflects a new and varied apostolate in whose service Guittone can now draw on the rich Latin patrimony of the *summe* and *compendia*, obedient to the precepts of an *ars dictandi* now applied to the vernacular. The prose letters furnish an anthology of models for sermons, congratulatory notes, obituaries, political propaganda; and the confrères, poets, and professional men to whom they are addressed testify to his confident assumption of the mantle of spokesman for the Gaudenti.

There is no conflict between his prose and his poetry. Several of the 'prose' letters are in verse and, but for their lack of a well-defined metre, would find their place among the post-conversion poems. These comprise forty regular sonnets, twenty-nine extended sonnets, six *ballate* and thirteen *canzoni*. I shall discuss them briefly in that order.

Guittone had taken over the Sicilian sonnet, first used for correspondence, *tenzoni*, and brief lyric statements, and had made it a link in a chain of courtly narrative. In the post-conversion poems the sonnet reverts to its original occasional role and, apart from two groups of sonnets, is used for miniature sermons and correspondence. The early innovation, which had deepened the expressive range of the sonnet, is replaced by another innovation which relegates the sonnet once more to its proper place as the least significant of the metres. The sermon in sonnet form is itself a novelty, best seen in the poems numbering from ss. 164–74. Yet these sonnets are reduced and fragmentary essays in a field which is worked more fully in the *canzoni*, and though a severe moral tone sounds through almost every post-conversion sonnet it is the *ballata* which was to draw from him his finest sacred verse.

The correspondence sonnets, which run from ss. 203–39, testify to the remarkable range of Guittone's friends and contacts,[12] from nobles and politicians to a host of contemporary poets. These sonnets also testify to a stylistic range which is responsive to circumstances and to the tastes of the recipient. The virtuosity, especially in replies 'per le rime' and the use of *rimas caras*, is most obvious when he writes to poets (e.g. ss. 205, 207, 209, 213, 220, 230, 231, 237). There are lively comic or satirical poems (ss. 223, 224, 227, 230) as well as sober moral lessons in which the language does not obscure the message (e.g. ss. 218, 228, 232, 236). Guittone is technically ostentatious only when he chooses to be, and the group of sonnets on the vices and the virtues (ss. 175–202) reveal him as a teacher, probably of novices in the Order, with a simple, clear manner. The sequence of ten vices followed by ten virtues[13] is iconographically presented. And, like the monochrome frieze in the Arena Chapel, the vices and virtues are conceived and addressed as personified emblems. There can be no room for doubt when the choice is presented as clearly as this, and the sonnets that frame the sequence (ss. 175, 186, 187, 199–202) proclaim the poet's faith in the power of reason to induce virtue.

In the other sequence of post-conversion sonnets, the *Trattato d'Amore* published by Egidi in 1931,[14] another iconographic device governs the order of the thirteen poems.[15] This time it is a painting of blind Cupid whose emblems (s. 241) become, one by one, the subject of separate sonnets. The poems that frame this sequence (ss. 240, 251) are addressed to a certain 'caro amico' and it is possible that this too is a diptych of which the matching sacred panel is lost.

The *Trattato d'Amore* is notable for its two variations of the regular sonnet metre. One is the opening sonnet (s. 240) with internal rhyme, one of only two examples among the post-conversion sonnets. The other is the double sonnet[16] of which there are two: the first a *caudato* of sixteen lines (s. 247), the second, a *rinterzato* of twenty-two lines (s. 248). Guittone's use of *rimalmezzo* at moments of thematic intensity in the courtly sonnet cycles is here confirmed by his using it at the head of this cycle. Here, as there, it is the sign of a deliberate authorial modification of the fabric of the metre, and it is a palpable Guittonian presence. Elsewhere, among the isolated and occasional post-conversion sonnets, there is no call for it in that form. It reappears in disguise as the double sonnet.

Fra Guittone's sonnets open with a group of twenty-five double sonnets. If the manuscript order, reflected in the printed order, is as reliable a guide to the poet's intentions here as it is elsewhere this probably means that he improved on the secular Sicilian metre to allow it to express, first among the sonnets, the superior themes of his new poetic. It means that even the sonnet has undergone a conversion and emerged more spacious, robust and versatile. The Sicilians had produced the sonnet; Guittone produces the double sonnet; and it stands at the head of his short religious poems as a proud claim to his continuing originality. However, the change in the metre is not entirely unheralded and we can see that he intended a development not so much of length as of rhythmic contrast and intensity. The key difference between the regular and the double sonnet is the insertion of heptasyllables between the hendecasyllables in both *fronte* and *sirima* — two additional short lines in each *pes* and one or two additional short lines in each *volta* — making a total of twenty or twenty-two lines.[17] The shorter line rhymes with the longer line it follows and the rhythmic pattern will vary according to several factors: the number of short lines introduced, whether the rhyme is *alternata* or *incrociata* and the number of rhyme sounds in the *volte*. Guittone's double sonnet thus resembles those longer stanzas in his post-conversion *canzoni* where the short line offers a strong if intermittent balance to the long line.[18] Added to this, each pair of long and short lines, the latter rhyming with the former, will recall the halting emphasis created by *rimalmezzo*, with a stronger pause at the second rhyme word. As a cross between the regular sonnet with internal rhyme and Guittone's most mature *canzone* stanzas, his double sonnet must have seemed to the *stilnovisti* a hybrid monster to be shunned at all costs. However, Guittone's zest to explore his metres did not let him settle for one standard pattern even here. He devised four variations of the eleven-plus-seven-syllable-line sonnet and has left four examples of a sixteen-line sonnet with two extra hendecasyllables added to the *frons*. His favoured form is the twenty-two line sonnet, of which we have twenty-two examples, and there is one of twenty-seven lines (s. 157), a *stravagante* even by his standards.[19]

The main body of double sonnets which heads the collection of post-conversion sonnets is also a sampler of Guittone's new themes and his enlarged audience. We find there letters to friends (ss. 154–9), sermons to confrères (ss. 146–9) and secular nobles (ss. 160, 161, 162), several exhortations to ladies (ss. 151, 152, 153a, 153b) and a palinode (s. 163).[20] The most remarkable is the first in the series, s. 139, a hymn to divine love which breaks out in a double sonnet with double internal rhyme.[21] Like the double internal rhyme in c. xxv it is reserved for the poem that heads a collection under the rubric 'Fra Guittone'. Guittone exalts the antithesis of that love which he had celebrated in the courtly sonnets and he produces for the first and only time a highly-wrought version of the metre especially devised for this purpose. 'O sommo bono e de bon solo autore' is to the post-conversion sonnets what 'Ora parrà s'eo saverò cantare' is to the post-conversion *canzoni*, a manifesto of sheer technical prowess which guarantees the validity and fecundity of Christian ethics as the most worthy subject for his poetic expression.

This raises a question about the *canzoniere guittoniano* which has not been examined and which I can only touch on here. If the double sonnets stand at the head of the post-conversion sonnets this does not mean that they were all written before them.[22] Like Dante's placing of certain of his early *rime* in the *Vita Nuova* to chart his spiritual and poetic development, the overall manuscript order of Guittone's *rime* reflects an ideal development in his sentiments and poetry — and it was meant to do so. Guittone's choice of metre is deliberate. The sonnet, the *ballata* and the *canzone*, which until the 1260s had been used only for secular subjects, are here forcefully applied to moral and sacred subjects. All his mature work is an attempt to wrest from 'Amore' his preroga-tive over the principal metres; and in each case Guittone expands and develops those metres to prove their virility at the service of the Christian deity. This may help to explain the presence of six *ballate sacre* among Guittone's *canzoni ascetiche e morali*, for the *ballata* is the one metre not present among the *rime d'amore*.

It is presumed that Guittone's *ballate* were written near the end of his career, perhaps in the late 1280s, and that they complete the ideal passage from courtly to religious themes through the central political and ethical phase.[23] This would make Guittone's *ballate sacre* contemporary with both Iacopone's *laude* and the *ballate* of Cavalcanti and Lapo. I suspect, however, that Guittone wrote his *ballate* somewhat earlier, perhaps in the late 1270s, and that the simpler metres to which Iacopone reverted, and the elaborate secular *ballate* of Cavalcanti and Lapo, are a reaction against Guittone's metrical sophistication on the one hand, and his bold assumption of the *ballata* for sacred subjects on the other. Guittone did not invent the *lauda-ballata* but his role in the development of this form, as in the others, was decisive.[24] The *ballata* appeared in the Italian lyric during the so-called Siculo-Tuscan transition, between the 1250s and 1270s.[25] This is also the period when the elementary early *lauda* metres, notably the four-line strophe of *doppi quinari* and *doppi settenari*, were being enriched by *ballata* forms suited to choral recitation by the new mendicant-inspired fraternities.[26] The Gaudenti, though founded in 1261, the year following the great *Devotio*, were neither Laudesi nor Disciplinati and it is unlikely that Guittone's *ballate* were written for performance by his confrères nor do they appear in any confraternity *laudario*. They are, in my view, a literary exercise to prove what the secular form in its major variants can do for the sacred subject; and in them I believe Guittone lent his weight and his prestige to the anonymous, modest writers of sacred lyrics who were then experimenting with the subtler singing forms of the secular *ballata*. Guittone's six *ballate sacre* are a synthesis of the thematic content of all Duecento *laude*, and at the same time they show that elaborate *ballata* metres can be harnessed to sacred themes.[27] The Passion meditation, 'O bon Gesú, ov'è core', c. xxxv (*ballata grande*), and the Marian hymn 'Graziosa e pia', c. xxxvi (*ballata mezzana*), present the two central figures of liturgical narrative and dramatic *laude*. In 'Meraviglioso beato', c. xxxvii (a *ballata minore* in honour of S. Domenic) and 'Beato Francesco, in te laudare', c. xxxviii (*ballata grande*), Guittone acknowledges the debt of his century to the founders of the two great mendicant Orders. 'Vegna, — vegna — chi vole giocundare', c. xxxix (*ballata minore*), and 'Ora vegna a la danza', c. l (*ballata grande*), invite the believer to a sacred dance in which the language of courtly love can now be released in spiritual joy. Guittone does not exclude from these poems the tense logic and dense syntax of his moral *canzoni*.[28] The verse and strophic pattern is different in each of them, and in four of them (cc. xxxvi, xxxvii, xxxix, l) he introduces internal rhyme. As a group these *ballate* give moral support and poetic respectability to their humble sisters, the confraternity *laude*, and they form an integral part of Guittone's positive adoption of a Christian poetic.

The dozen remaining *canzoni*, written between 1265 and 1294, reveal, with the prose letters, the scope of Guittone's activity as 'portavoce' of the Gaudenti. They cover a wide range of subjects; they are directed to lay people as well as clerics, women as well as men; and technically they are as varied a group as any in the corpus. This diversity alone fulfils the promise he had made in the manifesto, 'Ora parrà s'eo saverò cantare', and several of these poems are, in their robust and austere dignity, the equal of any in the *canzoniere*. If conversion closed off one lyric avenue it is clear that it opened several new ones, and his major post-conversion poems can be read as the first substantial exploration in Italian of those lyric genres excluded from the Sicilian canon. Guittone demonstrates the existence of God (c. xxxi) and the supreme value of honour (c. xliii). He laments the death of a close friend (c. xlvi) and attacks corruption in his native city (c. xxxiii). He sends commendatory verses to confrères (cc. xl, xlii, xlv), as well as sermons and warnings to celebrated civic and military leaders (cc. xli, xliii, xliv, xlvii). The preacher's voice, restrained in the post-conversion sonnets, here dilates freely, but nowhere so strongly as in the three *canzoni* which draw on his early poetry by way of contrast. 'Tanto sovente dett'aggio altra fiada', (c. xxxiv), is a moral *plazer* which offsets the values embodied in his love poems. Guittone here lays down a code of conduct for every rank of society and invites laymen to emulate the knights of the primitive Christian church. In the two remaining poems, which are among his longest, Guittone returns to what he sees as the canker in courtly literature, its polite glorification of concupiscence. In 'Onne vogliosa d'omo infermitate' (c. xlviii), he strips love of its sentimental bookish trappings in a sustained attack on that 'follor' which turns men into beasts. The uncompromising duality of body and soul implied in his argument could make this a very late poem, although it recalls inevitably some of the phrases in the palinodes. There is an explicit echo of an earlier poem (c. xx) in 'Altra fiata aggio giá, donne, parlato' (c. xlix), which is addressed to women who want to preserve their honour and which may have been written not long after the conversion poems. This *canzone*, which should be read with the double sonnets 151, 152, 153a and 153b,[29] as well as c. xx, is Guittone's most mature expression of his own moral sensitivity to those ladies who up till now had figured only as paragons in courtly lyric. We shall see that this is present in his earliest poems and that it led him to abandon the courtly lyric altogether.

In the remarkable second *congedo* of c. xlix, Guittone reflects ruefully on his need to write long concentrated poems ('gran canzon faccio e serro motti', line 167) which are difficult for his readers and from which he must exclude some of the things he wants to say.[30] In his view only the 'gran canzon' can do justice to 'gran matera', and it is noticeable that the shorter poems in this group (cc. xl, xli, xlii, xlv, xlvi) are occasional, dedicatory pieces, whereas the great themes of public rectitude and private virtue are left to the longer poems (cc. xxxi, xxxiii, xxxiv, xliii, xlvii, xlviii, xlix). In only one of these poems does he use internal rhyme (c. xliii), although each of them (the stanza length varying from fourteen to twenty-seven lines) has its own particular balance of seven- and eleven-syllable lines, including the *canzone* with *coblas unissonans* (c. xliv). The phrase 'serro motti' has been taken as Guittone's claim to and admission of an axiomatic and concentrated style. But it goes hand-in-hand with 'gran canzon'; and the two together seem to me to embody Guittone's ideal of doctrinal and structural substance enlivened by the mobile and flexible rhythm which his use of the short line and internal rhyme gives to the stanza, and which is already present in his earliest *canzoni*.

A careful reading would show that Guittone's *canzoniere*, like Dante's, is marked by a frequent recapitulation of themes and styles, and by a constant meditation upon elements present from the start. The conversion poems are the best known examples of this, but they are not the only examples, as we shall see. They are signs not so much of change as of renewal and it is this renewal which gives seriousness and coherence to Guittone's entire literary production. It should make us wary of the dislocated reading which his prominent poems invite, and of the neglect which large areas of his corpus continue to suffer.

In this study much use is made of the terms 'poet' and 'persona' as if they were different voices in the poems. This is simply a way of coming to terms with the individual and received elements in Guittone's poetry, and of using the difference as a key to the interpretation. This will become clear in the following chapters but for the present the vocal range can be shown in several examples.

When Guittone re-creates the charmed circle of *fin' amors* his 'I' is a standard lover cast in the courtly mould; an anonymous subject of commonplace emotions:

> Spietata donna e fera, ora te prenda
> di me cordoglio, poi morir mi vedi;
> che tanta pietá di te discenda,
> che 'n alcuna misura meve fidi.   s. 3, 1–4

[Cruel and pitiless lady, take pity on me since you see me dying. May such mercy flow down from you as will in part revive me.]

> Gioia ed allegranza
> tant'hai nel mio cor data, fino amore,
> che pesanza non credo mai sentire   c. v, 1–3

[O noble love, you have filled my heart with such joy and gladness that I am sure I shall never feel heaviness there again.]

As well as being the unself-conscious hero of a sentimental struggle, the lover is often presented as the chronicler of his own experience, a persona-poet through whom the author shapes his fictive discourse:

> Amor, verso e canzone
> e ciascuna ragione
> che de solazzo sia,
> lass'eo per* tutta via,
> mentre ch'esta rea doglia
> non torna in bona voglia.   c. ii, 51–6

[Love, I shall stop writing lines and songs and any discourse that may console me, until this undeserved suffering is replaced by your favour.] (* Egidi's text emended by insertion of 'per'.)

A renformare amore e fede e spera
e bon conforto entra noi, bella gioia,
e per intralassar corrotto e noia,
e che 'n trovar lo saver meo non pera,
me sforzeraggio a trovar novel sono.   c. viii, 1–5

[To strengthen the love, loyalty, hope and solace that we share, lovely joy;
to banish lament and suffering, and to ensure that my skill as poet is not lost,
I shall try to write a new song.]

However, in the central poems of the *canzoniere* where Guittone records his own
change of life, he writes *in propria persona*. There can be no doubt that the 'I'
is Guittone himself, speaking directly through his verse:

ni 'n mia spezialitate a far li aveva,
ni la guerra voleva;
la casa e 'l poder ch'eo
li avea era non meo,
mai lo teneva dal comune in fio   c. xv, 61–5

[There was no scope there for my particular competence, and I wasn't
interested in the war. The house and property that I had there was not
freehold; I only rented it from the council]

e dove piú d'onor degno m'ha fatto
esso meo car Segnor, la sua merzede,
piú me biasmate matto,
dicendo pertenevame gaudere,
poi tempo, agio, podere
e bella donna e piacentera avia;
e ch'è grande villia
e fera crudeltá disnaturata,
la qual non fu trovata
in fera alcuna, und'om parlasse mai,
ch'abandoni figliuol che picciol vede,
com'io tre picciolelli abandonai.   c. xxxii, 81–92

[and in that separation by which my dear Lord in his mercy has made me
worthy of honour, you reproach me all the more for being mad and say
that I had every reason to be happy since my time was my own, I had a
property and an attractive and comely wife. And you say that it's disgraceful,
a depraved and bestial cruelty; that it's unheard of that any wild animal
known to man will leave its young offspring the way I deserted my three
little children.]

Guittone's early verse is by and large nondescript as poetry, nor shall I
claim for it a beauty that it does not have. It fulfils its promise only later.
There, among the poems of his maturity, we catch the unmistakable cadence of
the first Italian *cantor rectitudinis*:

Legno quasi digiunto
è nostro core in mar d'ogne tempesta,
ove pur fugge porto e chere scoglia,
e di correr ver morte ora non resta.   c. xxxii, 66–9

[Our heart is like a ship cast adrift at the mercy of every storm. It shuns the haven and sets course for a reef, unfaltering in its rush towards death.]

Come a lavorator la zappa è data,
è dato el mondo noi: non per gaudere,
ma per esso eternal vita acquistare   c. xxvi, 73–5

[The world has been given to us like a mattock to a labourer: not to enjoy but, by using it, to win eternal life.]

CHAPTER 2

Fra Guittone reviews his love poetry

Guittone's return to faith 'nel mezzo del cammin' sets a precedent in Italian literature. He is the first Italian poet to draw on his own experience, and his work, as it has come down, is arranged to reflect well-defined stages in his poetry and in his life. He is now better understood than ever before and any fresh study will begin where the more penetrating reassessments leave off.[1] My own observations, which are limited to the pre-conversion poetry, take as their starting point certain ideas in three important recent studies devoted to the 'sottile ragionatore in versi'. The shortest of them is Achille Tartaro's article 'La conversione letteraria di Guittone'.[2] He takes the order of components in the prime manuscript, Laurenziano Rediano 9,[3] as a reliable guide to the overall structure Guittone intended for the *canzoniere*. He reads the opening poem, c. xxv, and the order it imposes on the *canzoniere*, as the poet's attempt to overcome 'la frammentarietà del discorso poetico tradizionale'.[4] The second and the most substantial of all is Claude Margueron's study where, among a wealth of patiently assembled material, he makes biographical deductions from certain poems and tackles the problem of chronology. The third, and in spite of its brevity perhaps the most balanced account of the poetry to appear so far, is Antonio Enzo Quaglio's essay 'L'esperimento di Guittone d'Arezzo'.[5] In this able synthesis the author questions the facile equation between life and literature imposed on the *canzoniere* by the manuscript bipartition into religious and secular poems; and he traces a more subtle consistency and maturation of style and thought in the corpus as a whole than the order in Rediano 9 would seem to allow.

Using these works as a point of departure I propose a fresh study of Guittone's early poetry in the light of his post-conversion palinode. I shall attempt to trace the development of Guittone's early poetry from its idealistic courtly beginnings to his final rejection of 'materia amorosa' in middle life. To show where my reading differs from previous interpretations, I shall broach in a discursive way the problem posed by Guittone's judgement on his love poetry, and introduce the terms used in my reading of the texts. This will lead straight to the poems written after conversion which in turn lead back to the sonnets and *canzoni* of Guittone's 'prima maniera'.

In several of the poems written at or just after his conversion, poems that have been called Guittone's manifesto, the poet reviews his earlier writing. He seems to ignore the poems on political and moral themes assigned to that period by Rediano 9,[6] and gives the impression that the only 'materia' which had occupied him up to that point was 'amorosa':

> Ora parrà s'eo saverò cantare
> e s'eo varrò quanto valer già soglio,
> poi che del tutto Amor fug[g]h' e disvoglio,
> e più che cosa mai forte mi spare   c. xxv, 1–4

[Now we shall see whether I can still write poetry and whether I can still command respect as before, since I now shun and reject Love completely and hate him more than anything else.]

That he should turn on 'Amore' was hardly surprising once he had reached that vantage point from which he was to direct his later work. His coming of age demanded a public confession of youthful error. It would make the process of conversion look like a dramatic leap from one ideal to another and create affinities with religious and literary conversions in the Christian tradition.[7] The poet's wish to mythologize the central act of his life was faithfully reflected in the most authoritative manuscript which, as has been noted, cuts the body of poems in half and sets the manifestoes proudly at the head of the poems assigned to 'fra Guittone'. Careful study by modern scholars has restored unity to that divided corpus and it is no longer possible to take the rigid manuscript dichotomy at face value. As Quaglio puts it:

una divaricazione così marcata, nonostante sembri incoraggiata dal poeta, tende ad una schematizzazione eccessiva del suo cammino poetico e della sua esperienza umana ... ribadisce in linea di principio, con la sua drastica e inaccettabile partizione (in sede critica s'intende, ché dal punto di vista editoriale il libro delle sue rime è tuttora bipartito), lo stretto collegamento di partenza tra vita e rappresentazione poetica, tra la storia e la letteratura, implicitamente riconducendo il magistero stilistico di Guittone alle sorgenti immediate del suo ardore passionale, che nei momenti più alti preserva la poesia dal rischio cerebrale insito nella sua poetica formalistica. Se non è dato di dubitare della sostanziale veridicità delle convinzioni guittoniane, si finisce per semplificare la sua storia poetica, e anche umana, quando se ne contrappongano le facce, e quelle soltanto, che le antiche sillogi separano esplicitamente. La crisi religiosa vera e propria, sottolineata dai versi stessi del poeta come il nodo fondamentale della sua vita con un'insistenza che sa di zelo letterario, non rappresenta l'improvviso e drammatico rovesciamento di posizioni ideologiche, quanto invece il coerente approdo di un'esistenza storicamente travagliata e tesa più che alla conquista del verbo divino alla ricerca di valori morali e spirituali certi e durevoli. (pp. 259–60)

Quaglio describes the continuity between the early and later poetry in this way:

Nella varietà discontinua dei suoi aspetti, ben visibile nella robusta ripresa dei modi tradizionali, la poesia guittoniana tende sin dai primi passi ad allargare, senza pregiudizi aulici, anzi con generosa mistione di modi, l'area ristretta della casistica amorosa, saldandola alla riflessione moralistica, frenando l'effusione lirica del sentimento negli schemi della logica oratoria. Qui si rispecchia non solo il sentire pratico, personalmente chiamato all'insegnamento, di Guittone, ma il buon senso borghese della classe cui egli appartiene; la quale reclama un adeguamento della tradizione siciliana e trovadorica alle esigenze concrete del tempo e incoraggia i suoi rappresentanti all'analisi ravvicinata del rapporto amoroso, all'inserimento dei problemi erotici nel tessuto concreto dell'agire e del comportamento umano. (pp. 267–8)

This is well said. Guittone's abiding concern was a moral one conditioned by his particular socio-historical background. Summing up fifty years of patient reassessment from Torraca to Margueron, Quaglio defines the scope and content of the true Guittonian manner, then finds a place for the courtly erotica in a broadening line that leads inevitably to the moral and political themes of the central poems, and beyond them to the religious poems of the last phase. This new perspective, or the clear restatement of it, is a salutary reminder that certain outdated critical judgements of the Guittonian corpus have gone unchallenged for too long and have merely worsened his already discouraging reputation. One could object that the total view presented by Quaglio is too comprehensive and not sufficiently detailed, and that it tends to focus on the courtly poetry from the end of Guittone's poetic development rather than from its beginning by picking out those features in the 'prima maniera' which come to maturity in the moral and religious writing. But this would be to quibble at the brevity of his essay, not its quality. My own reading, which supports the view of a maturing process at work and is confirmed by Margueron's chronology, starts at a point midway in that overall perspective redrawn by Quaglio and traces the author-persona relationships in the early poetry up to the poems that first appear under the rubric 'Fra Guittone'.

To reach the programmatic *canzoni* in logical order one must work through a formidable repertoire of traditional troubadour poetry, predictable in its emotional content, often difficult in style — which Guittone then treats as if it traced a history of his own unregenerate life:

> Fra gli altri miei follor fo, ch'eo trovai
> de disamor, ch'amai:
> pregiai onta, e cantai dolze di pianto;
> ed ingegnaime manto
> in fare me ed altrui saccente e forte
> 'n perder perdendo nostro Dio e amico.   c. xxvii, 26–31

[Among my other follies I wrote about unlove, which I loved: I prized shame and sang blithely about tears, and I contrived to the utmost to make myself and others knowing and single-minded for failure by losing our God and friend.]

One can simply reject his biographical assumption; or else ask why Guittone should have made it at all. Conjecture on this score may not require the reader to look closely at the love poems; yet Guittone himself took them seriously and apparently feared their continuing harmful effects on his readers. That is, he took as substantial poetic statement precisely those elements in his 'poesia d'amore' which apparently did *not* anticipate his conversion and his later poetic manner. This invites several observations. We recognize in the conversion poems the clear ring of Guittone's personal voice. We can presume that the 'I' who speaks is the poet himself. In those passages where he reflects on his earlier writing he presumes an identity between his present speaking voice and the speaking voice of his love poems. He speaks now as if he had once written and acted under the sway of 'Amore'; he assumes now, in his own person, moral responsibility for the actions and intentions of his courtly 'I', and for that literary activity by which he 'destroyed virtues and embellished vices'.[8] The uniform sobriety of his judgement suggests a more restricted vocal range in his early poetry than in fact there is. The 'I' can be the dogged lover weathering the peaks and troughs of joy and despair.[9] It can be the voice of a teacher dissecting a hypothetical amatory situation. It can be the voice of male raillery, provoking an equally abrasive female response — to mention only three major keys. The love poems offer not only a range of thematic content and courtly idealism. They also reveal differing degrees of identity between the voice of the protagonist and that of the poet, various levels of enthusiasm for his 'materia', and degrees of seriousness in his presentation of *fin' amors* ideals.

One could dismiss as rhetorical exaggeration fra Guittone's reflections on his love poetry. I prefer to explore the question of identity between the later and earlier authorial voice which these reflections pose. I shall try to show that in his early poetry Guittone grappled with what he saw as a problem of authorial sincerity in the inherited body of courtly literature. Far from being an undifferentiated block of poems promptly left behind for more serious and topical concerns, they show a definable movement towards that direct authorial voice which was to find satisfactory expression in ascetical themes and a thoroughgoing didactic manner.[10] This assertion wants proof but for the moment serves to open a fresh way into a neglected and difficult area of Guittone's verse — its most influential portion if we are to take at face value the wholesale imitation by his secular contemporaries and the antagonism of the *stilnovisti*.[11] Since this way begins with the poet's self-consciousness in the central poems, we must see what he says there about his early writing.

Fra Guittone refers to that body of work several times in cc. xxv, xxvii, xxviii, xxxii, and in ss. 164, 210, 211 and 237. In the *canzoni* his comments introduce or support wider arguments. By and large they present new credentials for a familiar literary figure. He is now entitled to proclaim a new life because he has publicly rejected his past; his confidence rests on a proven ability to write well; what he says is born of experience. In the *canzoni* he harmonizes variations on the theme of regret which the sonnets present separately and in more self-contained form. The length of the *canzone* makes for a spacious and even rambling line of thought in which criticism of the past plays only a minor part. It is not easy to judge from *canzone* to *canzone* what point of time each one represents in relation to the period or event of conversion. On the other hand the brevity and neatness of the sonnet form seems to have encouraged him to explore various introspective paths one by one. As a result the poet's stance and a given poem's proximity to the event of conversion are more easily definable in the sonnets than in the *canzoni*.[12] The terms 'introspection', 'poet's stance' and 'proximity to the event of conversion' need to be clarified in the context of Guittone's poetry. I have used them to suggest ways, discernible in the text, by which Guittone refers to his past life and his past poetry, and as interpretative guides to the critical problem of the love poetry posed by the moral slur he casts on it. By levels of 'introspection' or 'authorial self-awareness' I mean the degree to which Guittone identifies his present activity as poet with his earlier writing, and the ways he identifies the 'io' of his courtly poetry with his present 'real' self. At one level he celebrates his conversion from unspecified 'mal' with no mention of writing:

> Vergogna ho, lasso, ed ho me stesso ad ira;
> e doveria via piú, reconoscendo
> co male usai la fior del tempo mio.   c. xxvi, 1–3

[I am ashamed, alas, and angry with myself, and I should be all the more, realizing how badly I used the prime of my life.]

> Vergognar troppo e doler, lasso, deggio,
> poi fui dal mio principio a mezza etate
> in loco laido, desorrato e brutto,
> ove m'involsi tutto,
> e venni ingrotto, infermo, pover, nuto,
> cieco, sordo e muto,
> desviato, vanito, morto e peggio:
> ché tutto el detto mal m'avea savore;
> ché quanto al prenditore
> piú mal piace, è peggiore.   c. xxvii, 5–14

[I ought to be very ashamed and much grieved for from my birth to middle age I remained in a filthy, shameful and repulsive state, wallowed in it and became sick, feeble, impoverished, stripped, blind, deaf and dumb, lost, empty, dead and worse; for I relished all this evil. The more a client likes what is bad, the worse it is.]

At another level of intensity the poet seems to claim not only that he wrote about illicit love but that his present self was the 'I' of his love poems. At this level Guittone seems to say that the previous persona was as direct a mouthpiece for his sentiments as is the present 'I' of the palinodes:

> Adonque che savere guidal quello
> che d'amare se pena e va forzando,
> poi tale acquisto facene per ello?
> Ed io che l'ho provato, el raccomando
> a cui el piace, ch'io son lui ribello   s. 164, 9–13

[Therefore what kind of judgement guides the man who exerts himself and strives to love, when by it he makes such a gain as this? Whereas I, who have tried and tested it, assure those who are satisfied with Love that I am in revolt against him.]

> Fra gli altri miei follor fo, ch'eo trovai
> de disamor, ch'amai:
> pregiai onta, e cantai dolze di pianto;
> ed ingegnaime manto
> in fare me ed altrui saccente e forte
> 'n perder perdendo nostro Dio e amico.   c. xxvii, 26–31

[Among my other follies I wrote about unlove, which I loved: I prized shame and sang blithely about tears, and I contrived to the utmost to make myself and others knowing and single-minded for failure by losing our God and friend.]

Between these two levels 'mal' may be specified as 'amor' or 'Amore', but with little obvious claim to identity between the present and past poet-persona:

> Ahi, como e quanto allegro esser deggio,
> poi da tua signoria, malvagio Amore,
> l'alma e 'l corpo mio francato veggio.   s. 210, 9–11

[Ah, how overjoyed I should be, now that I see my soul and body freed from your control, accursed Love.]

> or torno de resia
> in dritta ed in verace oppinïone:
> e, se mostranza di viva ragione
> valer potesse ai guerrer ditti amanti,
> credo varraggio lor, ché 'n modi manti
> demosterrò la lor condizion rea.   c. xxviii, 10–15

[now I return from heresy to the upright and truthful view: and if a sound and rational argument can help those warriors who go by the name of lovers, I believe that I shall help them, for in various ways I will show that their condition is a dishonourable one.]

We shall see that one guide to Guittone's envisaged relationship between the post-conversion poet and the pre-conversion persona will be whether and how he speaks to an audience, and what stress he gives to conversion as an actual turning-point in his life.

By 'authorial stance' I mean the way Guittone faces his subject-matter and his envisaged audience. In some passages identity between author and persona 'drives' him to an inward re-creation of the struggle between conflicting ideals and behaviour, which may echo the language and style of the love poetry itself:

> Allor tornò lo mio travaglio a poso
> e a saver lo mio folle desio,
> allora presi cor d'esser gioioso,
> en guisa tal, ch'onni tormento obbrio.   s. 210, 5–8

[On that day my torment changed to calm, and my mad craving to steady judgement. On that day I resolved to be joyful with such good effect that I have forgotten all that anguish.]

In other passages the poet assesses the effect of his past writing or warns others against the dangers in it:

> E poi de' pomi miei prender vi piace,
> per Dio, da' venenosi or vi guardate,
> li quali eo ritrattai come mortali   s. 237, 9–11

[And since you like to choose from among my apples, for God's sake be careful of the poisoned ones which I have rejected as deadly]

or he may substitute for 'personal experience of love', sententious teaching directed at a 'chi' or 'omo' who will enter the snares of love in the world at large rather than in his poems:

> Ahi, como matto è ben senza questione
> omo che mette sua voglia 'n amare,
> ché tutti soi misteri 'n obria pone.
> E' tanto lo distringe in ciò pensare,
>   che doglia e danno sempre han lui stagione,
>   che 'n mante guise lo face mal trare   s. 164, 1–6

[Ah, how stupid, without any shadow of doubt, is the man who fixes his desire on loving, for he forgets all his obligations. It forces him to be so preoccupied that grief and worry fill his every moment, and it makes him attract evil under various guises.]

A single passage may weave together these separable strands, especially in *canzoni*, but some notion of the variable quality of Guittone's stance and introspection helps to explain why the sense of conversion as an event is not so near the surface in each poem, even though they were all probably written between 1265 and 1266.[13] At times it seems to have just taken place. He stresses the verbal activity of change, the wonder of his new state, the menace of the old. There is scope for word-play, especially antithesis; little room for overt teaching. The poet discourses inwardly on a struggle still fresh in his experience and imagination:

> Non piò l'amaro tuo sami dolciore,
> ché ben cerno da male e mal da peggio,
> mercé Lui, d'onni mio bono fattore.   s. 210, 12–14

[No more does your bitterness taste sweet to me for I clearly distinguish good from bad and bad from worse, thanks to Him, the maker of my every good.]

> Ahi, quant'ho che vergogni e che doglia aggio,
> e quant'ho che sbaldisca e che gioire,
> se bene isguardo, col veder d'om saggio,
> u'so, u' fui, u' spero anche venire!   c. xxvii, 1–4

[Alas, how much I have to be ashamed of and to mourn, and how much to celebrate and rejoice when I consider carefully with the eyes of experience, where I am, where I was, and where I hope to be!]

When Guittone warns poets, patrons and lovers of the mortal dangers lurking in his love poetry, conversion as an event looks comfortably behind him. He may or may not admit responsibility for the actions of the protagonist in the verses, and may do no more than admit a continuity of simple authorial activity, yet he does reject them on moral grounds and contrasts them with the themes of his new writing:

> E tu vietal, bel conte, in cortesia
> li traiti miei e perigliosi motti,
> und'eo vertude strussi e vizi ornai.   s. 211, 12-14

[And you, noble count, must please shun those treacherous and dangerous sayings of mine by which I destroyed virtue and embellished vices.]

At a further remove from the event, he can offer the new poetry (as if it were already a sizeable body of work) as counter to the old. Didactic intention mutes the sharpness of re-lived 'personal' experience and he abandons the teasing intricacies of word-play:

> E poi de' pomi miei prender vi piace,
> per Dio, da' venenosi or vi guardate,
> li quali eo ritrattai come mortali;
>   ma quelli, che triaca io so verace,
> contra essi e contr'ogne veleno usate,
> a ciò che 'n vita voi* siate eternali.   s. 237, 9-14

[And since you like to choose from among my apples, for God's sake be careful of the poisoned ones which I have rejected as deadly. But against them and all poison make use of those which I know to be a reliable antidote, that you may have eternal life.] (* Egidi's text emended by insertion of 'voi'.)

As an event conversion appears most remote when Guittone reduces amatory experience to the axioms of a sermon *de miseria humanae conditionis* preached to an unseen audience. Conversion as personal experience matters little in this context because his argument rests on the bloodless logic of clerical maxims launched from a pulpit built on that traditional language:

> e tutte gioi, che 'n ciò amore oppone,
> mister è pur che 'n nòi deggian finare.
>   Adonque che savere guidal quello
> che d'amare se pena e va forzando,
> poi tale acquisto facene per ello?   s. 164, 7-11

[and any joy that love provides* must of necessity end up as affliction. Therefore, what kind of judgement guides the man who exerts himself and strives to love, when by it he makes such a gain as this?] (* Another reading of the second half of line 7 is 'che cria amore o pone'.)

To illustrate and draw together these partial observations I propose to look first at the four sonnets from which I have been quoting. In them the variations I have noted seem clearly distinguished by Guittone himself, and they help to show in the *canzoni* where Guittone synthesizes his attitudes to conversion. Let us begin with s. 164, which seems to me an early failure to bind together two separate kinds of statement. Moralizing in the grand manner quenches any spark of personal experience the poet might have claimed:

> Ahi, como matto è ben senza questione
> omo che mette sua voglia 'n amare,
> ché tutti soi misteri 'n obria pone.
> E' tanto lo distringe in ciò pensare,
> che doglia e danno sempre han lui stagione,
> che 'n mante guise lo face mal trare;
> e tutte gioi, che 'n ciò amore oppone,
> mister è pur che 'n nòi deggian finare.
> Adonque che savere guidal quello
> che d'amare se pena e va forzando,
> poi tale acquisto facene per ello?
> Ed io che l'ho provato, el raccomando
> a cui el piace, ch'io son lui ribello,
> merzé de lui, ch'a mal vammi lungiando.   s. 164, 1–14

[Ah, how stupid, without any shadow of doubt, is the man who fixes his desire on loving, for he forgets all his obligations. It forces him to be so preoccupied that grief and worry fill his every moment, and it makes him lead a life that is wretched in so many ways; and any joy that love provides must of necessity end up as affliction. Therefore, what kind of judgement guides the man who exerts himself and strives to love, when by it he makes such a gain as this? Whereas I, who have tried and tested it, assure those who are satisfied with Love that I am in revolt against him, thanks to Him who is drawing me away from evil.]

It is difficult to read the last *terzina* as following naturally from what precedes it.[14] Between the language of clinical moral dissection of love's effect on others, and a first-person retreat from love which still holds him, 'a mal vammi lungiando', there yawns a gap too wide to be closed by mechanical juxtaposition of the two styles in one short poem. This uncertain conjunction of styles and stance is not evident in s. 210:

> Deo, con fu dolce e ben aventuroso
> lo giorno che da me gioia partio,
> ch'allora departi' d'esser noioso
> e despiacente a ragione e a Dio.
> Allor tornò lo mio travaglio a poso
> e a saver lo mio folle desio,
> allora presi cor d'esser gioioso,
> en guisa tal, ch'onni tormento obbrio.
> Ahi, como e quanto allegro esser deggio,
> poi da tua signoria, malvagio Amore,
> l'alma e 'l corpo mio francato veggio.
> Non piò l'amaro tuo sami dolciore,
> ché ben cerno da male e mal da peggio,
> mercé Lui, d'onni mio bono fattore.   s. 210, 1–14

[God, how sweet and fortunate was the day on which I banished joy from myself, for on that day I ceased to be irksome and repugnant to reason and to God. On that day my torment changed to calm, and my mad craving to steady judgement. On that day I resolved to be joyful, with such good effect that I have forgotten all that anguish. Ah, how overjoyed I should be, now that I see my soul and body freed from your control, accursed Love. No more does your bitterness taste sweet to me, for I clearly distinguish good from bad and bad from worse, thanks to Him, the maker of my every good.]

There is no doubt that the 'I' who is now pleasing to God (lines 3–4) was only a short time ago completely subject to 'Amore' (lines 10–11).[15] Guittone captures the moment of conversion first by a series of contrasts (lines 1–8), describing his inner condition before and after 'lo giorno', and then, in an apostrophe to 'malvagio Amore', by a celebration of his new-found freedom. The insistent past verbs and triple 'allora' of the *quartine* underline an irrevocable change.[16] The personified deity apostrophised in the *terzine* shows that the poet's 'moral deformity' came entirely through amatory experience seen in archetypal terms as the 'signoria d'Amore'. Could this 'Amore' be the same one who figured in Guittone's own early love poems? Could the 'I' now free in body and soul be the 'I' of those poems? He does not say so but his audience will have noted the similarity of language and style between this poem and certain of Guittone's courtly poems in circulation. That day, 'lo giorno', is like the day the lover met his lady, or the day she desisted from her scorn;[17] and, but for the fourth line, the two *quartine* could celebrate his return to 'madonna's' favour,[18] with the same repetition and obvious contrasts. What he now sees as moral 'tormento' could easily be the emotional agony that is such a hackneyed motif in the courtly sonnets; and with one or two slight changes the *terzine* could equally well express the lover's joy at being received into the 'signoria d'Amore'.

These similarities are not fortuitous nor proof of a poverty of means. If the same language fits either situation then the lover's torment was as real as is the poet's sense of new-found tranquillity. A style that may be facile or contrived in the courtly context will find a new validity in the context of religious conversion. When Guittone the convert-poet describes his own change of heart in the formal language of his most derivative love poetry, he presumes, and asks us to presume, that the 'io' of his new state is the same person as the 'io' of those poems in which he first used that language.[19] However, when he engages in literary correspondence on the effects of his earlier writing, he has no need to show a continuity of person between the old and the new poetry, as s. 211 makes clear:

> Alcun conto di te, conte Gualtieri,
> mi conta, ché gradir m' è te audire,
> sí che non poco en te so, e volentieri,
> tanto m'agrada forte ai bon gradire:
> e voi siet'esso; homi alto mistieri
> non piò tardar, ma servo al tu' desire:
> francamente in allegrezza chieri
> quanto al mio Signor posso servire.

Ché servir me né te for Lui non dia,
ma vietar deggio — ed io lo vieto a tutti —
ciò che senza lui, lasso, operai.
E tu vietal, bel conte, in cortesia
li traiti miei e perigliosi motti,
und'eo vertude strussi e vizi ornai. s. 211, 1–14

[Count Gualtieri, any word of yours I value, and it is a pleasure for me to hear from you that I have been of some influence on you. I accept the task gladly, so much does it please me to please those who are good: and you are that. I hold it a noble duty to delay no longer; rather, I submit to your wish. You have asked plainly how I can possibly serve my Lord wholeheartedly. For neither you nor I should serve anyone but Him; hence I must reject — and I proscribe it publicly — whatever I did, alas, without Him. And you, noble count, must please shun those treacherous and dangerous sayings of mine by which I destroyed virtue and embellished vices.]

Presumably Gualtieri had written to the acknowledged master of love poetry, asking how he could reconcile his religious vocation with his secular verse,[20] no doubt praising the poet in the *quartine* and leaving the question for the *terzine*. Guittone observes this format in his reply and shows by *replicatio* and other devices of the old style that rejecting the 'materia' of his earlier poetry has not diminished his *ars*.[21] But the frankness of the question must have nettled him, because presumably the circulation of his earlier poetry even among local litterati was out of his control, and those poems would remain *the* public statement of his 'creed' until new poems took their place.[22] His two-pronged reply in s. 211 was meant to settle doubts about the sincerity of his conversion (by a public confession of *all* his amoral activity, lines 10–11), and to disown the creed propounded earlier. As elsewhere, and in a typical reasoning process from the general to the particular, 'mal' undefined, 'ciò che senza lui, lasso, operai' (line 11), becomes synonymous with his earlier 'traiti e perigliosi motti'.[23] And by binding himself and his correspondent to the same obligations (line 9) Guittone obliges Gualtieri to shun his love poems as a logical consequence of the poet's public disavowal of them.[24] This sonnet is normally paired with s. 237.[25] In both poems Guittone warns a correspondent about the danger in his writings, and in the latter as in the former he reserves the message for the *terzine*. But the difference between the two is more noteworthy than their likeness:

A te, Montuccio, ed agli altri, il cui nomo
non giá volontier molto agio 'n obrio,
a cui intendo che savoro ha 'l mi pomo,
che mena il piccioletto arboscel mio,
non diragio ora giá quanto e como,
disioso, di voi agio desio;
ma dico tanto ben, che nel meo domo
con voi sovente gioi prendo e ricrio.

E poi de' pomi miei prender vi piace,
per Dio, da' venenosi or vi guardate,
li quali eo ritrattai come mortali;
    ma quelli, che triaca io so verace,
contra essi e contr'ogne veleno usate,
a ciò che 'n vita voi* siate eternali.   s. 237, 1–14[26]

[To you, Montuccio, and to the others, whose name I never willingly forget
for long, who like, I believe, the taste of the fruit which my little tree bears, I
can never express the longing I have for you; but I'll say this much, that in
my home, with you, I have often found and recaptured joy. And since you
like to choose from among my apples, for God's sake be careful of the
poisoned ones which I have rejected as deadly. But against them and all
poison make use of those which I know to be a reliable antidote, that you
may have eternal life.] (* Egidi's text emended by the insertion of 'voi'.)

Addressed to a school of admiring poets, 'A te, Montuccio, ed agli altri',
the language is, for Guittone, decidedly flowery, with its two related metaphors
(trees/fruit, poison/antidote) and its roundabout sweet nothings in the *captatio*.[27]
In its bland praise and self-deprecation Guittone seems to be reassuring them
that he is the same Guittone as of old, a man of letters and not some crabbed
religious maniac, a hospitable companion and not an austere mentor. Yet the
captatio presumes that since nothing has changed between them, and since they
admire *all* his verses, they will be as open to the new themes as to the old. The
easy formalities of the *quartine* lead unerringly to this assumption made con-
fidently in the first line of the *terzine*, 'E poi . . .' (line 9).

In sonnet 211 Guittone could only warn off Gualtieri from his 'traiti . . . e
perigliosi motti': he had no alternative to offer him. Now he can point to a body
of poems which offsets the love poetry as neatly as the new antidote counteracts
the old poison (lines 10–13),[28] a body of work equally serious and equally
compelling as poetry. If his new poetry matches the old because it is an equally
comprehensive statement of his new ideals, his colleagues and admirers can
now take it as their model, to repair the damage his love poems will have done
them.

I am not necessarily challenging the accepted chronology for s. 237, though I
would place it later than the year immediately after his conversion and would
take its position at the end of the *sonetti morali* as a possible sign of later
composition. What is clear in the sonnet is that conversion as a motif is non-
existent and can only be inferred by reading line 11 with s. 211, lines 9–14,
for example. In s. 211 the strident quality of Guittone's palinode suggests that
the past is still too close for comfort; in s. 237 conversion seems to be well
behind him and is simply noted as an aside.[29] He has no need to effect an
identity between present and past personae when he makes no equation in the
poem between his religious conversion and the disowning of his love poetry;

and in this sense s. 237 is clearly more remote from that event than either s. 210 or s. 211.

These four sonnets suggest that the degree of moral responsibility which Guittone assumed for his love poetry was not uniform. At its most intense he speaks as if he had been the *fin' amors* protagonist, as if his religious conversion were a liberation from slavery to 'Amore' (ss. 210, 164, lines 12–14). When he admits guilt for the harmful effects of his love poetry (ss. 211, 237), his rejection of courtly literature is one result of religious conversion, concomitant but distinguishable from it. Guittone betrays little suspicion of guilt when he turns the 'sentimental life' of courtly poetry into the impersonal material of moral maxims (s. 164). To some extent the particular theme of a poem and the audience he has in mind (whether general or particular, cultivated or uninitiated), will dictate the degree of personal culpability he cares or needs to admit.[30] But the three guidelines I noted earlier — levels of awareness, the poet's stance, nearness to the event — help us to define particular aspects of the general sense of guilt that pervades his judgement of his earlier writing.

This can be put another way. When Guittone claims identity between himself as a convert-persona and the 'I' of his love poetry, the poems will tend towards a private celebration of his escape from the clutches of Love, still so fresh in his imagination that he can hold in balance the opposing deities and systems: the drama of the personal event eclipses all sense of an outside, public world. That world comes into focus when the event recedes and the poet can take stock of a large body of writing which runs counter to his new ideals — writing that was once an important facet of a life now changed, writing which continues to wreak moral havoc on unwitting readers. The style of these authorial retractions suggests a point midway between introspective discourse, not yet free from the modulations of love poetry itself, and the extroverted assault on sexual *mores* which lifts *fin' amors* experience out of its aristocratic and formulaic context and measures it by the pulpit yardstick of right and wrong. In such passages Guittone's message for Everyman grows more assured and rigid the less his sense of personal conversion comes to the surface; and as it recedes so there is less need for a show of continuity between poet and persona, past and present.[31]

Turning from the sonnets written after his conversion to the *canzoni* which proclaim his new life and which stand at the head of his work in the manuscript tradition, one has the impression that the sonnets preceded the *canzoni* as short occasional statements awaiting a more mature synthesis. The technical demands of the *canzone* form could well have inclined Guittone to pause before attempting a definitive palinode. And the harmonious integration of literary conversion in his general moral conversion, as shown in the three *canzoni* we shall study now, xxv, xxvii, xxviii, suggests that Guittone reflected on his various attitudes to the earlier poetic, as distinguishable in the sonnets, so as to find the most forceful and definitive way of setting a new course. One of the most celebrated passages in the whole *canzoniere* is the opening to c. xxv, the *canzone* that heads the collection in the prime MS. Laur. Rediano 9.

> Ora parrà s'eo saverò cantare
> e s'eo varrò quanto valer già soglio,
> poi che del tutto Amor fug[g]h' e disvoglio,
> e più che cosa mai forte mi spare:
>   ch'a om tenuto saggio audo contare
> che trovare — non sa né valer punto
> omo d'Amor non punto;
> ma' che digiunto — da vertà mi pare,
> se lo pensare — a lo parlare — sembra,
> ché 'n tutte parte ove distringe Amore
> regge follore — in loco di savere:
> donque como valere
> pò, né piacer — di guisa alcuna fiore,
> poi dal Fattor — d'ogni valor — disembra
> e al contrar d'ogni mainer' asembra?
>   Ma chi cantare vole e valer bene,
> in suo legno a nochier Diritto pone
> e orrato Saver mette al timone,
> Dio fa sua stella, e 'n ver Lausor sua spene   c. xxv, 1–19

[Now we shall see whether I can still write poetry and whether I can still command respect as before, since I now shun and reject Love completely and hate him more than anything else. I have heard it said by one held wise that no-one can write poetry or be of any worth unless he is pierced by Love; but if he means what he says, he is, in my view, far from the truth, for wherever Love fixes his grip there reigns madness instead of wisdom. Therefore, how can he have any worth or have any beauty whatever when he turns away from the creator of all worth and conforms to its opposite in every way?

But he who wants to sing well and be truly worthy must set Justice as pilot in his boat and put honoured Wisdom at the helm. He must make God his star and true Praise his aspiration]

The poem opens with Guittone's famous rejection of 'Amore' as source of poetic inspiration and inner worth. 'Cantare' and 'valere' will complement each other in the future because they did so in the past. Subject to 'Amore' the lover finds worth and a voice and he gives utterance to his own sentimental experience (lines 6–7). The man who seeks true worth must not fear he will lose inspiration if he commits himself to the Christian code for he too will give compelling utterance to his own 'moral' experience (lines 16–17). Or will he?

By the end of the first stanza, line 12, 'cantare' slips behind 'valere' and after the opening line of the second stanza disappears altogether. There, the impetus of the poem's opening equation is felt again for a moment, but the 'io' has now changed to a 'chi'; autobiography has become teaching. The equation 'cantare' = 'valere' is of no use to Guittone when he proposes moral standards for *others*. It serves only to define the strength and security of his *own* new-found didactic voice in terms of an experience, now behind him, in which the persona was also the poet. Sure of his present 'I' (author as protagonist, direct voice) Guittone takes as 'real' the fiction of poet-persona identity in courtly poetry (lines 5–7). His own love poetry becomes in turn a biographical statement for which he as author must now accept moral responsibility. It is biography not so much in its events as in the certainty with which Guittone as author, now translating his private ideals into verse, accords to his love poetry the same colour of biographical disclosure.[32]

It is easy to see incidental parallels between these lines and the *quartine* of s. 210.[33] But compared with this stately passage from the madness of love to true Christian dignity, the neat antitheses in s. 210 look facile in their brevity. Compared with the sonnets we have just read, Guittone here blends with relative ease his sense of conversion as an event, with his implicit claim to be both the author and protagonist of his poetry; and he integrates these two 'subjective' elements into the wider context of his universal moral message. He conveys the urgency of conversion more vividly than in s. 210.[34] And the 'follore' which afflicts those subject to Love becomes a symptom of that disregard for reason which brings chaos to individual and social life, instead of being merely a private addiction turned sour, as he described it in s. 164. As nowhere in the sonnets, he here displays a sure and integrated grasp of his multiple role as former devotee of 'Amore', as accomplished poet and as neophyte with a mission to spread the word. It is this maturity of vision which justifies his confidence in the opening challenge and assures for c. xxv its place at the head of Rediano 9.

In c. xxvii Guittone turns from a 'mostranza' of the true human values to an extended meditation on his conversion and his religious vocation. The second stanza is of special interest to us:

> Quanto Deo, sua merzé, dato m'avea
> di senno, di coraggio e di podere,
> solo a sua lauda ed a salute mea
> ed al prossimo meo prode tenere,
> ad oltraggio di Lui ed a mia morte
> ed a periglio altrui l'operai, lasso!
> Fra gli altri miei follor fo, ch'eo trovai
> de disamor, ch'amai:
> pregiai onta, e cantai dolze di pianto;
> ed ingegnaime manto
> in fare me ed altrui saccente e forte
> 'n perder perdendo nostro Dio e amico.
> Guai a me, lasso, dico,
> e guai a chi nemico
> ed omo matto crede, e segue legge
> d'omo ch'è senza legge!
> Però fugga lo meo folle dir como
> suo gran nemico ogn'omo,
> ch'eo 'l vieto a tutti e per malvagio il casso.   c. xxvii, 20–38

[All that God in his goodness had given me of intelligence, vitality and strength, to keep solely for his praise and for my salvation and to help my neighbour, I used, alas, to insult Him, to bring about my death and to harm others. Among my other follies I wrote about unlove, which I loved: I prized shame and sang blithely about tears, and I contrived to the utmost to make myself and others knowing and single-minded for failure by losing our God and friend. Alas, a curse on me, I say, and a curse on those who trust an enemy and a madman, and follow the law of someone who is lawless! Therefore let everyone avoid my mad writing as he does his worst enemy, for I publicly disown it and condemn it as damned.]

There can be little doubt that Guittone as author celebrates in verse his own personal conversion: this is clear from the certainty with which he balances past against present experience. A new life has begun when the old can be judged for what it was and shown to be left behind: hence, as in s. 210, the symmetrical matching of past shame and present joy (c. xxvii, 1–2);[35] hence the clear sense of a present vantage point from which past and future are both in view, line 4. This also helps to explain the congeries of past 'moral' infirmity described as physical sickness (lines 5–12),[36] where the disfigurements include a ritual maiming by Love, 'venni cieco muto e sordo' — the topos now taken seriously.

But his conversion has been, and must be shown to have been, a total experience embracing inner life and outward activity, that is, Guittone in himself and in his relations with his fellows. Having admitted his past illness he will now confess his past abuse of divinely-given gifts (lines 20–5). Here too he projects his present sense of duty into the past, and, as before, his exhaustive contrast of ideal with practice stamps the past with the actuality of the present. As in s. 211, lines 9–14, the argument clarifies itself step by step, first the general 'mal', then an example as if 'trovar' were one of many activities he could have chosen: 'Fra gli altri miei follor fo, ch'eo trovai' (line 26). Yet as we saw in s. 211, where all the 'mal' lies in the 'motti', so here, writing poetry was obviously *the* culpable activity (lines 22–3), because it made him and others lose God. First-person past verbs, 'trovai', 'pregiai', 'cantai', 'ingegnaime', hammer home his activity as poet; but more than that, what he now sees 'objectively' as former subject-matter, 'trovai/de disamor' (lines 26–7), is what the same 'I' had given itself up to, 'ch'amai' (line 27) — not merely in the writing of it but in the living of it. His love poetry was an internal as well as external advocacy and adoption of courtly ideals. In these four lines Guittone chooses to concentrate the whole of his personal activity and sense of guilt in the poetic function; and if the 'I' is the poet himself, so in his *fin' amors* poetry the poet was also the courtly protagonist.[37] The echo of lines 22–3 in lines 30–1 confirms this identity of voice now recognized in its effects on an audience. As in lines 26–7 the two verbs suggest at once the double role of the single voice: 'ed ingegnaime manto' ('trovai de disamor') — Guittone as author; 'in fare me' ('ch'amai') — the poet as hero of the sentimental experience he relates in the courtly poems. He will have depraved others because his own *fin' amors* experience made compulsive reading. It influenced his audience in the past just as he means to influence his audience in the future.[38]

At this point (line 32) self-reproach gives way to warning and for three lines Guittone adopts the stern declamatory tone so characteristic of his *rime ascetiche*. The impersonal style balances the introspection in the preceding lines, while the identical rhyme, 'legge' (lines 34, 35), invites the reader to search for the spirit beneath the letter of the law.[39] Cheek by jowl the soul-searcher and the moralist show how close the convert saw the two roles, and how close he is in this poem to his most natural form of self-expression. The terms in the conclusion which rounds off the stanza are not entirely coherent with the rest of the passage,[40] the shape of which is more obedient to rhetorical argument than to a strictly syllogistic pattern.[41] The first member (lines 26–31) is a particular confession which identifies the poet with the persona in the earlier poetry; the second (lines 32–5) is a general warning not to follow false advocates; and the third, 'però fugga . . .' (lines 36–8) is a conclusion which resolves general moral exhortation ('fugga . . . ogn'omo') in personal self-reproach ('lo meo folle dir'). The *canzone* ends in a remarkable passage which confirms the continuity of past with present poet-persona as established in the second stanza:

> E voi, Amor, pur acolto m'avete,
> e de vostra masnada ormai segnato;
> però merzé; le man vostre mettete
> ne la zambra del figlio vostro onrato,
> e me fornite voi ben sofficiente,
> che, non mancando, fornir pote ogn'omo.
> O donna mia, non mi faite carizia
> di sí tragran devizia;
> né, perch'eo sia for merto, amor sdegnate,
> ma stringavi pietate,
> che pria vi strinse for mertar eo nente.
> E se ch'io merti, Amor meo, pur volete,
> di che darmi dovete,
> ché null'aggio, savete,
> ma' che miseria e male; unde ben faite
> se, ch'eo vo dia, me date,
> non per me, ma per voi; ché s'eo non merto,
> voi pur mertate certo
> ciò ch'eo mertar vorrìa; ma posso como?   c. xxvii, 77–95

[And yet you, Love, have welcomed me and have now marked me as one of your household. Therefore have pity on me. Put your hands into the secret room of your noble son* and fit me out with all I need, for anyone can equip others if he has a ready source of supply. O my lady, do not starve me of such exceeding riches, nor withold your love because I am unworthy. Rather, let that compassion rule you which once ruled you when I was totally undeserving. And if, my Love, you should still want me to be worthy you must

give me the wherewithal, for you know that I have nothing except wretched-
ness and evil. Hence you do well to give to me that I may give to you, not for
my sake but for yours. Since even if I am undeserving, you constantly deserve
that which I should want to deserve; but how can I on my own?] (* The
literal translation is meant to catch the doubting Thomas echo present in the
Italian.)

With no by-your-leave Guittone switches to fulsome Provençalized diction[42]
and addresses himself to the Virgin as if she were first the Ovidian deity who
has at last numbered the poet among his elect (lines 77–82), and then, as if she
were the harsh beloved who might be persuaded to 'recognize' her lover (lines
83–95), to show mercy for her own sake if not for his.[43] The language of this
stanza represents two styles, two periods of time (one later, the other earlier) in
relation to the central act of conversion. In the first two stanzas of the *canzone*
Guittone had looked back at his past poetic activity and lamented it in a way
that equated the actions of persona and author. In the fifth stanza, which could
have been lifted from one of the *fin' amors canzoni*, iv or viii for example, the
love poet looks ahead to embrace a religious vocation in the language of
'archaic' love poetry with its evocation of the Court of Love.[44] This interplay
of moral tone and religious parody reveals the pivotal position of the conversion
manifestoes in Guittone's poetic career and the identity of poet and persona
which they now impose on the whole corpus.[45]

In the third canzone, xxviii, Guittone attacks the ideals of *fin' amors* literature
in their most substantial form — the person of 'Amore' holding sway over his
devotees and promising an alternative system of human perfection:

> O tu, de nome Amor, guerra de fatto,
> segondo i toi cortesi eo villaneggio,
> ma segondo ragion cortesia veggio
> s'eo blasmo te, o chi tec' ha contratto.
> Per che seguo ragion, non lecciaria,
> und'ho già mante via
> portato in loco di gran ver menzogna
> ed in loco d'onor propia vergogna,
> in loco di saver rabbi' e follia;
> or torno de resia
> in dritta ed in verace oppinïone:
> e, se mostranza di viva ragione
> valer potesse ai guerrer ditti amanti,
> credo varraggio lor, ché 'n modi manti
> demosterrò la lor condizion rea.   c. xxviii, 1–15

[O you, Love by name, war in fact, according to your devotees I am acting
basely, but according to reason I am the one who displays courtesy when I
upbraid you or anyone who has dealings with you. For now I pursue reason
not the lusts of the flesh, as when once I often chose a lie instead of a noble
truth, personal shame instead of honour, anger and madness instead of
discretion. Now I return from heresy to the upright and truthful view: and if a

sound and rational argument can help those warriors who go by the name
of lovers, I believe that I shall help them, for in various ways I will show that
their condition is a dishonourable one.]

'Amore' as personified deity was already an old-fashioned notion to litterati
of the mid-thirteenth century. He plays a minor role in Guittone's earliest
sonnets and it was only later, with a book-illustration or painting in mind or at
hand, that the poet attempted a serious analysis of 'la figura del carnal amore'.[46]
The idea of the 'dio alato' remained important for anti-courtly argument because
it masked unregulated emotion with religious ritual; it encouraged ambiguities
and euphemism in love literature; it was a key to a code of behaviour still seen
through clerical eyes as a rival to the Christian code. 'O tu, de nome Amor,
guerra de fatto' is, however, a full-throated tirade and not a schematic, alle-
gorical *descriptio*, because the poet is still uncomfortably close to 'lo periglioso
mal del detto Amore' (line 89).

The poem opens (lines 1–4), with a rigidly balanced statement that covers the
whole field in the comprehensive grasp of its two extreme terms. The destructive
reality is pitted against the sweet words of sentimental experience (line 1);
blunt reason against civilized manners (lines 2–3). In the *frons* the critic stands
outside his neat axioms, but in the *sirima* he describes in miniature his conversion
and identifies the new critical self with the persona of his literary 'fatti d'amore'
(lines 5–11). By a now-familiar pattern of contrast between present (ideal) and
past (practice) he expatiates on the 'lecciaria' he had extolled in his love poems.[47]
Lines 7–9 recall earlier complaints against Love's destructive power and echo
the former effects of his dominion.[48] The poet who now follows reason once
indulged in 'lecciaria'; the 'vergogna' was his *own*, 'propia' (line 8). Guittone
will have something to say to lovers (line 13) because he too was one of them.
Other lovers will feel guilt for what he now describes as 'lecciaria' because the
joyful/suffering 'I' of his own love poems was his own self. The whole stanza
establishes at the outset of his attack on 'Amore' a continuity and identity
between critic (lines 1–4), the 'I' of love literature (lines 5–9), the convert
(lines 10–11), and the teacher (lines 12–15), in an argument that circles backward
from present, through remote past, to near past, to present again and future.
His attack on Love will carry weight only because he makes it clear that *he* in
his present, belligerent person was once in the band of Love's 'cortesi'. Once,
he believed the doctrine he taught; now, he holds another creed which will also
be the stuff of poetry: 'or torno de resia/in dritta ed in verace oppinïone'.

If the courtly poetry were all that had survived one would be inclined to fall
back on the standard, unsympathetic critical judgements which Quaglio mentions only to set aside for a more persuasive reading of the 'materia amorosa'.[49]
I have already noted that, sound as that reading is, there is room for fresh
observation in the less easily definable area of author-persona relationships in
the courtly poems which is, understandably, not a key issue in Quaglio's

synthesis. But his early warning still holds good, that in spite of the order in Rediano 9 and Guittone's claims to the contrary, conversion does not cut off one poetic from another. Guittone's moral judgement of his love poetry becomes a stumbling block to what should be a fictional interpretation of the pre-conversion poetry. Without it, his courtly verse is a thematic repertory of the *fin' amors* poetic, derivative in sentiment and situation, and with faceless, anonymous protagonists. With it, we begin to ask not why he should have taken it so seriously but whether it is a static statement, or whether the conversion poems are a *terminus ad quem* of any definable movement within the love poetry. I have tried to show that we can accept the conversion poems as direct and sincere expressions of Guittone's personal sentiment. He tends to read this authorial sincerity back into the love poems, though none of them sounds as direct or convincing as c. xxv or c. xxvii. To see whether the love poetry deserved his palinode we must examine how Guittone tried to use traditional materials for a personal re-statement of courtly idealism; we must examine how he made his 'parlare' reflect his 'pensare'.

Just as there are good reasons for ignoring the *canzoniere* bipartition as an over-simplification, so one might be tempted to argue that Guittone was not so culpable as he made out, not even culpable at all. In both cases a moderate critical position throws more light on the poems. The break in his work, as shown in the manuscript, has been healed by showing a growth (and presence from the start) of ethico-moral interests and intellectual analysis. Likewise, the poet's claim to full authorial seriousness in his early work can be interpreted by tracing a growth towards the obvious sincerity of the post-conversion poems, and by showing how Guittone sought to give a fresh stamp to his traditional themes. If he was always in some degree moralist and didact, we shall see that from the start he also sought for a way to speak directly through his 'materia'. My reading of the love poetry will try to establish how Guittone set about making the stock sentiments of the *fin' amors* poetic pass for his own.

CHAPTER 3

Order in the 'prima maniera' and two early narrative experiments

The order and the grouping of the love sonnets, which corresponds in the two manuscripts, Laurenziano Rediano 9 and Vaticano lat. 3793,[1] has been taken to show that Guittone conceived and wrote the courtly poems in well-defined families. Quaglio sees these groups of poems as a testing ground for the 'onne mainera' Guittone boasts of at the end of c. xi:

L'ingegnoso suo 'trovare' si manifesta non meno che con invenzioni metriche, prosodiche, retoriche, con innovazioni strutturali, mediante le quali le tendenze didattiche tentano di superare la frammentarietà del discorso poetico così articolato nella organizzazione di cicli lirici narrativi: i primi sonetti (nn. 1–18 dell'ed. Egidi) espongono la storia di un amore infelice; segue una collana (sonetti nn. 19–30) che trattano della lealtà in amore; un folto gruppo di sonetti (nn. 31–80) insieme a varie canzoni sviluppa, nelle forme del 'contrasto' e delle 'noie' (non manca la donna-schermo), il motivo della gioia, quasi riequilibrato dal contrasto, realistico e popolaresco, tra l'amante e la donna villana. E si aggiunga anche una sorta di ars amandi (sonetti 87–110), condotta sulla falsariga di Ovidio e Andrea Cappellano ... (pp. 265–6)

His debt to earlier studies is not hard to see, and the synthesis he makes of them is appealing. He accepts the groups of sonnets first proposed by Pellizzari[2] (who 'improved' on the grouping suggested by Pelaez in his review of the Pellegrini edition of the *rime amorose*)[3] and retained by Margueron with two minor changes in his first appendix;[4] he also uses Margueron's phrase 'cycles lyrico-narratifs'. To this he adapts Tartaro's phrase 'superare la frammentarietà del discorso poetico',[5] and with it the concept of an intended structural symmetry which Tartaro confines to his discussion of the conversion manifesto, c. xxv. For Tartaro the traditional discourse is broken into secular and religious 'experience', and c. xxv imposes a total unity on the two halves of the *canzoniere*. For Quaglio 'la frammentarietà del discorso poetico' lies in its multiple courtly themes and situations, which Guittone links together in families of poems. Quaglio is careful to avoid noting specific *canzoni* in his narrative cycles, though he does mention 'varie canzoni' in the third group (ss. 31–80). He distinguishes between the first three groups of sonnets ('cicli narrativi'), and the *ars amandi* (ss. 87–110); and he sees the 'contrasto realistico e popolaresco' (ss. 81–6) as a kind of balance to the 'gioia' motif in the third group. His reticence pinpoints difficulties in the groups as defined by Pellizzari, difficulties recognized in part by Margueron.

There is no manuscript evidence of any organic growth in the *canzoni*. They have been attached to the first three cycles on the basis of thematic likeness and could only be said to correspond to certain static points in the sonnet 'stories'. This is particularly true of the third cycle where the Pellizzari/Margueron outline of six episodes applies solely to the sonnets.[6] The general title 'lyrico-narrative cycles' offers no explanation for the fifth and sixth groups which are decidedly non-narrative, nor even for the fourth group, the 'tenzone con la donna villana', which is a narrative only in the sense that it has first-person protagonists, where the first three cycles describe changes in a situation.

The drawback in Pellizzari's grouping is his reliance on thematic content as the sole criterion of likeness, and it seems to me that the inadequacy of this criterion, if used on its own, has prevented any serious interpretation of the sonnet families as provided by both the most authoritative manuscripts. It is clear that the fourth, fifth and sixth sonnet groups are non-narrative, and that the fourth and fifth represent different attitudes to the *fin' amors* ideals from those revealed in the first three groups. It is equally clear that the affinity which is perceived between the *canzoni* and the sonnets is based on their serious presentation of *fin' amors* ideals and not on narrative elements common to both. The narrative element in Guittone's sonnets, rudimentary though it may be, is synonymous with a 'straight' presentation of traditional courtly language and sentiment; while the anti-courtly experiment is reserved for two genres, low-style 'contrasto' and the didactic *ars amandi*.

We saw in the palinodes that Guittone's view of his courtly poetry was not uniform, and that both his degree of moral responsibility for the sentiments in that poetry and the vividness of conversion as event, depend on the poet's sense of identity with his courtly persona. These distinctions are relevant to the love sonnets which, from preliminary observation, fall into two broad categories — narrative/courtly, and non-narrative/anti-courtly.[7] In so far as 'narrative' means an attempt to draw a sustained and changing line of events (as distinct from the static and occasional motifs of troubadour lyrics, self-contained and unconnected), it would seem that he tried to infuse life into those motifs by forging them into stories told in verse. If my earlier equation between identity of present and past persona and the 'reality' of the event is correct, it seems reasonable to suggest that the linking of sonnets into well-defined families was an attempt to represent as a real event what individual lyrics would pass off as imaginary or fictive.

I shall try to show that the printed, that is, manuscript, order of the *sonetti d'amore* — 'serious' narratives, and anti-idealistic genre groups — does in fact reveal and correspond to a discernible process of disengagement from the *fin' amors* ideal as a literary inspiration, and that the sonnet families are steps towards the self-criticism of 'Ora parrà s'eo saverò cantare' and the other poems written after conversion. I shall argue that Guittone's early development, prior to the central phase, begins with an attempt at a primitive and pure statement of courtly sentiment (where the author is assimilated into his persona), then moves to a more knowing manipulation (authorial) of the genres and the lexical range (where the roles of poet and persona are clearly separated).

I shall argue that each family of poems represents an experimental advance in this line of development, and that each experiment reveals a deeper authorial grasp of the relationship of non-courtly to courtly elements in the poetry as experience. Beginning with an outline of the thematic unity in each sonnet family, I shall try to show that they display specific styles and stages in Guittone's early poetic. I shall argue that in them Guittone attempted a deep and thorough search of his antecedent material for its stances and attitudes to *fin' amors*, and that he gradually moved away from what he saw as the classical and direct self-projection of an archaic and pure stage in lyric idealism. His hind-sighted rejection of the 'prima maniera', expressed in moral terms, simply completes and crystallizes a process that had been in motion from the beginning. And I shall suggest that the variety of genre and style in the pre-conversion poetry is not the result of an *a priori* decision to experiment with 'onne mainera' but is the result of an authorial search for a 'sincere' voice in the courtly poetic, which drove him to try every 'mainera' that the inherited poetic offered him.[8]

Such an interpretation would support the view which sees Guittone's later didactic-intellectual manner and moral pre-occupation as already present in the love poetry.[9] That view explains what happens in the early poems, in the light of Guittone's socio-historical background, as an expression of his 'sentire pratico e buon senso borghese'. I would see the early poetry as revealing a constant tension between two levels of reality — the literary tradition conceived in its feudal purity, and the non-courtly formation of a latter-day practitioner — which can be traced from beginning to end of the 'prima maniera'. I would show Guittone at grips with the formalistic elements in courtly poetry, trying to appropriate its ideals by turning stock sentiment into the stuff of real experience. And, instead of a hind-sighted anticipation of later concerns in the early poems, I would see the sonnet families (and then the *canzoni*) as a series of provisional 'answers', as a constant re-appraisal of the courtly ethos, as a sign of dynamic if not always vertical growth in the *canzoniere*, and as a necessary preparation for his open rejection of *fin' amors* in middle life.

Guittone's sonnets offer the most promising opening to this kind of study because, as thematically coherent cycles, they provide him with an extended and consistent first-person persona; they make use of a wide range of traditional themes and styles; and their idealism ranges from archaic purity of *fin' amors* to 'modern' cynicism. I shall study them first not to suggest chronological priority over the *canzoni* but to show them as a background to the whole courtly range in the *canzoniere*, against which the *canzoni* will stand out as individual statements which can be related to points in the total development traced by the sonnets. The chronological order of most of the pre-conversion poems is unknown,[10] and if there is any order at all it will have to be deduced from internal evidence. Though there is a risk of imposing a trajectory on the mysterious processes of thought,[11] I am led to my interpretation by what seems to be a development in the early poems towards the authorial voice which characterizes the later poems; and by the need to offer some insight into many poems which escape the anthologies and which, to my knowledge, have not been studied in the context guaranteed them by the best manuscript sources.

Over and above the narrow thematic range which defines the boundaries of his narrative cycles, Guittone uses several linking devices to ensure continuity and forward movement within each group. At certain points he refers to the previous or following sonnets to give them a coherence and perspective they lack as individual poems. The opening *quartina* of s. 12 refers to the six or seven sonnets of complaint against the cruelty of love which open the first cycle. In the opening lines of s. 21 he recapitulates the promise of love he made in ss. 19 and 20. Sonnet 49 marks the end of the *tenzone* in the third cycle and introduces a new episode in the story. These are only a few examples, but they suggest that Guittone uses a narrative technique and that it centres on points of climax within each family, which give an undulating line to each story rather than a steady, forward progression. A closely-related device is his use of past verbs to recapitulate the action and to provide a springboard for the next movement. The past verbs in the opening *quartina* of s. 50 summarize the *tenzone*, ss. 37–49, and lead down into a series of complaint/abuse sonnets. In a similar way the past verb 'so stato' at the outset of s. 19 puts a new complexion on the first cycle (ss. 1–18), as if its serious protestations had been false. Close attention to the change in verb tense will reveal Guittone's awareness of the temporal unity of each cycle, the moments of stasis, and the likely new turn of events. At other events within each cycle there is an obvious continuity of movement from sonnet to sonnet, as between ss. 12 and 13, 20 and 21, and 36 and 37; a continuity occasionally underlined by a verbal echo of the *coblas capfinidas* type, as between ss. 9 and 10. These devices are more noticeable in the unwieldy third cycle. They serve to string the episodes together and keep the eye roving back over the earlier twists in the narrative line. Sonnet 62, which comes early in a fresh impulse of 'gioia', consciously matches s. 54, which lists in *plazer* form the lover's disillusionment with love. Sonnet 76, which echoes the incipit of s. 72, 'gioia amorosa amor', seems in that recapitulation to round off the 'lontananza' motif explored in ss. 72–5.

These devices within the poems themselves tend to confirm the order of sonnets within each cycle as given by the two manuscripts. I shall support them with many observations on the shifting nature of the author-persona identity within each cycle and from cycle to cycle, and shall suggest that Guittone's narrative experiments were more serious and self-conscious than the mere grouping of thematically related poems could ever show. They are Guittone's attempt to identify the traditional voice of the love lyric with his own, through the cumulative effect of a consistent persona identifiable throughout a given series of extended situations (the story of each cycle) which, by interlacing and self-reflecting devices, creates the illusion of personal biography. If we look at the narrative as a coherent theme *and* a consistent first-person protagonist, we shall see that whenever the narrative line changes direction or tone, the tension between Guittone's inherited language and his private vision of courtly values becomes acute, and threatens a breakdown in the carefully fostered illusion of identity between the poet and his persona.

THE FIRST NARRATIVE CYCLE, ss. 1–18

The one narrative development in the first cycle, a sudden and complete change from 'woe to weal' which takes place halfway on, reveals the essential problem of creating a lyric 'story' out of the sentimental polarity of joy and fear in courtly lyric literature. As a narrative the cycle develops by repeating the two classic sentiments of the serving lover, and it sets the pattern of naive *fin' amors* idealism by which the other cycles will be judged. The salient features of that pattern are Guittone's presentation of 'Amore' and the lady, and the kind of language he uses.

The lover speaks from within a given situation, in this case unfavourable at the outset. When not addressing himself alternately to 'Amore' or to his lady, he is locked in an inner monologue of self-encouragement. 'Amore', though he is only vaguely personified as the Ovidian deity, plays the standard part given him in high courtly literature. He rules the lover's physical, emotional and intellectual life, dispensing the passion of love as he wills and deciding when that love should be, or seem to be, reciprocated:

> Spessamente lo chiamo e dico: Amore,
> chi t'ha dato di me tal segnoraggio,
> ch'hai conquiso meo senno e meo valore?   s. 1, 9–11

[Often I call him saying, 'Love, who has given you such power over me that you have taken possession of my wisdom and my inner strength'?]

> che for m'hai miso di mia possessione,
> e messo in quella de la donna mia,
> e sempre mi combatti onne stagione.   s. 2, 3–5

[for you have dispossessed me of myself and given me over to my lady, and you keep warring against me endlessly.]

> Pietá di me, per Dio, vi prenda, Amore,
> poi sí m'avete forte innaverato;
> da me parte la vita a gran dolore,
> se per tempo da voi non sono atato   s. 8, 1–4

[For God's sake take pity on me, Love, since you have severely wounded me: if I am not soon helped by you my life will slip away with much pain.]

'Madonna' remains a shadowy figure, the butt of an intense and balletic play of emotions on the lover's side. She is his unseen mover, 'orgogliosa e fera', who may grow 'dolze e pietosa' if he persists in his service and in his plea for 'merzé':

> Spietata donna e fera, ora te prenda
> di me cordoglio, poi morir mi vedi;
> che tanta pietá di te discenda,
> che 'n alcuna misura meve fidi.   s. 3, 1–4

[Cruel and pitiless lady, take pity on me since you see me dying. May such mercy flow down from you as will in part revive me.]

> E tutto ciò non cangia in lei talento,
> ma sempre sí n'avanza il fero orgoglio;
> ed eo di lei amar però non pento.   s. 6, 12–14

[But none of this has any effect on her will; rather, it only hardens her cruel pride all the more. In spite of this I don't regret loving her.]

> E la merzé, ch'ognor per me si grida,
> de dolze e de pietosa umilitate,
> piacciavi l'orgoglio vostro conquida.   s. 8, 12–14

[May the pity that comes from sweet and kindly gentleness, and which I keep on crying out for, conquer your hard heart.]

> Ed eo lo provo per la donna mia,
> ch'è fatta ben piú d'ogne altra pietosa
> de piú crudel che mai fosse, ni sia   s. 11, 9–11

[And I have experienced this in my lady who, from being the most cruel imaginable, has become more kindly than any other lady.]

And just as Guittone assigns to 'Amore' and 'madonna' their traditional and characteristic roles in what is formal, derivative courtly verse, so he writes that verse in an equally traditional and 'archaic' manner.

These early sonnets are a mine of rhetorical figures,[12] but their syntax is on the whole straightforward and the *ornatus* is *facilis* rather than *difficilis*.[13] Especially noteworthy as typical of writing based on troubadour models are the endemic constructions for synonym and repetition,[14] and the nominal *conversiones* which can give a calm stateliness to what is often a sentiment of anguish.[15] Tied to this construction, which is essential to the troubadour concept of courtly ideals and a *forma mentis*,[16] is the phraseology which the earliest Italian poets took over from Provençal and Old French lyric and which gives an archaic patina to entire sonnets in this earliest expression of Guittone's 'prima maniera'.[17]

In spite of the formulaic and make-weight style of Guittone's inherited diction (which he will have seen as the style fitting his persona's situation), and in spite of a certain staccato quality which comes from obvious matching or separation of *quartine* and *terzine*,[18] Guittone presents his persona 'straight', committed to an experience of courtly love. His persona is unself-conscious in his pursuit of the *fin' amors* male ideals; he is at once the hero and the chronicler of the events related in the poems. It is the lover's constant and unmitigated introspection which turns this chain of sonnets into an embryonic *storia animae*:

> Fero dolore e crudel pena e dura,
> ched eo soffersi en coralmente amare,
> menòmi assai sovente in dismisura,
> e mi fece de voi, donna, sparlare. s. 12, 1–4

[The harsh pain and the bitter suffering that I experienced from loving with all my heart often led me into indiscretion and made me abuse you, my lady.]

> Ben l'ha en podere e la ten conoscenza,
> com'eo giá dissi, la madonna mia,
> che, senza chieder lei ciò che m'agenza,
> m'ave donato e miso me en balia. s. 18, 1–4

[Wisdom truly governs my lady and guides her, as I said before, for without being asked she has given me my delight and put me under her sway.]

Yet there are signs in this first cycle that Guittone baulked at the troubadour assumption that the poet spoke 'as if' he were the persona of his poem. Several sonnets amount to authorial asides on the biographical quality of the poems that surround them, and give the impression that Guittone, temporarily detached from the sentimental experience he is describing, passes judgement on his suffering and rejoicing lover. These asides reflect the real world of non-courtly ethics[19] and foreshadow the rationalizing and quasi-logic of Guittone's later manner. In them he seeks to strengthen the lover's resolve and straighten his conduct, as if to overcome the stumbling-blocks that had kept literary lovers on their long-suffering knees for more than a century. At the same time what will be seen to be authorial incursions into an ideal and closed biography suggest that the persona, as passed on to Guittone by the Provençal/Sicilian tradition, was not on his own a sufficiently clear spokesman for Guittone's questioning restatement of the *fin' amors* lyric ideal.

Early in the cycle, s. 5 introduces non-courtly elements which affect the intensity of first-person narrative. The sonnet comes between two mildly contorted poems on the familiar motif of the contrast between the lover's dogged devotion and the lady's harsh disregard—both of them sonnets of self-encouragement where the 'io' is locked in self-communing discourse:

> Malgrado vostro e mio son benvogliente,
> e serò, ché non posso unque altro fare s. 4, 12–13

[In spite of your reaction and my hurt feelings I still love you, and I'll continue to do so because I can't do otherwise]

> Ch'eo l'ho servita a tutto 'l me podere,
> e 'n chererli mercé giá no alento s. 6, 5–6

[For I have served her to the limit of my powers and I never cease to implore her pity.]

The form of s. 5, a strict balance between general principles and their particular application, interposes a distance between the persona of the poem and his sentimental condition:[20]

> Ahi! con mi dol vedere omo valente
> star misagiato e povero d'avere,
> e lo malvagio e vile esser manente,
> regnare a benenanza ed a piacere;
>   e donna pro cortese e canoscente
> ch'è laida sí, che vive in dispiacere;
> e quella ch'ha bieltá dolze e piagente,
> villana ed orgogliosa for savere.
>   Ma lo dolor di voi, donna, m'amorta,
> ché bella e fella assai piú ch'altra sete,
> e piú di voi mi ten prode e dannaggio.
>   Oh, che mal aggia il die che voi fu porta
> si gran bieltá, ch'altrui ne confondete,
> tanto è duro e fellon vostro coraggio!   s. 5, 1–14

[Ah, how I suffer when I see a man of worth discomforted and deprived of possessions while the evil and base man is rich, living in comfort and pleasure. And I suffer when I see a worthy, gracious and intelligent woman remain un-courted just because she is ugly, while the one with charming beauty is unbelievably base and arrogant. But the suffering I feel in your regard, lady, is mortal because you are more beautiful and more cruel than any other lady, and what concerns me most is the good and the harm that come from you. O, cursed be the day that such great beauty was bestowed on you, for your heart is so hard and cruel that you torment others with it!]

Guittone sets out to combine general ethical considerations (lines 1–8) with a first-person complaint against 'madonna'. To offset the sonnet's natural tendency to remain a mixture of two separate styles of address, one in the *quartine*, the other in the *terzine*, he attempts to give the ideas a coherent inner growth. The second *quartina* matches the first in reverse order[21] and pulls the opening mercantile image (a contrast between worth and material possessions) on to a plane of courtly social behaviour (a contrast between physical appearance and inner disposition), from which the lover can apply that abstract state of affairs to *his* lady. If the 'donna ch'ha bieltá' can be 'villana ed orgogliosa', it is only a simple transition to 'voi, donna, sete bella e fella'.

In several details of construction Guittone shows how he tried to tighten the sonnet as it moved towards a conventional closing curse on 'madonna's' bewitching beauty. The paratactic 'e' with which the second *quartina* begins (line 5), suggests that 'donna' and 'omo' are weighed on the same pair of scales.[22] The second *quartina* balances the first and highlights Guittone's negative statement of ideal conduct in both the man and the lady.[23] But by the second *quartina* emphasis has shifted from material possessions to sentimental attitudes. The strongly adversative 'ma' of line 9 accentuates a fluent and logical application of general principles to his particular case. The paired contrasts, 'bella-fella', 'prode-dannaggio' of lines 10–11 echo and condense, in reverse order, the key qualities of the *quartine*. By comparative progression his lady (line 10) is *more* beautiful and *more* harsh than the standard lady in lines 7–8; his profit and loss in her regard (line 11) is greater than that of the standard man in lines 2–4. The two *quartine* find their climax and synthesis in lines 10–11.[24]

Yet these linking devices and the binomial formulae scattered throughout the sonnet, [25] which give it the look of archaic homogeneity, fail to conceal the non-courtly bluntness of the opening *quartina*. It could be argued that those lines denounce the way things are in real society — the contemporary urban commune where only the 'fellon' prospers — and echo a key idea in the Guelph anti-feudal polemic, that inner worth ('valore') merits material reward and that wealth can be won only by the truly worthy. As a logical appeal to a practical order of merit it has little in common with a courtly and literary ideal where 'valere' is always the sign and guarantee of respectable social and amatory *mores* — and not of profit and loss. To lay down an ethico-mercantile principle as model for the lover's behaviour and as touchstone of the accord between female grace, worth and beauty, is to question the courtly social ethos. In earlier days a woman could have been beautiful and pitiless — bad luck, one just whined and cursed as the lover does at the end of this sonnet. But to suggest that inner worth (line 5) can reside in an ugly subject (line 6)[26] and that ignorance of that hidden worth, or the lady's flaunting of her physical appeal, are wrong on the analogy that material wealth is *not* an index of inner worth in the possessor, seems to me an example of Guittone's pragmatism at odds with the sentimental values his persona should be upholding at this stage.[27]

In the context of the first sonnet cycle Guittone probably meant to do no more than apply to his lover's case the evident disparity between appearance and reality, between merit and reward. The lover's worth goes unseen; the lady is lovely but hard. Yet Guittone seems in this sonnet unaware of the strength and breadth of his analogies, which are more sweeping than he needs for his example. The analogy is too objective and 'modern' to be the observation of the archaic lover himself. In this sense the 'mi' of 'con mi dol vedere' (line 1 — an incipit that anticipates 'opening' reflections in the later poetry),[28] is the 'mi' of Guittone as *author*, and not the persona 'mi' of 'm'amorta' (line 9). What the lover has on his mind (lines 9–11) would prevent him worrying about the 'malvagio manente' and the 'donna cortese ch'è laida', who are real figures outside the framework of courtly ideals.[29] The didactic *exempla* of the *quartine* betray Guittone's private concern for values outside those pertinent to the event described in the first *terzina*, and for a moment they shatter in their realism the poet's illusion of courtly biography.

In s. 5 Guittone gives a hint of his difficulty in pitching the courtly tone exactly. This gives way quickly to the safe and familiar lover's complaint which within five sonnets works its way round to the antithetical moment, the lady's response and the lover's 'gioia'. But before that resolution of grief into joy, the lover's anguish reaches a climax in s. 9 and for the first and only time in this cycle Guittone breaks into the halting metre of a sonnet with internal rhyme:

> Se Deo — m'aiuti, amor, peccato fate,
> se v'allegrate — de lo male meo:
> com'eo — piú cher merzé, piú mi sdegnate;
> e non trovate, — amor, perché, per Deo!...
> Tegno eo — tanto ch'eo merzé trovasse,
> che mai non fasse — piú per me, de fede,
> che dir: merzede, — amor, merzé, merzene!   s. 9, 1–4, 12–14

[As I hope for God's mercy, love, it is wrong of you to rejoice at my misfortunes. The more I beg your pity the more you scorn me, and, by God, you have no reason to do so, love!... I am so obsessed with finding pity that I do nothing, I swear, except cry: 'have pity, love, pity, pity!]

The *rimalmezzo* is not a random exercise but the turning point in the first cycle. The dolorous commonplaces in the preceding sonnets are here compressed into a tense and bewildered cry by a religious devotee. Yet the lines are broken after the third and fifth syllable with a formal mastery that foreshadows an immediate change in the lover's case. This is Guittone's first attempt to enter the story by stylistic means alone. It is as if he were breaking the lover's knot by a show of force, and it is a clear sign that his technical virtuosity is not haphazard but is applied for precise effects and at calculated moments. When the final cry is taken up at the beginning of the next sonnet, and the taut repetition has subsided into a narrative link-line, the crisis is over, and after two religious celebrations of the power of 'merzé', in ss. 10 and 11, the lover contrasts past with present experience and seems to anticipate in a lower key, and from within the courtly framework, his literary self-criticism in the conversion poems:[30]

> Fero dolore e crudel pena e dura,
> ched eo soffersi en coralmente amare,
> menòmi assai sovente in dismisura,
> e mi fece de voi, donna, sparlare.
> Or che meo senno regna 'n sua natura
> sí, che dal ver so la menzogna strare,
> conosco che non ment'om ni pergiura
> piú ch'eo feci onni fiata 'n voi biasmare,
> Ché non vive alcun che tanto vaglia,
> dicesse che 'n voi manchi alcuna cosa,
> ch'eo vincer nond'el credesse in battaglia.
> Non fo natura in voi poderosa,
> ma Deo pensatamente, u' non è faglia,
> vi fe', com fece Adamo e sua sposa.   s. 12, 1–14

[The harsh pain and the bitter suffering that I experienced from loving with all my heart often led me into indiscretion and made me abuse you, lady. Now that I have returned to my senses, so that I can tell a lie from the truth, I acknowledge that no-one lies or perjures himself more than I did whenever I criticized you. For there isn't a man alive so strong that I wouldn't be confident of defeating him in battle if he said that you were imperfect. Nature played no part in your creation. Instead, God, whose intention cannot err, created you directly, the way He made Adam and his spouse.]

When the persona reproaches himself as poet (lines 3–4, 7–8), he sets the contrasting moments of anguish and joy into a narrative perspective.[31] There can be no doubt that the sentiments of the preceding sonnets were uttered earlier in time, that one led to the other, and that the persona is responsible, as poet, for his own utterance. As a self-critical stance it has its counterpart in the palinodes which identify past poet with past persona,[32] yet the difference in depth is obvious. In the later *canzoni* the self-aware convert-poet was to confess as his 'follor' *all* the writing in which he, as poet-protagonist, was subject to 'madonna's' scorn and favour. In this sonnet, 'dismisura' (line 3) is the excess of language to which she drove the 'unself-conscious' lover-poet. Here, the persona speaks from within a courtly fiction with pretensions to narrative depth; there, Guittone gives that fiction a moral dimension because he judges it as an outsider.

At the end of this unwitting anticipation of later conversion there are signs that Guittone does question the identity between persona and poet affirmed in the *quartine*. To compensate for his past 'sparlare' and 'biasmare',[33] the lover makes the bold claim that her creation was willed directly by God without natural mediation, 'the way He made Adam and his wife' (lines 12–14). This could pass for pre-stilnovist praise of 'madonna's' angelic nature; yet the simple comparison[34] is closer to the scriptural defence of womankind in c. xx, lines 61–8, where Guittone attacks cynical male exploitation of the role fixed for ladies by courtly literature. It also suggests an early variation on the defence of female chastity in c. xlix, lines 21–7, where he claims that women can make good the harm done by Eve. In s. 5 Guittone broke his spell by evincing a more modern and ethical awareness than the situation allowed. Here, his religious hyperbole foreshadows a later concern for the *equality* of man and woman before God, and, with it, a practical respect for real women outside the paragon context set for them by literature. It is as if his need for a climax of praise — one *terzina* that will make up for all the scorn that the lover had heaped on his lady — makes Guittone forget the lover's restricted situation and limited formulae, both of which he *does* recall in the chivalric challenge in the first *terzina*, lines 9–11. If the final pious comparison (line 14) has a decidedly non-courtly ring,[35] it is because a domestic and 'bourgeois' statement is ludicrous on the lips of a *fin' amors* lover.

These two examples of tonal discord within a sonnet may betray only a lapse of narrative coherence or the unconscious intrusion of ideas that were to mature in Guittone's later writing. Yet they point to his recurring uneasiness with the limited conceptual and vocal range[36] of the courtly 'io', as if he would broaden and deepen the lover's experience with more realistic insights, and root the lover's sentiment into the firmer soil of non-courtly principles.

The lover's self-criticism in s. 12, which orders the previous eleven sonnets into a loose narrative with one simple change of direction, effectively blocks any further change in the story line. In this early experiment, marked by its simple vision of the bare essentials, there are only two alternatives — the lover's woe ('donna orgogliosa') or weal ('donna pietosa').[37] Once the lover-poet has recognized her acceptance of him in ss. 10, 11 and 12, praise can only repeat itself and the story loses momentum. So when Guittone experiments with the persona's stance, and shifts, in the short compass of three sonnets, ss. 11 to 13, from unself-conscious monologue to literary self-criticism and then to didacticism, he seeks at this point of stasis in the story line to extend the narrative in a way that is more natural and 'honest' for him than pseudo-biographical discourse.[38] The immediate effect of the two changes of stance (from ss. 11 to 12, and from ss. 12 to 13) is a progressive withdrawal from immersion in the emotionally turbulent event to a serene and reflective detachment from it, which Guittone makes up for by an even purer courtly idealism than in the narrative sonnets. The didactic mode triumphs in the six sonnets that follow s. 12, and apart from several nagging references to his own experience as a guarantee of his teaching,[39] and an echo of s. 16 in s. 18,[40] the narrative line all but disappears. What takes its place is an enlightened courtly male self-interest, couched as advice to other lovers:

> Ho da la donna mia in comandamento,
> ch'eo reconforti onni bon servidore,
> ched è disconfortato ed ha tormento,
> perché inver lui sua donna ha fero core   s. 13, 1–4

[I have been ordered by my lady to reassure every loyal lover who is troubled and suffers because his lady is hard-hearted towards him]

> Donque chi vol d'amor sempre gioire
> conven ch'entenda in donna de valore,
> ché 'n pover loco om non po aricchire.   s. 18, 12–14

[Therefore the man who wants always to rejoice in love should pursue a woman of worth, for a man cannot draw riches from where there is poverty.]

The teaching fiercely upholds 'madonna's' paramount place, is suitably feudal in its heavy use of the master-servant analogy, and is properly archaic in its 'provenzaleggiante' diction.[41] A first reaction to this change may be worth noting down. If the speaking voice seems suddenly at ease,[42] it may not be so much because the persona's problems are over but because Guittone is particularly sure of his words and style when teaching others. The speaker's complete trust in the viability of the best male virtues *because they have worked*,[43] seems to me the most glaring effect of Guittone's personal pragmatism on his inherited literary taste. The *fin' amors* lover locked in his experience was never satisfied with himself — *amorosus semper est timorosus* — and was always ready to launch into self-reproach. Should a change of stance do away with that saving diffidence?[44]

The colour of pastiche given by the addition of a group of teaching sonnets to a rounded if limited sentimental experience, and the uneasy extension of the narrative line, can be verified in detail. The logic in Guittone's didactic celebration of courtly service, and its self-contained certainty,[45] work against his attempt to make the lover-cum-poet also pass for teacher, because they work against that narrative coherence in which Guittone might have found a suitably versatile persona for his own voice. Just as the modern awareness in s. 5, lines 1–8, clashed with the more limited conceptual possibilities open to the courtly lover, so the feudal teaching in ss. 13–18 clashes with the events as already outlined in the previous poems. A few details will make this clear.

When in s. 13, lines 9–11, the lover-turned-teacher takes for granted the unfailing power of 'amore', 'servir'[46] and so on, he forgets that according to s. 12 *he* was the scorned suppliant of ss. 5, 6, 7 and 8, and that at that stage in his story those virtues were of no avail:

> Ch'eo l'ho servita a tutto 'l me podere . . .
>
> E non mi val; und'eo tormento e doglio   s. 6, 5, 9

[For I have served her to the limit of my powers . . . to no avail; this is why I suffer and grieve.]

The discretion and reserve he demands of a true servant in ss. 15, lines 5–6, and 17, lines 12–14, ought to have sounded inconsistent to Guittone after his clamorous appeals for mercy elsewhere (s. 2, lines 1–4, s. 8, lines 1–4, and especially s. 9, line 14, and s. 10, line 1) — inconsistent, that is, if he saw a natural continuity from lover to teacher in the same narrative cycle.[47] Praise of the lady's initiative, in s. 18, lines 3–4, reads strangely after the lover's conscious application of 'umiltá' to break her 'orgoglio', in s. 10, lines 9–14. The *quartine* of s. 14, which not only repeat the classical equation between madonna's 'bellezza' and 'saggezza' but deride the man who desires a 'donna laida o vil',[48] show just how unsentimental and non-courtly are the lines in s. 5 where the 'donna laida e cortese' stands as a reproach to the blindness brought on by the *fin' amors* pursuit of beauty at all costs.[49]

One could object that it is futile to seek narrative cohesion in a teaching genre, yet the opening *quartina* of s. 13 makes it clear that Guittone was setting the narrative on precisely that new course:

> Ho da la donna mia in comandamento,
> ch'eo reconforti onni bon servidore,
> ched è disconfortato ed ha tormento,
> perché inver lui sua donna ha fero core   s. 13, 1–4

[I have been ordered by my lady to reassure every loyal lover who is troubled
and suffers because his lady is hard-hearted towards him.]

The discrepancies in narrative consistency which I have touched on merely
point to a more fundamental problem already outlined, namely of finding in a
restricted number of stances or modes of delivery a convincing and sustained
identity of voice with the first-person protagonist. Narrative, or at least the
superficial linkage that gives an impression of continuity to thematically related
single poems, which passes for narrative in Guittone's earliest sonnets, is difficult
because the troubadour models which embody his inherited notions of lyric
literature[50] are occasional poems, each one separate and self-contained and,
within certain ritual limits, capable of endless variation — 'un dramma che
non conosce scioglimento'. The situations are given and defined by genre
traditions. They are not open to change by Guittone's personal pragmatism,
which only succeeds in opening a gap between author and persona whenever
and however it enters a poem. The narrative shortcomings of the first cycle
suggest that at the beginning of his 'prima maniera' Guittone was able to cope
with only one variation of the sentimental range and that, once he had exhausted
its possibilities, teaching was the only course left to him, in the absence of
stylistic and lexical resources which had yet to find expression in the sonnets.
The didactic and priestly role may be the reverse side of the devotee's experience
in occasional lyrics,[51] but it destroys a narrative illusion because it presumes a
vantage point remote from the 'experience' which the narrative seeks to create
— so remote that the confident maxims of courtly teaching contradict at every
turn the restless and uncertain history of the lover this teacher is supposed to
have been.

There is, however, another side to this group of teaching sonnets which is
worth noting now for what follows. It is in germ an *ars amandi* and foreshadows
the *ars amandi* proper which is probably Guittone's last extended experiment
with the sonnet before the conversion poems. Although in these early 'insegnamenti' he does not invoke Andreas Capellanus, there are already signs of that
male solidarity and self-satisfaction which characterize the later work, though
as yet no cynical exploitation of female complicity. Here the lover's desire to
teach is dictated by the lady and he shares his experience to comfort his peers,
sufferers like himself. In the later *ars amandi* he will set himself up to enlighten
the less well-informed as a self-appointed expert in theory and practice; and
his protestations of modesty at the end of that treatise will serve to underline
his academic grasp of the subject and his superiority over his pupils. The courtly
teaching poems are, in turn, the forebears of those later sermons to ladies, such
as c. xlix and ss. 151, 152, in which Guittone will demonstrate supreme confidence in the male prerogative to interpret another morality. The serene
didacticism which marks his later work is not absent from his earliest poems, and

it is a sign of that seriousness and consistency which marks his whole production and makes up for the incidental mistakes and failures in his early narrative experiments.

THE SECOND NARRATIVE CYCLE, ss. 19–30

Clearly, Guittone was not satisfied with his first experiment; and it seems more significant that s. 19 resumes the first-person narrative stance discontinued since s. 12, than that the theme should change from 'amore corrisposto' to 'lealtà in amore'. The change of motif and the resumption of inward discourse would seem to signify a fresh attack on the narrative problem. Guittone commits the persona once more to the harsh experience of *fin' amors*, and once again he presents him as uncritical of the code and immersed in his monologue. However, s. 19 reveals a lover more critical of *himself* at that point than at any moment in the first cycle, and this calls for some comment. We saw that s. 12 drew the earlier sonnets into a 'narrative' of blame and praise, and I suggested that the lover-poet stance in that sonnet represented a middle stage of self-awareness in Guittone's movement from monologue to teaching. Sonnet 12 was an embryonic phase in that self-criticism which, in the conversion manifestoes, fixes *all* the courtly poetry in its baleful stare. Compared with his self-reproach for verbal 'dismisura' in s. 12, the persona's confession in s. 19 looks decidedly moral, and closer in spirit to that of the conversion poems:[52]

> Sí como ciascun omo, enfingitore
> e, ora, maggiormente assai ch'amante
> so stato ver di lei, di bieltá fiore;
> e tanto giuto ei so dietro e davante
>   con prego e con mercé e con clamore,
> facendo di perfetto amor sembiante,
> che me promise loco en su' dolzore
> adesso che lei fusse benestante.
>   Eo, pensando la mia gran malvagia,
> e la gran fede in lei dolce e pietosa,
> sí piansi di pietá, per fede mia;
>   e fermai me di lei non prender cosa
> alcuna mai, senza mertarla pria,
> avendo forte e ben l'alma amorosa.   s. 19, 1–14

[Just as every man nowadays is much more a deceiver than a lover, so have I been towards her, the flower of beauty, and I so importuned her from every direction with clamorous entreaties and supplications, that she promised me a place in her affections as soon as she found herself well disposed. Reflecting on my deep deceit and on her unsuspecting trust, sweet and compassionate as she is, I wept tears of compunction, I swear it, and I resolved never to take anything from her without first deserving it by having a heart steadfastly and truly full of love.]

In this new beginning the lover brands as deceitful the 'perfetto amor' he displayed in the first cycle.[53] This backward glance places the experience of ss. 1–18 as an earlier and more innocent phase and betrays a sense of the reality beneath courtly euphemism which was nowhere present in the first cycle. Now, no man is sincere when it comes to the hallowed language of praise and entreaty (lines 4–5).[54] If this is an attack on the male abuse of the courtly code it is a remarkable confession considering that Guittone was only at the beginning of his disengagement from high *fin' amors* idealism; and it foreshadows the exploitation of female gullibility he will teach in the *ars amandi* sonnets. The change from complacent teaching (s. 18) back to first-person monologue, is achieved by an exaggerated self-reproach which now enables the lover to pursue *fin' amors* afresh, as if he were starting from scratch.[55] Self-reproach is a potent marshalling element in Guittone's narrative structures, as the conversion poems have shown. Sonnet 19 is to the first cycle what s. 12 is to the sonnets that precede it and what c. xxv will be to the entire body of courtly poetry. And s. 19 hints at a later and deeper identity between moral sensibility (the poet's) and the persona's 'fatti d'amore'.

An outline of the movement in ss. 19–30 will show how in the second experiment Guittone stretched the limbs of his narrative out of their given, cramped position. After a fresh start, ss. 19, 20, which wins at once a token promise of reward, s. 20, lines 12–14,[56] the lover drops into familiar hyperbole of self-dedication, s. 21. He seeks to enter Love's service and 'madonna's' favour as if for the first time,[57] vaunting his chances against the failure of others in ss. 22, 23 and 24:[58]

> cioè l'amor, ch'ogni om ch'el signoria
> guaimenta e dice che per lui si more,
> e pur se pena di trovare via
> como de sé islocar possa lo core.
>
> Ed eo pur peno di condurlo a mene
> e di venir de sua corte servente   s. 24, 5–10

[that is, love; for every man whom it masters laments and says he is dying because of it, and does nothing but torment himself to find a way of removing his heart from its control. Yet I do nothing but try to draw it to myself and to become a retainer at its court.]

He then resigns himself to a failure, s. 24, lines 12–14, which at once reflects on his poetic worth:

> Ben saccio de vertà che 'l meo trovare
> val poco, e ha ragion de men valere,
> poi ch'eo non posso in quel loco intrare
> ch'adorna l'om de gioia e de savere.   s. 25, 1–4[59]

[I am fully aware that my poetry is of little account and by rights should be worth even less, because I cannot enter that place which graces a man with joy and wisdom.]

As in s. 12, where the lover's reflection on his role as poet signalled a staging point in the first experiment, so now the lover-poet draws away from the static and hopeless state outlined in his downward plunge from s. 19 to s. 24, and after one last stab at winning Love's mercy (ss. 26–7), he moves outwards to a public appeal (ss. 28–30) in which the persona-poet is now unequivocally Guittone himself.[60]

The pattern of growth resembles that in the first cycle, but it would be rash without a closer look at the evidence to presume that Guittone's answers and possible mistakes will be the same as before. Now, the initial degree of self-awareness is deeper; the situation is, if anything, more limited; the style is a little more varied; and the rounding off of the experiment more dramatic. However, we can expect the weak or uncertain spots to show up as discords of tone and logic, and we must fix our attention on those sensitive areas to build up the emerging picture of Guittone at grips with his early persona.

The knowing start might lead us to expect a new spirit of self-searching vis-à-vis 'perfetto amore', reflected throughout this short sequence. What do we find? 'Madonna's' reported acceptance of the lover at the end of s. 20 obliges him to resume the correct postures of self-reproach and self-encouragement:

> Ed ella disse me che 'n mia possanza
> s'era sí misa, che, s'ormai vetasse
> lo meo piacer, li torneria 'n pesanza.   s. 20, 12–14

[But she replied that she had already committed herself to me and that if she were now to refuse my wishes it would weigh heavily on her.]

> Ma tuttavia l'amor quasi è neente
> ver quel ch'eo so ch'ad amare convene,
> che prendere e donar vol giustamente.
> Ma, como in ferro piú che 'n cera tene
> e val entaglia, varrá similmente
> amor, ch'è 'n me piú che 'n altro servene.   s. 21, 9–14

[Nevertheless my love is almost nothing compared with what I acknowledge to be necessary for a love that wishes to take and give merely what belongs to it by right. Yet, just as an incision is more lasting in metal than in wax, so will that love be, which is more sincere in me than in others.]

When he does recall the less sentimental behaviour of other men, in the *terzine* of s. 22,[61] he rejects their worldly wisdom for a waiting game which is in line with his desire in s. 19 to wipe the slate clean — though it does smack of the male complacency of ss. 14–18. So far so good. But in the next three sonnets one senses that by deliberately trying to bypass the common harsh experience and by turning his persona head-on to the most demanding ideals of love service, Guittone lost sight of that male resourcefulness and its implied degree of sophistication which had been his starting point and term of reference:[62]

> che m'è dolor mortal vedere amare
> piacent'omo talor donna non bella,
> e non amerá lui, ma le dispare;
>   e trovo me che non guari amo quella
> che m'ama forte e che piacente pare
> in tutte cose ove bieltá s'apella.   s. 23, 9–14

[for it pains me deeply to see a handsome man love a plain woman, as sometimes happens, and her not love him but, rather, dislike him; whereas, I find that I simply cannot love the one who loves me passionately and is so gracious wherever beauty is invoked.]

> Ahi Deo, chi vidde mai tal malatia
> di quella che sorpreso hame lo core?
> ché la cosa ch'altrui par venen sia
> è sola medicina al meo dolore   s. 24, 1–4

[Ah God, whoever saw a sickness like the one that has overtaken my heart? Yet the only cure for my pains is that which to others seems poison.]

What began as the persona's experience coloured by Guittone's moral sensibility, becomes a struggle to master the traditional literary experience of suffering in love. The initial subtlety of self-perception, which marked the second experiment as an advance over the first, founders in a trough of conventional despair.

The *terzine* of s. 23 bring to mind ss. 5 and 14. His attitude to the lady is predictably closer to that of s. 14, lines 3–4[63] though in line with the governing sentiment of self-reproach, lines 12–13, which now puts on the lover all the onus for not loving. The 'mortal suffering' he feels comes from an exalted male fidelity to the moral code imposed by *fin' amors*. A man *can* love an ugly woman if she reveals noble inner attributes. Here she is apparently more mindful of the code than he is, for she loves him in spite of his ugliness presumably because she recognizes his virtue. Guittone's instinctive trust in the ideal of female superiority reasserts itself in the *terzine*, which presume a relationship not based on physical attraction. He could have incorporated the insight of s. 5, lines 5–7, into s. 23, lines 9–14, had he retained the more realistic sympathy for women which s. 19 implies. In his will to embrace what is harmful to others (s. 24), other men (lines 5–8) are once more the playthings of love, and not the knowing manipulators they had been in ss. 19, line 3, and s. 22, lines 9–11. By s. 24 the narrative torment of not loving is deadlocked in a dilemma where Guittone plays the persona's hopeless aspirations against the common experience of frustration. The doggedly 'provenzaleggiante' diction in ss. 21–3 (the ideal as narrative reflected in the most archaic style) is offset by a heavy use of adversative particles (the narrative caught in hopeless alternatives). But the line of growth returns in s. 25 — just as it did in s. 12 — when the lover reflects on the worth of his poetry. Yet now there is this difference that where, in ss. 13–18, Guittone broke his narrative deadlock by lifting the lover on to a podium, in ss. 25–30 he invokes the public context of genuine literary correspondence, which gives biographical and hence narrative credence to his exchange with Bandino:

> Ben saccio de vertà che 'l meo trovare
> val poco, e ha ragion de men valere,
> poi ch'eo non posso in quel loco intrare
> ch'adorna l'om de gioia e de savere . . .
>
> per ch'eo rechiamo e chero lo savere
> di ciascun om ch'è prode e canoscente
> a l'aiuto del meo grande spiacere.   s. 25, 1–4, 12–14

[I am fully aware that my poetry is of little account and by rights should be worthless, because I cannot enter that place which graces a man with joy and wisdom . . . For this reason I beg and implore the advice of whoever is upright and wise, to help me in my great affliction.]

The poet's call to all worthy men, 'ciascun om', seems to contradict the opening lines of s. 19. There, men in love had been deceivers and manipulators of the code; yet by s. 24 they are at the mercy of an irresistible force. In s. 22, lines 9–11 other men are *carpe diem* cynics who scoff at his naivety; now, in s. 25, there are trustworthy counsellors at hand who may show him how to enter that place 'ch'adorna l'om de gioia e de savere'. The banal sentiments in s. 25, which I would see as an attempt by Guittone to compensate for narrative break-down, are marked by a particularly heavy use of the make-weight, repetitive style.[64] It is a kind of verbal relapse after the all-out effort in s. 27, where the lover's subtle striving is reflected in the awkward syntax and rare end-rhyme, and which, together with s. 26, logically precedes s. 25:

> ma quant'eo più recheo, lor men pare
> ch'eo presso sia di voi trovar mercee,
> e veggio vo a fedel desiderare
> tal, che non vol, e che v'odia e descree.
>   Donque deritto n'ho, s'eo meraviglio,
> che voglio e deggio e posso esser servente
> e, com'eo sia, m'ingegno e m'asottiglio;
>   e tutto ciò non vale a me neente.   s. 27, 5–12

[but the more I beseech you the further I seem to be from finding compassion in you, and I see that the kind of servant you want is someone who won't long for you, but rather, will despise and mistrust you. Therefore my bewilderment is justified, for I long to serve you — I must and I can — and in spite of my shortcomings I rack my brains to find a way; yet none of this gets me anywhere.]

This slight change of order better serves a steady movement outwards, from s. 25, lines 12–14, to s. 28, lines 1–2, and accentuates the shock effect of the proper name after the vague 'ciascun om' of s. 25, line 13. The deadlocked lover-poet of s. 25 is now Guittone himself. It is clear from the exact summary of the earlier dilemma (ss. 21–4, 26–7) in s. 28, and his desire there to avoid the common dire experience, that Guittone saw the exchange of sonnets as an integral part of the second narrative cycle:

> Mastro Bandino amico, el meo preghero
> vòi ch'entendiate sí ch'a onor vo sia.
> Amare voglio e facemi mistero,
> che non son degno, e'n gran ben n'averria,
>   ché, senza ciò, aver onor no spero;
> e pur d'ennamorar no ho bailia.
> Unde sovente vivonde in pensero,
> ché meraviglia sembrame che sia,
>   vedendo manti stanno innamorati,
> sí che tutt'altro poneno in obbria,
> en tale loco, u 'son sempre isdegnati.
>   Però vo prego m'assenniate via,
> ch'a ciò mi guidi, a guisa de li amati,
> ché credo bene aggiatene bailia.   s. 28, 1–14[65]

[Mastro Bandino, my friend, I want you to answer my plea in such a way as will do you credit. I desire and need to love someone of whom I am not worthy, but I'd achieve much good if I could, for without that love I have no hope of winning honour; yet I am unable to make her fall in love with me, and for this reason I am often distressed. For it seems to me incredible when I see many other men loving, to the exclusion of everything else, women who constantly spurn them. Therefore I beg you to show me the way that will lead me to become like those who are loved, for I am sure that this lies in your power.]

My earlier remarks about levels of self-consciousness point to certain conclusions one can draw from the last three sonnets in the second cycle. I would argue that if Guittone introduces a real correspondence at this point and relates it to the emotional problem explored in the preceding sonnets, he does so to give an illusion of biography to those earlier sonnets. The persona's anguish must be real and must be Guittone's, because now, in his own name, he seeks solace for it from another living poet. The primacy of narrative content, and Guittone's attempt to enter the person of his protagonist, affect the quality of the closing exchange itself, deleting some of the customary formalities and making the letters more lifelike. Guittone's reply (s. 30), is not 'per le rime', and his *captatio benevolentiae* in both sonnets is held to an absolute minimum,[66] both features highlighting the message at the expense of the form. In the last poem of the cycle Guittone folds the real exchange of sonnet-letters back into the persona's story when he makes Bandino's counsel of restraint and secrecy, s. 29, lines 9–14, look like an actual acceptance, by the lady, of the persona's pleas:

> Ormai sta solo e in loco celato,
> e sol bellezza pensa e canoscenza
> de la tua donna, ed altro non pensare.

> D'amor ragiona, se se' accompagnato;
> a le 'tu, o' sta' con ella, gioi né 'ntenza
> tutto cela: sí porai amare.   s. 29, 9–14

[For the meantime avoid company and conceal yourself, and fix your mind on your lady's beauty and wisdom, to the exclusion of other thoughts. If you find yourself in company speak about love; but if you should be with her, hide your joy and love from her completely: this is how you will achieve love.]

> Mastro Bandino, vostr'e d'Amor mercede,
> or aggio ciò che tant'ho disiato,
> sí che lo core meo non se crede
> esser de gioia mai apareggiato,
>   pensando quanto è 'n lui d'Amor fede,
> e quanto è preso el suo servire in grato,
> e qual è quella donna en cui el crede,
> e com'ha pregio 'l suo ben acquistato   s. 30, 1–8

[Mastro Bandino, thanks to you and to Love I now have what I so longed for, and my heart cannot believe that its joy was ever equalled when I consider how my heart now trusts Love and how its service has been so gladly received, and the quality of that lady it is devoted to, and how valuable is the good that it has gained.]

What was sought as advice in s. 28 becomes a way out of the impasse in ss. 21–7 and the lover, now as Guittone himself, can at last return that devotion which the lady admitted in s. 20, lines 12–14.

It will be seen that Guittone handled his second cycle with more originality and expertise than the first. The opening stance is less naive and he breaks the stock dilemma by an attempt to realize and appropriate, in the public terms of a genuine literary correspondence, his persona's 'fatti d'amore'. The sentimental range is as restricted as before and merely reverses, in a different balance of sonnet numbers, the change from 'dolor' to 'gioia'; but the authorial entries are more pronounced and the central static phase looks like a desperate bid to hold on to pure *fin' amors* in the face of creeping cynicism and overt authorial control.

I have noted that both experiments are centred on the stance of the persona as a point of assimilation for Guittone himself. By consciously modulating the interaction of persona and poet with thematic content, Guittone seems to draw the anonymous persona of courtly lyric into his own person, and turns the static and isolated moments of troubadour poetry into simple, biographical narrative. He seems more confident in the second cycle, which is less jerky than the first in linear movement and quite unabashed in Guittone's final claim to biographical identity with the narrative 'I'. Yet both cycles betray conflicts between the poet and his literary inheritance which the narrative fails to resolve; conflicts which break out when the story-line changes direction or intensity and when the biographical claim is explicit. It also seems clear that Guittone's handling of *fin' amors* argument or teaching can provoke serious, if unwitting, authorial criticism of the *fin' amors* code, particularly of the erotic idealisation of the lady.

As experiments the cycles reveal two opposing tendencies in the early stages of Guittone's 'prima maniera'. On the one hand there is a growing detachment from primitive courtly idealism and an increasing awareness of later exploitation of the code. This amounts to the glimmering of an historical perspective of courtly lyric, and is a foretaste of his subsequent disenchantment with the amoral presumptions in that tradition. On the other hand there are germinal signs of an improving technical skill and a greater expressiveness in the 'provenzaleggiante' style, which follows Guittone's more confident self-projection as the persona of his sonnets. It is this latter development which will lead him to a more testing and extended experiment, more complex in its range of ideas, language and style than anything attempted so far. If Guittone switches to a bravura display of *replicatio* in s. 31, he is justified in narrative terms because as author he has just proved his identity with the lover-poet in the most unequivocal fashion. In this way the third cycle follows the second, with the authorial self-consciousness now translated directly into the verbal texture of the poetry. By the same token the dominant word play at the outset of the third cycle gives it the look of a literary programme rather than a narrative of events— a celebration not of 'madonna' nor of love for her but of the incantatory power of 'gioia' and 'noia' to express two contrasting states of soul. We shall see in the next chapter how Guittone proceeded from that dazzling incipit and with what success he conducted his most ambitious narrative experiment.

CHAPTER 4

The third sonnet cycle

In the previous chapter I touched on certain discords of tone and inner logic which seemed to me evidence of Guittone's difficulty in creating convincing biographical narrative, and hinted at his disenchantment with the *fin' amors* tradition. That disenchantment, sporadic and muted though it is in the early cycles, finds expression in a double tension, already noted, which can be restated now because it is endemic to Guittone's entire narrative experiment and leads straight to the third and major cycle.

One tension is set up by Guittone's effort to recapture a primitive courtly idealism in spite of his instinctive objection to its unreality and amorality. Repeated variations on one theme from sonnet to sonnet, and the fresh narrative beginnings of the second and third cycles, argue a dogged will to grasp a core of pure literary sentiment. Guittone relies heavily on the choice of a deliberately archaic language and style and the essential, ideal situation, adversative and testing to the lover. The other tension grows out of a conflict between the persona's ritual veneration of the shadow lady, and Guittone's sympathy for real women seen from within the courtly framework, who become objects of male satisfaction when the code is exploited. These cross-currents will be most violent in the central episode of the third cycle, the *tenzone*, but first we should look at the cycle as a whole to see whether it is a sequence, and if so, whether it shows greater mastery of narrative and an easier authorial assimilation of the persona's voice.

The first two cycles are marked by a simple change from sorrow to joy and neither is long enough to allow a further change of sentiment.[1] The first cycle changes halfway through when the anguished lover wins his lady's 'pietá', and the positive gain is held to the end by a didactic celebration of courtly service. The upward movement springs from the sudden disappearance of her un-provoked cruelty. The second cycle opens with the lady's acceptance (s. 20), which sets the lover longing to merit her favour, his desire being met only in the closing sonnet (s. 30). In both cycles the change follows a moment of climax in the lover's despair — the danger of death, in s. 10, and his hopeless resignation in s. 25.[2] A graph of these movements would show little gradation between high and low points.[3]

The third cycle promises in its opening sonnet to be more complex, and its length of fifty sonnets allows and demands more variety of event than do its predecessors. The six episodes summarised by Margueron[4] presuppose two consistent characters throughout and a familiar basic movement from refusal to acceptance. Yet the cycle is more coherent than the episodes would lead us to believe. The opening 'gioia'–'noia' group, ss. 31–6,[5] alternating between praise and fear, breaks the certainty of his possession of the lady, given in s. 31. This leads to a 'contrasto', ss. 37–49, in which she rejects him. The lover's reproach and self-pity reach rock bottom in the downward plunge of sentiment and produce familiar motions of despair and hope which lead, in s. 59, to the reappearance of the lady and her qualified acceptance. Sonnet 59 acts as a keystone to the whole structure, as will be seen, and allows a forward movement of loosely connected sentiments. Undulations of hope and fear, possession and loss, which alone make Guittone's cycles feasible, are caught and rendered in a chain of traditional genre poems. The lover's praise and joy (ss. 60–2), which follows her invitation in s. 59, is threatened by jealous outsiders (s. 63), recaptured in feudal veneration (s. 64), protected in the 'donna-schermo' motif (ss. 65–6), and vaunted again in 'gioia' hyperbole (ss. 67–8). Sonnet 69 brings in a theme related to the 'malmaritata' complaint, as if their love were threatened by her relatives. In s. 70 he affirms the Guelph principle of inner worth as compensation for his low birth; and in s. 71 the motif of self-mutilation brings back the current of fear and jealousy. 'Lontananza' (ss. 72–5, 80) injects new impetus and generates the self-pity and hope which carries him through s. 76 to the closing virtuoso pieces in which he once more attains the lady.

Compared with the clumsy shifts of persona stance and vocal intensity in the first two cycles,[6] the story line of the third experiment is notable for its richer use of early linguistic resources and for the greater range of its traditional situational genres. The poet's more confident grasp of courtly sentiment goes hand-in-hand with a less ambiguous projection of his own voice through the mouth of his persona. This can be shown in the transition from the second cycle to the third. I noted at the end of the previous chapter how Guittone's sudden intensification of verbal self-consciousness in s. 31 could be read as an effect of his personal assumption of the lover's problem in the correspondence sonnets, ss. 28–30. Guittone is now free to test the expressive possibilities of language without having to show that such language is the persona's. And the persona can set in motion a new cycle of events with a poetic outburst that seems natural to him, and not imposed by the author. In this sense the more artificial *trobar clus* displays of the third cycle express Guittone's increased confidence in his absorption of the archaic manner and, with it, the primitive courtly ideals of that figure who is the centre of events.

Yet this advance on the previous experiments is matched by a much clearer grasp of the moral implications of courtly lyric seen, as Guittone sees it, out of its feudal context. Guittone's reconstruction of the courtly lyric tradition, which at the same time puts that tradition in perspective, begins now to take on a fascinating complexity. By the third cycle we begin to see how each narrative experiment marked a step away from unquestioning acceptance of pure *fin' amors*, towards a total rejection of it in the palinodes. In the first cycle the tradition was taken at face value both for the lover and the lady. It was a naive assay at unsullied sentiment, pared to its kernel and unadventurous in its expressive range. The second cycle began with the knowledge, on his side, that men use the code to deceive women. The woman remained, as in the first cycle, shadow paragon, unseen mover of the lover's inner life, as yet unaware of male cynicism. The whole downward plunge of purification in the second cycle took on the air of reparation to her for his deceit, and compensated for his earlier insincerity. The *tenzone* in the third cycle (ss. 37–49) shows that by now women are aware of the male hypocrisy which the lover had confessed in s. 19. Women can now appeal to the code, and thus stand aside from it, to test the sincerity of the lover's professed altruism. Guittone has come a long way from the archaic unself-consciousness represented by the first cycle, and every later sonnet that returns to naive sentiments will be coloured by the successive hints of disenchantment which Guittone as author scatters through the sonnet families from the beginning. The doubts and criticisms I noted earlier ring out loud and clear in the *tenzone*, which seems to me not simply crucial to the narrative of the third cycle but a crossroads in Guittone's career as courtly poet; and it comes, paradoxically, when his growing mastery of 'onne mainera' — the fuller range of Provençal language, style and themes — first makes itself felt. The *tenzone* calls for closer examination, but since it forms less than a quarter of the cycle and only one link in a chain, it cannot be isolated without violence to the whole structure. Its function and force will stand out as we look more closely at each of those links in turn.

The sonnets that lead to the *tenzone* (ss. 31–6), carry us back to a lost world of primitive *fin' amors* where 'gioia' and 'noia' as motif-words register the myriad fluctuations of the lover's sensibility to a cypher lady, now close, now far away. Once the correct 'tension of distance' has been reset and the vestiges of a situation recalled:[7]

> Oimè, lasso, com'eo moro pensando,
> gioia, di voi ver me fatta noiosa!
> Perch'eo non so veder como né quando
> eo v'affendesse fior d'alcuna cosa.
> Ch'al comenzar, gioiosa gioi, ch'amando
> ve demostrai de me fed'amorosa,
> voi foste dolce ver di me, sembrando
> de darmi gioi in voi sempre gioiosa.   s. 32, 1–8

[Alas, how I suffer when I think that you, joy, have become ill-disposed towards me! For I cannot see how or when I could have offended you in any way whatever. In fact at the beginning, joyful joy, when in my love I showed you my loving trust, you were sweet to me and seemed to give me a joy in you that promised to be always joyful.]

the story line is free to move slowly forward as the lover boosts himself to speak to her:

> (però soffrite ch'eo dicave quello
> che v'è diritto nome, ed è nascoso,
> e che meve non par propio ni bello,
> secondo el fare de voi amoroso)   s. 34, 5–8

[(for this reason bear with me if I call you by a name that is suitable yet preserves your anonymity, even though in my view it is not a true or worthy reflection of your loving deeds)]

> Ahi dolce gioia, amara ad opo meo,
> perché, taipino, ho voi tanto dottare,
> ch'orso non sete, né leon, par Deo,
> ma cosa che no po né sa mal fare?   s. 36, 1–4

[Ah sweet joy, bitter in my regard, why should I be so afraid of you, wretch that I am, for you are no bear nor lion, for heaven's sake, but something incapable of doing harm?]

In this preface to a face-to-face encounter, where the beseeching lover is once again on his knees in classic pose, there are two familiar and recurring notes that are significant for what follows. The first is the lover's request for an appointment, s. 32, 9–11,[8] which is met by the appearance of the lady in person, in s. 38. In a moment she will lose her shadowy reticence and cease to be a mere excuse for a contorted display of emotions on his side. That she will say anything at all is more remarkable than what she will say or how she will say it. Thus, what in courtly lyric is a stock longing ritually denied, becomes, in Guittone's concatenation of genres, a narrative bridge to the *tenzone*, losing some of its banality in retrospect and smoothing the way for a plausible change of tone to the realism of the debate genre.

The other recurring note is the lover's heightened sense of verbal inadequacy, offset by the new confidence Guittone displays in using a rare rhyme coupled with relatively fluid syntax:

> loc 'e stagion donateme sovente,
> ove posso dir ben ciò ch'opo m 'hae,
> ma pur non dico giá, sí son temente;
>   e non dispregio me, ch'amor me 'l fae:
> or, poi sí sete in tutte cose gente,
> datemi 'n ciò argomento e securtae.   s. 34, 9–14

[you have often given me the opportunity to say clearly what I wanted to say, yet I am so nervous that so far I have said nothing. Don't despise me for I am tongue-tied out of love: but now that you are well-disposed in every way prompt me and give me the confidence to speak.]

Such contrasts are frequent enough in modesty figures, but if that forced union of author and persona at the end of the previous cycle helped to explain the

fresh authorial *élan* of s. 31, it seems a tactical blunder to let the persona
indulge in sentiments that betray a lack of confidence — because they open
again a gap between poet and persona which had, in a sense, been closed when
the cycle began. The opening lines of the cycle are echoed in the following sonnet
where the lover seems to have gained the confidence he longed for and breaks
into a renewed cry of joy:

> Gioiosa gioi, sovr'onni gioi gioiva,
> onni altra gioi ver voi noia mi sembra,
> perch'eo n'ho tanto l'anima pensiva,
> che mai de cosa null'altra mi membra,
>   che a vedere como porto o riva
> prender potesse intra le vostre membra,
> poi senza ciò non mi sa bon ch'eo viva,
> tant'a lo cor vostra beltá mi membra.   s. 35, 1–8

[Joyful joy, more radiant than any other joy, all other joy seems to me an
affliction compared with you. Because of you my soul is so brimming over
that I can think of nothing else except how to find a haven between your
thighs*: without that there seems no point in living — this is how your beauty
haunts me.] (* or are the 'membra' in question merely arms?)

Carried away by his eloquence and as yet unchecked by any rejoinder he makes
an alarming admission that strips away all the euphemism of the previous
sonnets. Once his lust is plain the appearance of his unseen lady is both logical
and necessary, and in hindsight we can see that it is imminent. Guittone's
problem at this stage in the cycle, with a *tenzone* on hand, is how to make her
entry seem a feasible development in a cycle that so far has remained a monologue. Part of the trouble in the opening sonnets is the proximity of the assignation motif to the fear-of-speaking motif. The lover cannot speak his mind until
he sees the lady face to face, as he says in s. 33, 12–14 and s. 34, 9–12. To form a
credible part of the narrative sequence the *tenzone* will need to be introduced
by a desire for a meeting: yet that stock desire comes hand-in-hand with its
companion topos, the fear of speaking, which spoils what might have been a
sound mixture of narrative need, archaic sentiment and clear authorial self-
awareness. The blatant eroticism in s. 35, damaging though it is to the lover's
pretensions in our eyes, is a suitable pretext for what will be an encounter with
the spectre of his self-deceit. Yet the lover's suit comes to a climax in s. 37 with
a fine show of male probity, and she will turn on him not as a coarse lecher but
as a smooth seducer:

> Tant 'è lo vostro cor cortese, amico,
> d'amor dolce, pietoso e naturale,
> perch'eo mi riconforto e di dir dico.   s. 36, 12–14

[Your heart is so gentle, kind, lovingly sweet, compassionate and humane
that I take courage and say that I will speak to you.]

Dett'ho de dir: dirò, gioia gioiosa,
e credo piaccia voi darmi odienza;
però ch'omo mentir e dir ver osa,
for prova non abbiate in me credenza:
dico che v'amo sí, ch'ogni altra cosa
odio inver voi di coral malvoglienza,
e no è pena tanto dolorosa,
ch'eo non soffrisse, in far vostra piagenza.
E me e 'l mio, e ciò ch 'i posso e vaglio
dono voi, cui fedel star piú mi piace,
ch'esser de tutto esto mondo amiraglio.
Voglio da voi sol che 'l portiate in pace;
che ciò, pensando, sia, tutto mi squaglio
del gran dolzor, ch'entr'a lo cor mi face.   s. 37, 1–14

[I said I would speak; now I shall, joyful joy, and I am sure you will agree to give me a hearing. And since men dare to lie and to speak the truth indiscriminately, put no trust in me without a trial. I declare that I so love you that, compared to you, I hate everything else with all my heart, and there is no suffering so painful that I would not undergo to please you. Myself and my possessions and all that is in my power I give to you, and I prefer to serve you than be lord of all this world. All that I ask of you is that you receive my homage kindly; and, trusting that this may be the case, I melt with the sweetness that this creates in my heart.]

The declaration of love (lines 5–11) is at once the end of the first episode and the beginning of the second. The loose *coblas capfinidas* coupling between ss. 36 and 37, which Guittone turns into a narrative device, ensures a workable transition to the *tenzone*. The closed circuit of 'gioia'/'noia' opens as the lover is pulled forward to face a real lady who will not take his old-fashioned protestations for granted:

Eo t'aggio inteso e te responderaggio
(però che volonter non son villana),
e non, com'altre fan giá, per oltraggio,
ma solo per ragion cortese e piana.
Dici che m'ami forte a buon coraggio;
or mira ben se la parola è sana,
ca per amor amor te renderaggio
e, del contrar, ciò ch'è ragion certana.
E te e 'l tuo voli me fedel dare;
or mira como cresce segnoraggio:
qual e' fedel, tu tal voli me stare.
Consiglia me, com'om leale e saggio,
ch'eo deggia ver del tuo dimando fare;
ché de leal consiglio nom partraggio.   s. 38, 1–14

[I have listened to you and I'll reply to you (because I have no wish to be rude) and I shan't reply to shock you, as others have done, but simply in polite and clear terms. You say that you love me dearly, with all your heart. Well, you must make sure you mean what you say for I shall return you love for love and hate for hate, which is only as it should be. You want to give me yourself and your possessions in homage. Well then, you must consider carefully whether this homage which you wish to pay me will not increase the distance between us.* Advise me, as a reliable counsellor, how I should meet your request, and I'll not reject trustworthy advice.] (*Pellegrini, p. 59, omits the colon after line 10 and prints line 11 'tale fedel qual tu vòli me dare'. I have preferred this reading in a difficult passage.)

I noted earlier Guittone's sensitivity to the role of women in the courtly fictions. Here she becomes a mouthpiece for his own doubts about the validity of *fin' amors* as a code of manners, and the *tenzone* turns into a debate between Guittone's hind-sighted idealizing tendency and his personal pragmatism. Sonnet 38 conceals its frankness in the respectful niceties of correspondence formulae, with a preamble (lines 1–4), a statement of the problem (lines 5–11), and a closing request (lines 12–14).[9] She gives the impression that his declaration of love in s. 37 was simply one side of a *quaestio* and that he, 'om leale e saggio', is a counsellor wise in matters of the heart. Guittone gives that impression on purpose and now works the *tenzone* into the narrative with considerable skill.

When the lady claims, in parenthesis, that she is not intentionally 'villana' (line 2), she parries the lover's complaint in the preface that she had cut herself off from him.[10] She identifies herself with the paragon-lady of those sonnets, and at the same time makes a clear distinction between herself and the base-born 'pastorelle' and other common girls of literature, who often refuse their suitors in the coarse language of low-style debate because they know nothing else. He thus gets no chance to take the whip hand and treat her as a social inferior, as the male protagonist will in ss. 81–6. Her 'ragion' will be polite, 'cortese' (he can't reject her as 'laida o vil'), but to the point, 'piana' (which should prepare him, and us, for her wit and logic). By a delicious sleight-of-hand she pinpoints the ludicrous inadequacy of his hyperbolic feudal service (s. 37, 9–11), in the contemporary terms of male 'segnoraggio' (lines 5–11),[11] and invites him to search his courtly formulae for their logical content, line 6. She puts the onus on the lover to win her round on *her* terms (lines 12–14), for she will respond only in so far as she judges his advice to be sound.[12] The dry and simple diction of her reply (lines 5–11) undercuts the repetitive, 'provenza-leggiante' lushness of his declaration in s. 37. It is clear from the beginning that the contrast of language and style — hers, crisp and argumentative; his, oblique and formulaic — mirrors a deeper contrast and constant play of reality against appearances, of self-questioning against self-satisfaction. Compared with the groups of sonnets in earlier experiments, the *tenzone* is a minor masterpiece of split-level argument, sustained irony, and of the poet's ability to play each attitude off against the other to the full.

In s. 38 she met him on his own ground by clothing her argument in decep-tively common garb. He sees the 'ragion cortese' in her reply but not the 'piana', and he loses sight of her repeated call to self-scrutiny, 'or mira . . . or mira', s. 38, 6, 10, in a welter of compliment and adoration. He even takes on the mantle of counsellor she had mockingly offered him:

> Grazie e merzé voi, gentil donna orrata,
> dell'udienza e del responso gente,
> ch'io non udio mai donna, altra fiata,
> parlasse tanto dibonairamente,
>   che non si dice per parola ornata . . .
> fedel son d'ubidir vostro comando;
> tal fede chero e tal amor m'avanza.
>   Consiglio vo che tosto e non dottando
> de mi' amar e de mia fe, fidanza
> prendiate, como sia vostro comando.   s. 39, 1–5, 10–14

[Thanks and blessing to you, kind and noble lady, for listening to me and for your gracious reply. I have never before heard a lady speak so nobly that words could not express it . . . I am at your service; this is the trust I seek and the love that overcomes me. My advice is that, without delay or hesitation, you should trust in my love and my constancy, whatever you may wish of me.]

She, in turn, counters his advice with a delicate and deadly mixture of rebuff and condescending encouragement. In her opening metaphors of poisoned cup and wolf in sheep's clothing[13] she labels his hyperbole as sham. He can't fool her, and she will keep him up to the ideal mark by taking his ritual language at its face value, as if he meant it:[14]

> Ma non te poi ver me sí colorare,
> che ben non te conosca apertamente;
> avegna ch'eo però non vòi lassare
>   ch'eo non te receva a benvogliente,
> secondo el modo de lo tuo parlare,
> intendendolo pur simplicemente.   s. 40, 9–14

[But you can't disguise yourself from me without my seeing you through and through. Though I don't want you to get the impression that I don't accept you freely according to the terms of your claim, just taking it literally.]

Lines 13–14 seem to me to lie at the heart of the wider debate which Guittone engineers in this *tenzone*. Literature, in the person of the lover, meets reality head-on, in the person of the lady, and Guittone makes each character understand the other 'simplicemente'. Into a narrative framework of traditional sentiment which opens with a familiar pattern of antithetical emotions, he inserts a *tenzone* — an occasional, unsentimental, potentially low-style genre — which ruptures the hieratic order of serving-lover and lady-lord. The lover stays locked in the closed world of *fin' amors*, weighed down by its attitudes and language. Unable to see his own literary formulae in the hard light of common sense, he hears in her words only what suits his courtly expectations.

He is a figure from the past shunted into the present where he is made to look like a paste-board dummy, a well of empty words, a liar, perhaps a seducer. The modern Miss of the *tenzone* has taken stock of the decline of literary *fin' amors* as a code of manners. She knows that no man could profess that code sincerely nowadays; yet in self-defence she projects him back into his historical setting, confronts him with the ostensible purity of his sentiments, then subjects his words to the rigours of a common-sense scrutiny, 'or mira ben se la parola è sana' (s. 38, 6). Guittone's lover, a century out of phase, cannot cope with common sense. An examination of conscience is not one of the functions assigned to him by the books, and he misunderstands the lady in the bliss of ignorance. She misunderstands him deliberately, toys with his ponderous verbosity and exploits the advantage and disguise which the narrative situation gives her. The forward flow of the *tenzone* depends on their mutual misunderstanding which slowly forces the protagonists further and further apart.

The irony of her reply in s. 40, 12–14 is predictably lost on the lover in s. 41, as he takes her criticism and acceptance at face value (s. 41, 3–6) and repeats the request for a meeting which had turned the *tenzone* into a narrative episode (lines 9–14). As his incomprehension grows so her logic hardens. Surely this debate is a suitable time and place, she argues. Has she not already given him all the chances to prove himself that he should ever need (s. 42, 1–8)? Her sharp questions argue that a face-to-face encounter is now in progress. The *tenzone* has lost its set-piece flavour and has become a true episode in this narrative. The adversative balance of the *terzina* (s. 42, 9–11) exposes the euphemism and self-deceit of his request and restores to the limp 'agio e loco' formula its original colour of illicit assignation:

> Però vo prego, per merzé, che agio
> e loco date me, du' pienamente
> demostri voi, s'eo son bon o malvagio.
> E, s'eo son bon, piaccia vo pienamente,
> e s'eo so reo, sofrir pena e mesagio
> voglio tutto, sí con voi será gente.   s. 41, 9–14

[Therefore I beg you, for pity's sake, to give me an opportunity to show you once and for all whether I am good or bad. If I am good I trust that I'll be completely acceptable to you, and if I'm bad I'm fully prepared to undergo whatever suffering and trial you think fit.]

> Deo, con dimandi ciò, che t'ho donato,
> e che 'n possibel t'è sempre d'avere?
> Non hai tu loco e agio, e ascoltato
> è diligentemente il tuo volere?
> E, folle o saggio ch'eo t'aggia trovato,
> resposto t'aggio sempre a pian parere?
> Dimostra se ragion hai d'alcun lato,
> ed eo son presta a prenderla in piacere.

> Ma se dimandi alcun loco nascoso,
> prov'è che la ragion tua no è bella:
> per che né mo né mai dar non te l'oso.
> Ora te parte ormai d'esta novella,
> poi conosciuto hai ben del mio resposo,
> che troppo m'è al cor noios'e fella.   s. 42, 1–14

[For heaven's sake, how can you ask for what I've already given you, and what you can have whenever you wish? Don't you have the opportunity already, and hasn't your request been scrupulously met? And, whether I found you sensible or stupid, have I not given you from the start a straight-forward reply? Show me whether you have any ground for complaint and I'll be willing to accept it gladly. But if you ask for a secluded spot, that will prove that your motive is suspect: I have no intention of giving you that now or in the future. So, drop this subject at once, since you will have understood from my reply that I find it extremely distasteful and offensive to my feelings.]

This is her first blunt rejection[15] and it drives him into the self-pitying accents of formal *planctus* — he has only two basic reactions, after all — 'oimè', 'lassome'. Sonnet 43 is a fine example of that constipated, archaic diction in which the lover submerges his hurt feelings. His will to believe the best of his lady and to leave his fate in her gracious hands, is tireless:

> Bene veggio che di partir potenza
> darmi potete, s'a voi piace bene,
> solo in disabellir vostra piagenza
>   e 'n dire e 'n far ciò ch'a spiacer pertene;
> ma se potete, e no 'l fate, è parvenza
> che vo piace ch'eo mora in vostra spene.   s. 43, 9–14

[I recognize that you can make me leave you, if you care to, simply by marring your beauty or by saying or doing something unpleasant. But if you can and don't, that's a sign that you want me to die still longing for you.]

Her abrupt reply, 'consiglioti che parti . . .' (s. 44, 1) cuts across his coy postur-ing, and the lover becomes in her words what he had been by his own admission in s. 19, an 'enfingitore' (s. 44, 3–4). The moral criticism of *fin' amors*, implied from the start, is now plain as the lady ties together strands of authorial criticism which had appeared in earlier cycles. She holds him to the code he had professed in s. 41, 12–14, forcing him to accept the logic of his alternative, 's'eo so reo'; and she claims that she *is* the 'laida' whom the lover, in s. 14, 4, had said was unworthy of love:[16]

> Parteti e, s'amar voli, ama cotale,
> ched è piú bella troppo ed è tua pare;
> non me, che laida son, e non te vale.
>   E sappeti che, s'eo dovesse amare,
> eo non ameria te, non l'abbi a male,
> tutto sie tu d'assai nobile affare.   s. 44, 9–14

[Leave me, and if you must love somebody love a woman who is much more attractive and is on your own level — not me, ugly and unworthy of you as I am. And you should know that if I had to love somebody I wouldn't love you — don't take it amiss — even though your manners are very refined.]

The courtly abhorrence of 'laidezza', physical and social, which she invokes, shows how detached this lady is from courtly *mores*. She applies fearlessly to herself precisely that epithet which would have been an insurmountable obstacle to a *fin' amors* suitor. With superb consistency she presumes that since he is the sort of lover who, in s. 14, served his lady only because she was beautiful, and therefore noble, he should at once lose interest in her. The closing palliative (lines 12–14) is doubly ironic because the issue at stake throughout the *tenzone* is not his manners, 'nobile affare', which are impeccable, but his honesty.[17]

He wallows deeper in hyperbole. She *is* the most beautiful of all, whatever she says, and infinitely his superior (s. 45, 9–14). Pulling out all the stops of his devotion he trips himself with every word. Meanwhile, her language grows more abrupt, more 'villana', and compounds with a new note of cruel teasing:

> Or non vòi dire ch'eo sia saggia nente;
> ma, quale son, tu non me poi 'ngegnare,
> ché né fu, né será tal convenente
> in mio piacer giá mai, per null'affare.
>   E poi che sí conosci il voler meo,
> no me far corucciar, parteti omai!
> ch'eo ti farea parer lo stallo reo,
>   tutto sie tu, dei tre, l'un ch'amo assai
> piú che cos'altra mai (fe chedo a Deo),
> ma non de quello amor che penser hai.   s. 46, 5–14

[Now I don't want to claim that I'm particularly astute; but, however simple I am, I'm not taken in by you, for a relationship like this never did and never will attract me, no matter how you try. And now that you know my intentions don't make me lose my temper, be off at once! For I could incriminate you if you linger about, even though, of the three, you are the one I love more than anything else (so help me God), but not with the love that you are thinking about.]

'Fin' to the end, he takes her words in s. 46, 10–11 'simplicemente', as if they concealed the choice of going or staying. In his endless ability to parry her crushing briskness with ritual niceties he turns her threat into a classical dilemma, as if the choice lay with him, as if both alternatives were still open:

> Ahi, come m'è crudel, forte e noiosa
> ciascuna parte, e 'l partir e lo stare!   s. 47, 1–2

[Ah, how cruel, hard and objectionable I find both alternatives, leaving and staying!]

She is still the remote 'madonna' holding her lover in cruel suspense,[18] and she sparks off the emblematic 'noia' motif with hints of difficult, self-indulgent word-play (s. 47, 9–13). The lover is fixed in an archaic pose, able to wrestle endlessly with his limited alternatives and happily torn between respect for her wishes and the need to serve her. She, on the other hand, is drawn by his immobility to more clear-sighted observations and, as if to heighten the un-reality of his position, begins to use the less gracious language of those creatures who are 'volenter villane' and speak 'per oltraggio' (s. 38, 2–3). In s. 48 she reduces his delicate dilemma to 'esto misteri' and 'esto fatto' (lines 8, 14), and dispatches him with one telling blow:

> Donque te parte; e se di' che non poi
> mutar la volontá del tuo coraggio,
> come mutar donque credi l'altrui?   s. 48, 9–11

[Therefore leave me; and if you say that you can't change the resolve in your own heart, how then do you imagine that you can change that of others?]

The *quartine* of s. 48, like those of s. 46, contain a surprising dosage of archaic words, disjointed lines and awkward syntax, as if to counter his lush, repetitive style with a more difficult and muscular address, complementary to her demand-ing and robust insights.[19] Right to the end it was her 'dilettoso audire' and 'fazon piacente' which captivated him (s. 49, 7–8), and which finally brought about his 'death'. Even more delicious is his closing threat to seek someone who will appreciate his noble qualities (s. 49, 12–14). His pre-stilnovist praise of her angelic beauty (lines 9–11) looks ridiculous in the light of her down-to-earth wit, but proves that the *tenzone* skirmish has left intact his store of banal hyperbole.[20] Before she materialized in the *tenzone* the lover had let slip his desire to find a haven 'intra le vostre membra', (s. 35, 6) — a slip which, as if overheard, had enabled her to ridicule his protestations of selfless love. Now that she has revealed herself in such blunt and unacceptable terms he can safely fall back on fulsome praise to gloss over his earlier indiscretion now painfully obvious to him.

By now it should be clear that the *tenzone* brings into conflict Guittone's two contrasting views of literature as life. Both views are equally remote in time from the courtly models, and both are critical of amoral deviations from the high standard of behaviour demanded by *fin' amors*. Although in narrative terms she hands out a severe drubbing to her suitor, the male figure represents Guittone's struggle to re-state and identify himself with past ideals of blameless love-service, where words can once again be taken 'simplicemente' because lovers are as honest as they seem. She embodies Guittone's certain knowledge that the ideals enshrined in the literary tradition have been debased in practice and are no longer tenable.

Guittone's criticism of the courtly code, which coalesces in the person of the lady, should have had a paralysing effect on the sonnet sequence if he had meant to create a narrative out of standard genre poems. Can his persona's words ever be persuasive now that their emptiness has been so ruthlessly exposed? Can the lady lose her flesh and blood practicality and fall back into her former shadowy role? Does the *tenzone's* demolition of *fin' amors* sentiment allow any forward movement of *fin' amors* event? In the first two cycles one saw that certain discords were not held but were swallowed up in a broader movement of each cycle towards a kind of identity between author and persona. In a similar way the poet now sets aside the implications of the *tenzone* and weaves it, as an episode, back into the general fabric of the cycle. It gives the story-line a downward plunge and holds out the promise of an eventual climb up the emotional scale. But Guittone makes the *tenzone* serve a deeper end, because it gives the lady once and for all a substance she never had before; and the authorial stance of disenchanted protagonist which he adopts in the second *tenzone*, ss. 81–6, and the *ars amandi* (as well as his full-blown moral criticism in the conversion poems) can be traced to the role he gives the lady in the first *tenzone*. If the lady is no longer unapproachable and speaks as a real person, the male persona can drop his courtly guard and treat her with a realism as open and as unsentimental as her own. However, this anticipates the next chapter. For the meantime we can look briefly at the sonnets which follow the *tenzone*, from his reply (s. 49) to her resumption of the dialogue (s. 59).

Pellegrini saw them as a kind of parenthesis[21] and Egidi notes that the only reason for not placing s. 59 straight after s. 49 is the order given in Rediano 9.[22] Yet one can justify their position in terms of narrative development. Sonnet 50 is a tailpiece to s. 49, tied to it by the thematic and verbal echoes that mark points of recapitulation and forward movement throughout the cycles.[23] Sonnet 50 also picks up the opening 'gioia'/'noia' motif in ss. 31–6, which means that the *senhal* lady of the preface sonnets and the lady of the *tenzone* are one and the same person. As the lover slips gratefully back into the balanced love–hate permutations of 'gioia'/'noia', the entire *tenzone* becomes, in retrospect, a crisis which ensures narrative tension.[24]

In the first cycle the turning point from introspective monologue to outgoing teaching came when the persona saw his 'fare' and his 'dire' as one function. In the sonnets that follow the *tenzone* the persona also speaks of his deeds and his words in the same breath[25] and this paves the way for a bout of verbal abuse. In his eyes the *tenzone* had been a meeting, an event in his story, 'fare' rather than 'dire'. Once he recalls his vocal role the emphasis can shift from his deeds, which were clearly inadequate in the *tenzone*, to his words. Yet Guittone is careful to disguise the change of stance by a face-saving appeal to a code of manners and to an unseen but solid company of copy-book lovers, to prove that *this* member of their company is not 'villano' by choice:

> Or non pensate voi che sí leggera
> fussemi villania dire o fare   s. 52, 5–6

[Now you must not think that I would find it easy to speak or act basely]

Ahi, mala noia, mal vo doni Deo,
che mal dicente a forza esser me fate;
unde ciascun per cortesia recheo
che mel perdon, poi ch'è for volontate.　　　　　s. 53, 1–4

[Ah, evil bitch, damn you for forcing me to speak abusively. Therefore I ask everyone to forgive my outburst, because it was not premeditated.]

The echo of s. 38, line 2 brings out a cluster of ironies that complement those in the *tenzone* itself. Since he cannot grasp the content of her objections, he relegates her to the ranks of those 'villane' to which she had claimed in s. 38 that she did not belong:

Ma de dire o de far più cortesia
a voi e a ciascun de vostra gente,
me guarderaggio ben per fede mia.　　　　　s. 52, 9–11

[But mark my word, I shall avoid speaking or doing any further courtesy to you and those of your kind.]

He levels at her the charge of duplicity which had been the unspoken core of her criticism (ss. 53, 7–9, and 55); then he contradicts himself in a confused attempt to maintain 'cortesia' (ss. 55, 9–14; 57, 9–14; 58, 9–11), by admitting that her words *are* kind and that she *is* beautiful. The *plazer* curse in s. 54 conceals the truth that the 'maggior mister' a courtly lover could ever face would be the soul-searching demanded by the *tenzone* lady, and that his courtly virtues *were* inadequate to the non-courtly task she gave him:

Deo, che mal aggia e mia fede e mio amore . . .

poi ch'al maggior mister ch'avesse mai,
o cred'aver, non m'han valuto fiore . . .

che 'n fidanza de lor debel valore
vincente senza fallo esser pensai
de ciò ch'eo son venciuto a desinore.　　s. 54, 1, 9–10, 12–14

[God, a plague on my constancy and my love . . . since they haven't served me one jot in the most demanding task that I ever had or could have . . . for, trusting in their feeble strength, I thought I would easily conquer that by which I have been shamefully defeated.]

As an episode or event the *tenzone* fades before the lover's stock response to his failure, but his continuing dependence on every cruel word that issues from her sweet mouth, s. 57, 9–11, is well in character with Guittone's reliance on cliché to keep the narrative issue alive. If the lover was incorrigible to the bitter end of the *tenzone*, and if he is to rise from the depths of that rebuff by means of complaint and the well-tried formulae of fear and hope, one must not expect him to have snapped up any of the lady's insights. The interlude of *planctus* drops to its lowest ebb in s. 58.[26] It recalls the fear-of-death climax in ss. 10, 3–4 and 24, 12–13, and points the way to an imminent change in his fortunes:

> Poi morir deggio, dirò che m'amorta
> quella, ch'onore e valor e piacere
> e beltate sovra tutt'altre porta,
> e crudeltate e fierezza e volere
> de darmi morte sí, che non mi apporta
> amor servire né pietá cherere.   s. 58, 9–14

[Since I must needs die, I want to say that my assassin is noble, worthy and beautiful above all others, yet she is so implacably set on killing me that my constancy and my supplication win me no return of love.]

> Certo, Guitton, de lo mal tuo mi pesa
> e dolmi assai, ché me ne 'ncolpi tanto,
> s'altri il suo ti difende, or fatti offesa,
> s'aver nol dia giá tanto ni quanto?
> Se per ragion sonmi de te defesa,
> donque perché di mei fai tal compianto?
> Ver è che la ragion tua non ho 'ntesa,
> como cheresti me in privato canto.
> Ma vene in tale parte e 'n tal stagione,
> e pensa di cherer securamente
> ciò che credi che sia di tua ragione,
> ch'eo tel convento dar ben dobbramente;
> ma non cherer, né sia la tua 'ntenzione,
> ciò che 'l chieder e 'l dar fusse spiacente.   s. 59, 1–14

[Guittone, I admit that the suffering you blame me for burdens and vexes me, but if someone refuses to give you what is his can you be upset if you have no right to it whatever? If I have withheld myself from you with good cause why then do you upbraid me so violently? It's true, I didn't grant your request when you sought to meet me in a secluded corner. By all means, come to a quiet place at a quiet time and prepare to ask with confidence for what you think will meet your request, and I promise to give it to you twofold. But don't plan, much less demand, what would be unbecoming both to seek and to give.]

The turn that comes in s. 59 may not be so dramatic as the sonnet exchange at the end of the second cycle, but thanks to the earlier experiments we can judge its effect as a narrative expedient and as a device for bringing together author and persona. It is the pivotal sonnet in the third cycle. It picks up the *tenzone*, which had been grafted on to the 'gioia' preface, and shows that the lady has been won round since s. 48 by the lover's plight as he gives vent to it in ss. 50–8.[27] The various echoes, in s. 59, of previous poems in the cycle[28] have, as in other cycles, a tightening effect which offsets any clumsiness in the juxtaposition of debate and complaint genres and argues against the suggestion that s. 59 should follow s. 49, as if the *tenzone* had been dislocated by a careless scribe.[29] Sonnet 59 binds together the first three episodes and establishes an intermediate staging-point from which to branch out again for the last sequence in the cycle.

The sonnet exchange between Guittone and Bandino (ss. 28–30) turned an anonymous narrative exercise into an autobiographical story. Guittone himself took up the lover's problem and Bandino's answer met the lover's desire. With a similar effect Guittone claims the lover's entire story for himself in s. 59. But since the lady mentions his name in the context of a *tenzone* where her reality is never in doubt, and since she is solid enough without a proper name, Guittone's claim to be the persona of his narrative is more assured and less studied than at the end of the second cycle. It is as if his name had been taken for granted all along. Conscious identity between author and persona at this stage suggests that Guittone chose to be identified with the *fin' amors* sentiments of the male protagonist, come what may. Yet it is curious that he should take the side which he had just demolished in the *tenzone* — because if the real Guittone comes through anywhere in the early sonnets, it is as the lady in the first *tenzone*.

We have already seen that the poet constantly failed to sustain personal insights which are, in a sense, the result of head-on collisions between the hallowed formulae of his literary models, and his own common sense. The *tenzone* is an extended example of that kind of collision. It is not a lofty moral indictment such as we saw in the conversion poems but is worked deftly into the debate and draws on the literary realism of low-style genres. The debate itself is worked into the courtly narrative, which remains, for the meantime, his prime concern. But Guittone's doubts about *fin' amors*, clearly formulated in the *tenzone*, herald the end of his serious attempt to recapture the courtly ideal. And in the poems that follow s. 59 we see that his increasing use of a wider lexical and genre range illustrates on another level his conceptual retreat from *fin' amors*, for the persona's sincerity soon evaporates in displays of authorial skill.

Since the function of s. 59 is to keep the narrative alive, it is not surprising that her reply resembles Bandino's (s. 29) in more than the first-line mention of the poet's name. Its structure and content are akin to the typical reply sonnet,[30] and it takes on a facile, archaic patina[31] which was noticeably absent from her *tenzone* sonnets. She has lost none of her objectivity — witness her unanswerable questions (lines 3–6); and her excuse (lines 7–8) could pass for an exquisitely ironic comment on his dogged request in s. 41, 9–11.[32] Yet Guittone sacrifices her integrity to the demands of a cyclic structure[33] and launches his lover into a fresh series of difficult variations on the theme of praise:

> Gioia d'onne gioi e — movimento,
> non mi repento, — se villan so stato,
> né curucciato — voi; che però sento
> a me 'l talento — vostro umiliato.
> Che 'n ciò fui dato — solo a 'ntendimento
> del valimento — quale è 'n me tornato;
> e ho parlato — contra sapimento,
> ché piacimento — sol ho en voi trovato.
> E se gravato — m'avete sovente,
> sí dolcemente — m'ave trapagato
> lo vostro orrato — dir, che son galdente.   s. 60, 1–11

[Joy and wellspring of every joy, I don't regret that I was base and abused you, for I sense that your obduracy towards me has been softened. I gave into abuse simply out of desire for that worth that has returned to me, and I spoke against my better judgement because I discovered beauty only in you. And if often you oppressed me in the past, your noble words have now so sweetly repaid me that I am overjoyed.]

The appearance of a sonnet with *rimalmezzo* at this juncture invites comparison with s. 9 where the internal rhyme had expressed a peak of anguish and a moment of emotional release. Here the 'gioia' incipit recalls the opening sonnet of this cycle and confirms the identity of the persona from that sonnet to this, Guittone then as now. And like s. 31 it signals his claim to have appropriated the lover's discourse to himself in a burst of technical finesse conveyed through the *rimalmezzo* and the persistence of the *fronte* rhymes in the *sirima*.

The twenty poems that follow s. 59 reveal more clearly than any other group within the three cycles that Guittone found the basic 'materia amorosa' too limited to sustain in a varied and convincing narrative line. In the course of previous experiments his wooden sense of structure and a weakness for black and white contrast between the language of joy and lament, had given way to a more able control of narrative linkage and more resourceful variation of genre and stance. These closing sonnets maintain that development; yet the command of 'onne mainera' which they display carries Guittone away from the unselfconscious assimilation of *fin' amors* which had been his aim in the earlier sonnet cycles, and underlines the failure of the narrative method to recapture that ideal in his own time. Several observations will make this clear.

The lady's invitation in s. 59 gives the story a new lease of life and lifts it to a new crest which may run on, but will probably curl downward into another trough. Once he had stamped his own name on the protagonist and thus re-charged the atmosphere with biographical energy, Guittone's problem was how to extract the maximum variety from his meagre resources and clinch his claim to be the persona. This, of course, had been the problem throughout, but new themes and styles had blossomed in the third cycle, and, unlike the second cycle, Guittone had already committed his name to the story while it was still in progress. The way he tackled this problem in the dying stages of the third cycle illustrates the ingenuity and shortcomings of his entire narrative experiment.

Setting aside for a moment the decline from praise in ss. 60–1 to lament in ss. 72–5, and the final recovery, ss. 76–80, the sonnets hold together as a robust mixture of ingredients which had already proved satisfactory one by one. He begins with a secure thematic coupling to the antecedent poems, varies the general style with virtuoso displays in the difficult manner, relaxes the first-person tension by an occasional didactic excursion, and, in a significant new departure, enlivens the praise motif with a series of genre poems which evoke real events. These ingredients are not necessarily complementary. Verbal bravura can kill narrative movement; a genre poem on its own may not have enough life to affect the story. But they seem to me his last attempt to co-ordinate various kinds of authorial intrusion into the closed circle of courtly fiction.

With a quick back-pedalling of past verbs, sign of imminent forward movement in the cycles,[34] ss. 60–1 recapitulate the lover's recent abuse of the lady and her change of heart.[35] They echo the opening 'gioia' refrain of the cycle in s. 31, which was in itself a response to the lady's acceptance of the poet at the end of the previous cycle (s. 30). By s. 62[36] the praise motif has compensated sufficiently for the abusive interlude of ss. 50–8 to allow the first of the genre variations, the *gilos* warning in s. 63, which relegates the *tenzone* to the past.[37] In s. 62, 2, the poet makes a precise reference to the *plazer* curse in s. 54, and now replacing it with a blessing he reaffirms that his narrative has a forward linear growth where simple flashbacks establish the sequence of events.

Though there are examples of verbal bravura throughout the closing sequence,[38] it is most apparent at the beginning and at the end. Otiose and contorted as they seem, these experiments are made to fit and reflect the particular theme in which they occur or the level of sentiment in a given sonnet, and they are of different kinds. In s. 60 Guittone experiments with line structure and internal rhyme. The range of end rhymes is much narrower than usual,[39] while the rigid caesura imposed by the rhyme plays havoc with the sense pause[40] and gives a stammering, bubbling effect to the lover's cry of joy. In s. 65 the bravura is built round a *replicatio* of the root 'par', with dense play of derived, rich, identical and equivocal rhymes.[41] The bewildering similarity and dissimilarity of the rhyme word accords well with the 'schermo' theme, where the lover delights in deceiving his enemies. Sonnet 78 is an exercise in *rimas caras*, those difficult end rhymes which assault the ear with their harsh sounds and rare words or word forms.[42]

In these three examples verbal display gives the sonnet a difficult texture, but Guittone manages to convey the sense of each sonnet readily enough, with only the occasional obscurity. For the last major variation, in s. 77 and to a lesser extent in s. 79, he contorts the words to render the sense as obscure as possible. In s. 77 the 'enigma forte' may somehow celebrate his salvation and his limitless devotion (lines 3–6), which only the most dense *replicatio* can convey.[43] In the other case (s. 79), the more modest *replicationes*[44] are tied to a vestige of the 'schermo' theme (lines 9–14), which partly explains their use (as in s. 65 on the same theme), and at the same time holds together the general sense of the sonnet in spite of the verbal juggling.

One is tempted to dismiss sonnets like these as a triumph of banality, but if we bear in mind the end of the second cycle where Guittone brought the lover's problem right into the present and *then* broke into the 'gioia' incantation of ss. 31 and 35, the resurgence of authorial self-consciousness after the mention of

Guittone's name in s. 59 follows that renewed biographical claim as its legitimate offspring, and shows that poet and persona continue to be one and the same person. We can also recall s. 9, at the centre of the first cycle, where Guittone's first experiment was not an overtly autobiographical insertion of his own name but an attempt to provoke and solve a narrative crisis by a stylistic intensification of the metre.

Just as the transition to formal virtuosity is less abrupt here than it was between the second and third cycles, so Guittone's didactic touch is lighter than before. I showed how in the first cycle he was driven outwards into a teaching stance to preserve the lover's good fortune (ss. 13–18); and that, notwithstanding the lyric persona's tendency to be devotee and celebrant at one and the same time, the dogmatic tone co-natural to Guittone lifted the persona from the toils of his emotional struggle. In the closing sonnets of the third cycle Guittone seems to find enough variety of event to keep him out of the pulpit, and it is worth noting that in those sonnets where it does occur, notably in ss. 63, 68 and 69, the sententious style weakens their power to convey action as a narrative event:

> Voi che penate di saver lo core
> di quei che servon l'amorosa fede,
> partite vo da ciò per vostro onore;
> ch'onne peccato è, 'nver de quel, mercede.
>> Ch'un omo ennudo e de lo senno fore
> or miri quel che fa, om che lo fede!
> Ché tal è quei, cui ben distringe amore,
> che d'occhi né di cor punto non vede.
>> Ennudo sta, e non se po covrire
> de demostrar la sua gran malatia
> a lei, che pote lui di ciò guerire.
>> Donque chi 'l vede, in sé celar lo dia
> e contastallo a chi 'l volesse dire,
> per star cortese e fuggir villania.   s. 63, 1–14

[You who strive to penetrate the secret of those who remain constant in love, for the sake of your own honour cease your probing; for any sin is a good deed compared to that. Consider what a fine action it is to strike a man who is stripped and out of his mind. For this is the plight of anyone in the clutches of love, blinded in his eyes and in his heart. There he is, naked, unable to shield himself from displaying his malady to the one person who can cure him of it. Therefore whoever sees him should keep it to himself and should warn anyone else who might want to publicise his condition, to preserve decency and avoid vulgarity.]

After a stern, magisterial incipit[45] the *gilos*/secrecy theme[46] turns into a metaphorical description not of this lover's helplessness but of 'those whom love constrains' (line 7); those, that is, who keep 'l'amorosa fede' (line 2). Is it the lover who shows such apostolic concern for others in that state, or has he been 'stripped and driven out of his mind' himself, line 5?[47] The cool analysis and tidy balance of the admonition[48] stifles any first-person life the *gilos* genre might have carried into the story.

Sonnet 68 celebrates his joy rather than an event. It is a good example of the use of *sententiae* recommended by the manuals of rhetoric,[49] and is a typical example of Guittone's liking for a balance of general law in the *quartine* with a proof of personal experience in the *terzine*.[50] However, the most striking clash between dogmatic style and genre situation occurs in the following sonnet, which introduces the lively notes of marital infidelity and the risk of discovery:

> Ben meraviglio como on conoscente,
> o ver omo che ama per amore,
> po ver cui ama istar croio e spiacente
> e farli a suo poder noia e dolore,
>   perché d'alcuno modo lui parente
> li sia la donna ch'ama l'amadore;
> poi sa che ciò li aven forzatamente,
> perch'ha 'n poder d'amor l'alma e lo core.
>   Donque faria merzede e cortesia
> e ben suo grande e de la donna maggio
> covrirli e darli a stagion agio e via;
>   che s'ello pur guardar vol lo passaggio,
> e l'om de gir soffrir non po, follia
> li gioca sí, che monta ont'e dannaggio.   s. 69, 1–14

[I am amazed that a wise man or one who loves for love's sake can be harshly critical of someone else in love and do all he can to make him suffer, simply because the lady whom the lover loves is in some way related to him.* What's more, he should know that because she holds the lover's heart and soul under the sway of love, he is not responsible for his condition. Therefore he would do a kindness and a service, to his own advantage and even more to the lady, by protecting the lover and giving him the chance to meet her. For if he persists in blocking the lover's access and if the lover cannot restrain himself from making a move, the lover will be so maddened by desire that shame and harm will result.] (*Pellegrini, p. 104, prints line 5, 'Perché moglieri, o sorore, o parente'.)

Guittone gives the impression that his lady is 'malmaritata', or over-protected by a jealous guardian. This should give a downward twist to the story after the joy of s. 68; yet it carries no narrative conviction whatever. The assumption that guardians are devotees of love (lines 1–2) and should therefore relax vigilance over their wards, gives an air of wry detachment to what is an academic discussion, instead of being the heart-felt cry of a frustrated lover.[51]

In these three examples one senses that Guittone adopted the didactic pose at random to tighten his speculative grip on the 'materia amorosa' of his narrative, apparently unworried if *sententiae* and situational genres turned out to be counter-productive devices. Yet the genre sonnets have another, more serious defect which further weakens their power to carry the story line. They lack a lead-in and are not assimilated into the context; they all skim over the ritual sentiments of the genre, none of them reliving the event proper to each. Interspersed with poems of straight praise,[52] the genre poems straddle the whole sequence and they introduce the themes of secrecy (ss. 63, 71); the 'donna-schermo' (ss. 65–6, 79); the 'malmaritata' (s. 69) — all themes where jealousy is the key sentiment; 'lontananza' (ss. 72–6, 80); and an actual correspondence (s. 75). These sudden plunges from hyperbole of praise into adverse situations and back again, give the closing sequence an untidy, non-linear appearance.[53] But they do not on that account nullify the narrative elements which I have tried to show do exist in the third cycle. Since Guittone fails to bring out the core of reality in each genre poem, he manages to avoid what otherwise would be a series of violent and inadmissible contrasts between verbal banality and concrete event.

In ss. 63 and 69 the event is smothered by teaching. In ss. 65 and 79 it hardly gets a chance against virtuoso opposition and is barely strong enough to hold the tumbling words together. Sonnet 66 opens plainly,[54] but the poet's trust in the shut world of the 'schermo' ritual allows him to discuss a possible objection to the lover's behaviour (lines 9–11), and leads to a stock *refutatio* in the last *terzina*. This is just another reminder that in spite of the narrative vistas opened up by genre themes, Guittone's lover remains locked in an untouchable, bookish experience. In s. 61 he dissects a traditional hypothesis[55] before a public audience (lines 1–4), but the pedantic order of his treatment gets tangled in less obvious subtleties of sense.[56] The 'lontananza' interlude (ss. 72–5, 80) is easily the most consistent in this sequence, and there is even an attempt in s. 73 to fill out the picture with a mercantile pretext for the lover's absence. But as a convincing event it is bedevilled by its abrupt opening and it fades out as the lover falls prey to the fear–hope syndrome:

> e muto, perché quando il suo coraggio
> demostrame madonna per figura,
> de la 'ntenzone d'esso eo fosse saggio.   s. 71, 12–14

[and dumb, so that when my lady shows me a sign of her affection I would perceive it without having to express my awareness vocally.]

> Con più m'allungo, più m'è prossimana
> la fazzon dolce de la donna mia,
> che m'aucide sovente e mi risana
> e m'ave miso in tal forsenaria,
>
> che 'n parte ch'eo dimor' in terra strana,
> me par visibil ch'eo con ella sia   s. 72, 1–6

[The further I withdraw, the nearer my lady's sweet face draws to me. She kills me and revives me again and again, and she has so distracted me that in this foreign land where I now tarry I seem to be visibly in her presence.]

By s. 75 the echo of 'lontananza' in the opening word is an excuse for a riddle sent by one poet to another; and in s. 80 the 'lontananza' motif (line 5) is sketched in to explain how from one extreme of the sentimental range (praise/ service, lines 1–4) the lover can plunge to the other (longing for death, lines 6–8). The polite hope in the closing *terzina*[57] shows that the physical separation which underlies all 'lontananza' poetry and gives it bite, was not uppermost in Guittone's mind when he wrote this sonnet.[58]

It is possible that s. 80 became separated from the 'lontananza' group (ss. 72–5), in which case it could well be read after s. 74, leaving s. 75 to bring the now attenuated genre sentiments into the authorial present of a genuine correspondence, as in ss. 28–30. However, the letter sonnet has a more delicate function at this point. Instead of capping the cycle by allowing Guittone to assume the lover's plight, as was the case at the end of the second cycle, it adds, as a variation within the 'lontananza' group, a riddle in letter form to a named recipient. In this way he builds up the 'reality' of his departure by adding an epistolary distance to the emotional distance already evoked in the preceding sonnets; and at the same time he creates the illusion that *he* is the 'fedel lontano'. One proper name is all he needs for this, and the absence of a reply from Gherardo is irrelevant:

> Messer Gherardo, di non saver saggio
> lo chiar e scuro: ben è meo convenente;
> deh, quel sguardate che non guardo, om saggio.   s. 75, 12–14

[Messer Gherardo, I'm in a fine state when I can't tell the light from the dark.* Come, wise man, elucidate what I find obscure.] (* I have followed Pellegrini, p. 112, for lines 12–13, 'Messer Gherardo, di non saver s'aggio/lo chiar e scur ben è meo convenente:')

We should recall the start of this cycle where s. 31 broke out triumphantly after the exchange between Guittone and Bandino. With the poet's presence in the story now re-affirmed the final burst of authorial virtuosity (ss. 77–9) should come as no surprise. And if s. 80 has wandered from its proper place among the 'lontananza' sonnets the cycle ends with a masterly display of the difficult style he had made his own. This would now leave Guittone free to experiment in the anti-courtly style of the 'tenzone con la donna villana'. This impression remains even when s. 80 is left in the given order as the last poem in the cycle. On the other hand we can account for the separation of one 'lontananza' sonnet from several that are grouped together by noting the scattered placing in this sequence of other sonnets with a common theme.[59] They would suggest that Guittone was more concerned with variety than consistency, and would not have judged improbable the lover's relapse into a past and apparently cured malady.[60] In its printed order s. 80 leaves the cycle poised on the classical note of 'speranza', which would be an ideal spring-board for a leap into yet another narrative cycle.

As far as we know Guittone did not write another narrative sonnet cycle, and the next group of sonnets marks an abrupt change to a decidedly low-style *tenzone*. Was this simply one more in a series of random experiments, unconnected to the first three families of sonnets? I think not. It is certainly a more abrupt change, both in its language and its attitude to *fin' amors*, than is the transition from the first to the second and from the second to the third narrative cycles, but it is a change in line with the increasing authorial control of his material which Guittone shows through the first three cycles.

As already noted, the third cycle is more eventful and more varied in its style, more assured and relaxed in its changes of pace and stance. Guittone's growing mastery of the linguistic and thematic range of his models, passes for a more thorough absorption of courtly ideals. Yet the divergence between his voice and that of the persona is wider in the third cycle than at any previous point. The *tenzone* (ss. 37–49) presupposed a modern, common-sense view of courtly literature, fatal to the serious intention which animates his narrative structures. If Guittone could organize his misgivings about *fin' amors* into an articulate broadside at the naivety and, worse, self-deceit, of a perfectly drawn *fin' amors* lover, he would not be able to pursue that lover's ideal for much longer. Each narrative cycle had been an attempt to break through the anonymity of individual courtly lyrics and raise the status of their 'materia amorosa' from fiction to biography; and in the cycles he tries to show the fine ideals of courtly literature as verified in his own actions.

The closing sequence of the third cycle marks the final breakdown of the narrative experiment. The gap between persona and author had been bridged only at several points in the course of the experiment, in an unstable and unconvincing union. By the end of the third cycle Guittone resorts to verbal juggling and a lifeless manipulation of genre motifs to carry the story line. It is possible that the difficult surface texture he gives that part of the cycle may have been Guittone's last effort to cover the *fin' amors* notions with a hard and contorted shell, thus obliging his readers to read intently before they could savour a kernel of sentimental truth. But it seems more likely, in my reading of the texts, that Guittone took over as poet when the persona had failed to provide him with an adequate and convincing voice. Sonnets 77–9 are not random examples of Guittone's celebrated *trobar clus*. They are his last serious *fin' amors* sonnets, a technical compensation for his imminent abandonment of the poetic notion of feudal devotion as a fit subject for lyric writing. He had begun by trying to extend the limited emotional range of his received material, in cycles which attenuated and made credible the sentimental polarities in occasional lyrics. Towards the end narrative experiment gave way to stylistic experiment as Guittone began to refashion in Italian the rich technical resources developed by the Provençal masters. Guittone now opts for a more cerebral and detached attitude to his work and abandons his efforts to vivify the vapid lyric sentiments he had inherited. Could this mark the point of Guittone's entry into active political life, with the *tenzone* that follows as a sign of his acceptance of popular motifs consonant with his new activity? A parallel with Dante and Forese Donati suggests itself at once, but here we can only surmise. One cannot say *when* Guittone abandoned his serious lyric persona: his rejection of narrative does not necessarily mark a turning point in *time*. But it seems clear that a change from belief in the poetic validity of the courtly ideals, to a deeper grasp of the traditional range of themes and styles and consequent detachment from *fin amors* as a serious motif, did take place before his religious conversion; and one could say that the emergence of Guittone in a purely authorial and virtuoso role at the end of the third cycle signals that change and opens the way for the anti-courtly experiments that follow.

CHAPTER 5

The 'tenzone con la donna villana' and the *ars amandi*

There are precedents for the 'tenzone con la donna villana' in the *tenzone*, ss. 37–49, and the abuse interlude, ss. 50–8, within the third cycle. The difference, however, is not merely one of degree.[1] It points to a more fundamental change in the poet's attitude to *fin' amors* as outlined in the previous chapter. In ss. 37–49 it was the lover's expectation of the lady's 'cortesia' which enabled her to expose the shortcomings of *fin' amors* sentiment. Within the serious and naive context of that cycle her words were brisk but not 'villane', except perhaps towards the end of their encounter. It was a dialogue between two levels of commitment to the values embodied in courtly language; it was not a dialogue between the *stilus tragicus* and the *stilus comicus*. In the sonnets that followed the *tenzone*, the lover was acutely aware of the clash between his base speech and the demands of 'cortesia'.[2] She was not a 'donna laida' to be abused at will but the most gracious creature in the world, s. 57, 3, whom he would sting into a more favourable mood. The scattered harsh epithets expressed his grief and confusion and led the narrative line downwards until it was lifted again by her favourable reply in s. 59. However, there is no overlap at the end of the third cycle and the 'tenzone con la donna villana' opens abruptly:

> Villana donna, non mi ti disdire,
> volendomi sprovar fin amadore:
> ch'eo fin non son, ver s'ho talento dire,
> néd essere vorrea, tant'hai ladore.
>
> Ca, per averti a tutto meo desire,
> eo non t'amara un giorno per amore,
> ma chesta t'ho volendoti covrire,
> ché più volere terriami disnore.
>
> Ché tu se' laida 'n semblanti e villana,
> e croia 'n dir e 'n far tutta stagione,
> e se' leggiadra ed altizzosa e strana,
>
> ché 'n te noiosa noia è per ragione,
> donna laida, che leggiadra se' e vana
> e croia, che d'alter' oppinïone.   s. 81, 1–14

[Vulgar woman, don't protest against my desire to prove what a courtly lover I am: for I long to tell you that by that standard I am not courtly at all, nor would I ever want to be, on account of your ugliness. For even if you were compliant to my wishes, I wouldn't love you one day for love's sake. All I wanted was to straddle you — to have desired more than that would have shamed me. For you are ugly and coarse in appearance, and unfailingly repulsive in what you say and do; and you are fickle, arrogant and odd. Ugly woman, you are clearly an offensive nuisance, for you are flighty, vacuous, evil and full of your own importance.]

In ss. 81–6 abuse is a literary exercise with no pretensions to narrative order.[3] The epithets that appeared singly in ss. 50–8[4] now crowd together in the thrust and parry of charge and counter charge. The players' roles are, in one sense, the reverse of those in ss. 37–49. He is the knowing, anti-idealistic figure, while she reveals a courtly hope of polite words from her suitor. But his knowledge is simply brutal frankness, s. 81, 5–8, and has none of the searching logic of the lady's replies in ss. 37–49; while in her hurt innocence, s. 82, 7–9,[5] she acknowledges his vulgarity then mockingly dismisses him as she protests her virginal fortitude to the end, ss. 84, 5–8, and 86, 1–2, 9–14. All the invective lies in their mutual attack on the other's *words* not motives.[6] He could have lampooned her claim to the martyr's palm in s. 84, 5–8.[7] Instead, for his parting shot (s. 85) he simply piles on the abuse and reverts lamely to a courtly rejection of her 'laidezza', as if he might have improved her, s. 85, 5–8. She gives as good as she gets (s. 86, 1–4) because this is an even contest, verbally speaking, but ends protesting her innocence (s. 86, 9–11), as if to retrieve the courtly expectations she revealed in s. 82, and which she surrendered to trade blows with him.

If the 'tenzone con la donna villana' is Guittone's first non-biographical experiment and a trial run in an anti-courtly genre following close on the heels of the third narrative cycle, one might expect some carry-over of the language he had used so consistently in the earlier groups of sonnets. Guittone seems uncertain of the roles his couple should play in the *tenzone*. Should they be out-and-out 'villani'; or one 'villan' and the other 'cortese'; or should each of them have both characteristics? He seems uncertain, too, of his verbal equipment. Apart from two lines (ss. 81, 7 and 84, 8) the vituperation is noticeably toothless and uneven in quality because the language itself is still 'provenzaleggiante' and not consistently vulgar or colloquial enough for the situation.

The *terzine* of s. 81 will recall Guittone's ambiguous attitude to 'donne laide' in the earlier sonnets. On the one hand, the virtues of the physically 'laida' could go unrecognized, s. 5; and on the other, men debase themselves when they pursue a 'donna laida o vil' (s. 14). Conscious reversal of the latter ideal in s. 81, a change from second plural to second singular address, and the causal link between her 'villania' and his desire to have his will with her (lines 7–11), place the *tenzone* squarely in the sensual anti-idealistic tradition. Yet the style and lexical range are much the same as before.[8] The only sonnet in the *tenzone* to show an increase in word-play comparable with that in ss. 65, 66, 77 and 79, is s. 85,[9] but like those earlier sonnets it suggests that word-play goes hand-in-hand with banal sentiment, and that virtuosity simply compensates for lack of feeling.

The protagonists use no dialect words or colloquial turns of phrase which might have given their debate the colour of a market-place exchange. It is as a piece of unvarnished fiction that the *tenzone* marks the end of Guittone's courtly biographies, where language harmonized with theme and modestly low-style digressions served a narrative purpose. The *tenzone*'s imbalance between realistic genre and traditionally sedate language indicates that although Guittone was held back by linguistic resources that had been developed so far only in the elevated direction, he was being drawn to experiment with literary attitudes he would not claim as his own, but which he recognized as an integral part of the inherited range.[10] It is even possible that the conservative language in the *tenzone* betrays a nostalgia for the civilities of *fin' amors*, as if Guittone were breaking with his narrative past as gently as possible.

Guittone was free to embark on anti-courtly experiments once he had the *fin' amors* tradition sufficiently in perspective to be able to set its ideals to one side. The *tenzone* follows the narratives because by the end of the third cycle Guittone had broken off his attempts to make real things out of his persona and the persona's 'fatti d'amore'. The *tenzone* extends the growing assertion of authorial control over 'materia amorosa' at the expense of authorial identification with it. It is a short, not altogether confident display of the poet's disengagement from courtly idealism. The *ars amandi* that follows it is another anti-idealistic experiment, this time longer and more assured. It is hard to imagine that this decisive change of direction can be fortuitous in a *canzoniere* where each stylistic experience is an experience of life. A parallel between Guittone's realistic experiments at this point and Dante's *tenzone* with Forese Donati in the mid 1290s seems to me unavoidable. I would see in these two closing cycles the beginning of a crisis that was to continue through the Guelph defeat at Montaperti and Guittone's exile from Arezzo, to be resolved only by his entry into the Gaudenti in the mid 1260s.

The last coherent family of pre-conversion sonnets is Guittone's final experimental step away from biography towards an exclusively authorial manner. In its length (twenty-four poems) and the range of its teaching it rivals the third cycle, and draws together attitudes that had put the earlier cycles into a kind of temporal order of progressively intense experiment. The didactic sequence at the end of the first cycle (ss. 13–18) urged archetypal values on all suffering lovers, because the wise and lovely lady was sure to reward her 'fedel'. At the same time it lifted the persona out of his emotional turmoil and onto a plane close to that of the controlling author. The persona's new-found certainty lay in Guittone's unquestioning acceptance of the code's most serene axioms. The following cycles revealed a tension between those simple ideals and the realities which make euphemisms out of courtly formulae. Guittone sought to recapture *amor purus* in the face of his increasingly sophisticated and outspoken awareness of the hard facts. Men ape courtly manners to deceive women (s. 19). A woman with her feet on the ground will turn down a man's request for a secret meeting (ss. 41, 42). The lover's actions contradict his words (ss. 44, 48). Finally, the open eroticism of the 'tenzone con la donna villana' strips away any coy pretence to courtly innocence. Each family of sonnets is an advance on its predecessor, in so far as each delves deeper into the realities of 'materia amorosa'. These are the intuitions which Guittone could not set aside once he had worked them into his sonnet structures. The lover can no longer resign himself to the extremes of anguish and elation; the lady has come down from her pedestal to become an object of sexual pursuit. 'Insegnamenti d'amore', in the perspective of Guittone's passage through the sonnets, turn the ennobling and mysterious process of 'amore' into a game of seduction whose rules can be learnt from books.

This is no place to describe Guittone's debt to his models in the *ars amandi* genre.[11] Nor should one expect a rigorous structure of internal logic from a loosely-connected series of textbook teachings. But Guittone's *ars amandi* seems to be complete and to be arranged in a typically Guittonian sequence. It can be interpreted on its own merits and in the light of the earlier experiments. In the context of his serious courtly sonnets the didactic stance is symptomatic of Guittone's definitive retreat from the 'poetic of first-person event', and there are several passages in the *ars amandi* which tellingly illustrate the dialectic between literary ideal and real-life practice endemic to each series of sonnet experiments:

> pur esser non porá ch'alcuno aiuto
> non doni altrui, che n'ostarie 'l penare.   s. 110, 13–14

[at least it should give someone some help to mitigate his suffering.]

The modesty trope with which the *ars amandi* ends seems directed to a band of suffering lovers. We would imagine from this sympathetic closing wish that the gentlemen concerned were in familiar dire straits, suffering through their fidelity to a ruthless, hidden lady. But this is hardly the world of the *ars amandi*, where she *is* available provided one goes about it the proper way, and where there is a teacher to explain the right tactics. Authorial asides throughout the 'insegnamenti' remind the novices that the chosen lectures are drawn from reference books and not from experience.[12] Since it is a pot-pourri of choice pieces and oscillates between earnest *fin' amors* idealism and bland cynicism, it confirms Guittone's stance as an authorial outsider, handling a selection of traditional themes with cool efficiency. One senses in the *ars amandi* that Guittone faced a problem not unlike the one in the narrative cycles: how to blend the need for variety of teaching, dependent on the range of his sources, with a practical knowledge of the realities beneath literary euphemism. In its own way the *ars amandi* also reveals a conflict between the old attitudes (embodied in the narrative persona and enshrined in Guittone's source books) and the new (the stance of the disenchanted author, now in control of his materials). The shape of the *ars amandi* grows according to these two factors, not meandering but responsive now to one area now to the other. The teaching opens in ss. 87–9 with second-hand definitions of love and its effects:

> Secondo ciò che pone alcuno autore,
> amore un disidero d'animo ene,
>   disiderando d'esser tenedore
> de la cosa che piú li piace bene   s. 87, 3–6

[According to one authority love is a desire of the soul that longs to be in possession of that which pleases it most]

> Esto amor non è tutti comunale,
> perché non sono d'una complessione,
> ché tal è che non mai di ciò gli cale,
> e tal che 'n sua cura altro non pone.   s. 88, 1–4

[This love is not the same for everyone because not everyone is made the same way. There are some who are not in the least interested in it, and others who think about nothing else.]

> istar doe; che l'un ama e l'altro nente,
> reo accident' è, in qual no è fattore.   s. 88, 13–14

[that someone should be in love and someone else out of love is a regrettable state of affairs for which no-one is to blame.]

>   e sua natura fa el conoscidore
> disconoscente e dá laida resposa,
> e 'l molto leal falso e traditore,
> e 'l pregiato deven villana cosa.   s. 89, 5–8

[it is in the nature of love to make the wise man a fool and to prompt vulgar retorts.* It makes the faithful man unreliable and treacherous, and the man of good name becomes a thing despised.] (* The text of line 6 is corrupt; MS. Laurenziano Rediano 9 gives 'disconosciente edala tua resposa'.)

According to the authors, love rises spontaneously in a physiological process. It depends on the make-up of its 'subject'; it is capricious and tyrannical in its power. Out of his depth once he approaches the textbook *effects* of love, Guittone passes to the more familiar territory of practical advice:[13]

> Ora eo no son per dir ciò che ne scende;
> ma pur lo modo sol semplicemente
> como po' faccia chi d'amor s'enprende.   s. 89, 12–14

[However, it's not my intention now to describe its effects; rather, I shall simply confine myself to a rule of conduct for those who engage in love.]

By trying to begin at the beginning with a scientific description of love in its essence he had landed up in that archaic, closed world where the lover was the plaything of 'Amore'. As a teacher with the whole gamut of love literature at his finger tips he is not concerned with a passive, literary lover's 'gioia e dol'. Love is not an irresistible force but a matter of coping with foreseeable difficulties,[14] and of literally grabbing the chance with both hands when it comes:

> Or torno a dir che l'amante ave a fare,
> da poi ch'è per sembianti assai provato.
> Entender dia ch'a lei possa parlare
> in alcun loco palese o celato.
>   Prenda loco, se po far dimandare;
> se no, dimandi cagion d'altro lato;
> ca, per ingegno e per forza, mostrare
> vol la donna che vegna tal mercato.
>   E s'è celato loco ov'e' l'aconta,
> basci e abracci e, se consentimento
> le vede alcun, è tutto ciò che monta.   s. 94, 1–11

[Now I turn to describe what the lover must do once the portents look favourable. He should try to speak to her somewhere, either in public or in private, it doesn't matter which. If he can ask her personally he should make an appointment. If not, he should find some pretext to be with her: for the lady wants to be shown that, either by astuteness or force, this business will come to a head. If he meets her privately he should embrace and kiss her, and if he senses any compliance in her that's all that matters.]

There is no sad insight here into what lies below the artifice of courtly manners; no ethical judgement of self-deceit, as in the first *tenzone*. The ritual play of difficult access is simply 'tal mercato'[15] which the tyro must learn to exploit because she uses its fictions to play her own sly game:

> Or se no po de sé far parlamento,
> parli per tal che sia privata e conta
> e sia sua par, se po, di valimento.   s. 94, 12–14

[But if he can't speak to her personally he should do so through someone discreet and prudent, and, if possible, someone her equal in worth.]

> Or chi dirá, o ver chi fará dire,
> da poi ch'avèn ched ha loco e stagione,
> s'è maggio o pare o menor de podere
> la donna, se vol guardi per ragione   s. 95, 1–4

[Now when the appointment takes place, the lover, or the lover's representative, should examine carefully whether the lady is his superior, equal or inferior in strength of character.]

Guittone at once suppresses the crudity in s. 94, lines 9-11, and restores the tremulous 'appointment' made against all odds, to work in the forms of address taught by Andreas Capellanus (ss. 95-9). It is noticeable that when he addresses his equal,[16] in s. 99, the lover is urged to see a logical connexion between his physical desires and his humble display of 'reverenza':

E lei ched è si par, com'aggio detto,
de' l'omo certo reverenza fare,
ch'omo nom po, secondo il mio intelletto,
verso d'alcuna troppo umiliare
    per conducere a ben lo suo diletto:
ch'umeltá fa core umele fare
e lauda le fa prender bon rispetto
e tollele de laida responsion fare.
    Dunque umilmente laudando lei faccia
dire, o ver dica, quanto po piú bene,
com'è suo tutto in far ciò che le piaccia;
    e pregando per Deo e per merzene
ritegnalo basciando infra sue braccia,
che ciò è tutta sua voglia e sua spene.   s. 99, 1–14

[As I've said the man must show a certain respect for the lady who is his equal, though, in my view, a man shouldn't lower himself excessively in front of any woman merely to satisfy his desire. Gentleness makes the other heart gentle, while praise obliges her to act courteously and prevents her from reacting basely. Therefore, gently praising her he should have his representative say, or say himself, as well as he can, that he is hers to do with as she will; begging her for pity's sake to take him into her arms with kisses, for that is all he longs and hopes for.]

This sonnet brushes aside the cult language addressed to a superior being in ss. 97–8, steers the teaching back to a discussion of her essential chattel value, and ushers in six sonnets, ss. 100–5, which outline further ways to win her over. The devious stratagems are reflected in passages of obscure syntax,[17] but there will be no doubt of her connivance,[18] nor that a frankly erotic undertow will pull each stratagem to its inevitable conclusion:

La donna poi se pensa, e 'l fatto sente;
e, se per altra guisa e' de' avenire,
però li avene a ciò che gli è piacente.   s. 102, 12–14

[If then the woman gives thought to it she'll see the reason for this. And if their meeting must take place in some other way, she'll make sure that it does so in a way that satisfies him.]

Se non s'avede, almen loco consente,
ove lei parle; e forse piú gli fae.   s. 104, 13–14

[If she doesn't catch on at least she'll give him the chance to speak to her and perhaps do even more.]

ch'a convento od a forza pur convene
far ciò che vol l'amante for ritegno.   s. 105, 13–14

[for eventually, either willingly or under duress, she will have to comply with her lover's wishes, with no holding back.]

The magisterial tone is absent from these sonnets. Guittone handles the situations in what is for him an animated fashion, by the occasional use of direct speech[19] and a staccato, verbal alternation of actions and reactions[20] — which suggests to me that he relished the vibrant confirmation of his advice, in thumbnail sketches from something approaching real life.

Guittone's description of specific situations shows a marked drop in vitality when he returns, in s. 105, to the old-fashioned theme of the go-between. As if shaken by his enjoyment of erotica the teacher reasserts his control in a recapitulation which affects to tie the new pragmatism to the old idealism, and ushers in a closing plea for feudal service of 'madonna', 'all'antica':

> Me pare aver ben dimostrata via,
> che chi la sa compiutamente usare
> che per necisitá quasi la dia,
> cui dura assai coralmente d'amare.
>   Ma d'essa como l'om vo la balia
> e come l'aggia, non se pena guare
> se no la parte; e so ch'è restia
> e con poco procaccio d'acquistare.
>   Com de' tal omo donna concherere,
> che sé dovria mai sempre blasmare
> quella che l'accogliesse in suo piacere?
>   Molto val om ch'a donna possa stare
> a difension, poi ch'om ben la rechere
> e li fa ciò ch'op'è ver quello afare.   s. 106, 1–14

[I think that I've shown a way which, when fully used, will almost inevitably bring her to the one who perseveres in loving fervently. But, however the man wishes to control her, and however he possesses her, he suffers no torment until he leaves her; yet I know that she is intractable and that there is little gain in winning her. What is the point of such a man pursuing a woman if he is only going to abuse her when she gives him her favours?* The man who shows true worth is the one who can defend his lady's honour, because this is the proper way to court her; and she will do for him what is right and necessary to bring them together.] (* Pellegrini, p. 174, notes that MS. Magliabechiano ii, iii, 492 has no initial 'che' in line 10, and that with MS. Vat. lat. 3793 gives 'se dovria' for 'sé dovria'.)

The sonnet is obscure and the text may be corrupt,[21] but in the opening lines the teacher looks back over his course with euphemistic satisfaction, glossing over the hard-headed subterfuge outlined in ss. 100–5. The sweet adverb, 'coralmente' (line 4), gives an oddly innocent air to the knowing games just rehearsed,[22] though 'l'om vo la balia' (line 5) makes it clear that he, and not she, is the one who exercises command.[23] Yet the *ars amandi* does not end here. There follow four sonnets in which the teacher drops his cynical mask to advocate that faithful male service which only the *fin' amors* 'madonna' could inspire. To understand this late flush of altruism we must look at the *sirima* of s. 106, and, obscure though it is, try to understand the question Guittone asks and answers in those lines. How can the pursuit of physical satisfaction be reconciled with 'madonna's' role as perfect, inaccessible being, object of praise and goal of man's highest virtues? After a bookish and undigested discourse Guittone suddenly admits the implications of realism vis-à-vis the courtly tradition. Women were not sexual objects and their availability was never mentioned as long as Guittone tried to immerse himself in the persona of the *fin' amors* lyric lover. As soon as she becomes an equal or less than equal, the way lies open for the abrasive language of ss. 81–6. *Fin' amors* demands an idealistic commitment out of keeping with everyday experience; sentimental realism destroys all that was exemplary in the courtly tradition. The question in lines 9–11 crystallizes the contrary tensions present in all the sonnet families and is a focus for Guittone's vision of love poetry. His answer is to echo briefly the virtues extolled in ss. 13–18, with a fine but hardly convincing upsurge of archaic language:[24]

> Con prego e con merzé e con servire
> e con pietanza e con umilitate
> e con esser piagente in fare e 'n dire
> ver lei e ver ciascun di sua amistate   s. 107, 1–4

[Beseeching, deserving pity, devoted, compassionate, gentle, pleasing in word and deed to her and all her friends]

> Al dire, e al dire fare, e al cherere
> si vol guardar e loco e stagione
> e lo stato di lei, sí che 'l volere,
> ch'ha bono, possa far bona ragione   s. 108, 1–4

[To speak, to get someone else to speak and to beg her favour, one must choose the right time and place and make sure that she is predisposed to turn her good will to good effect]

> e gran promettetor star li convene,
> e far che l'om bon celador lo tegna
> e largo ver la donna ov' è sua spene
> e 'n arme avanzator de la sua ensegna.   s. 109, 5–8

[he should be ready to pledge himself and win a reputation for discretion; be generous to the lady he longs for and the valiant champion of her colours.]

An authorial recapitulation replete with modesty figures ends this last-minute attempt to salvage propriety for the *ars amandi*:

> Sempre poria l'om dir en esta parte
> trovando assai che dicere di bono,
> en tante guise departite e sparte
> la parte d'essa e le condizion sono:
>   però da ciò mi si faccio disparte
> con quel ch' ho detto; avegna che ciascuno
> me piace che 'n ciò prenda 'ngegno ed arte
> e veggia avanti piú ch'eo no li sòno.

> Tra ch'eo so poco, ed ho piccolo aiuto
> loco ed agio de dire tanto afare,
> so che lo detto meo non ha compiuto;
>   ma tuttavia però no mi dispare:
> pur esser non porá ch'alcuno aiuto
> non doni altrui, che n'ostarie 'l penare.   s. 110, 1–14

[One could go on talking about this subject and find much good yet to say, because the elements and circumstances of love are divided and dispersed under so many aspects. However, what I have already said will have to suffice; though I should like everyone to consider my discourse carefully and apply it beyond the point to which I have taken it. What with my ignorance and the lack of help and opportunity to discuss such a big subject, I realize that what I have said is far from complete. Nevertheless, I am not ashamed of it: at least it should give someone some help to mitigate his suffering.]

The entire courtly experience, which had been lived out in the narrative cycles, is here reduced to a textbook subject whose parts and conditions are 'en tante guise departite e sparte'.

As a direct extension of Guittone's poetic range the *ars amandi* is an academic exercise. Since the 'diversi casi' he raised and analysed were derived from events such as those in the narrative cycles, now seen from the teacher's desk as set moves, the *ars amandi* boasts an objectivity that would have been impossible to the persona absorbed in those events, his own events. The recurring note of archaic sentiment and language seems intended as an antidote to modern vulgarity; and the pious wish of the last lines (s. 110, 13–14) implies a new generation of lovers suffering like those of old. But as an expression of Guittone's new-found detachment from *fin' amors* as a life-style the 'insegnamenti' teach a novice in the literature how to profit by the amorous experience enshrined in the lyric tradition, and urge him to seek what Guittone had left unsaid in the first flush of his narrative sonnets.

The remaining sonnets in Egidi's edition do not seem to form an integral part of the experimental background to Guittone's early development. The seven sonnets that follow the *ars amandi* are grouped together because they belong to none of the other families;[25] and of the twenty-one sonnets that follow s. 117 it would seem that possibly only three or four can be attributed to Guittone.[26] This reading of the sonnet cycles that represent in Guittone's *canzoniere* the two main streams of secular lyric, does not pretend to provide for them a *terminus a quo* and *ad quem* in time. It does suggest, however, that Guittone did not achieve a sure command of the themes and styles of courtly lyric poetry all at once. It could well be that while he was experimenting with anti-idealistic genres in the sonnet form so well suited to them, he was also opening the *canzone* to the wider range of political and moral themes that occupied him in the early 1260s. If these last pre-conversion sonnets *are* the first obvious symptom of a gathering crisis in Guittone's life, they are also a poetic commitment to a change that leads directly to the *sirventesi*, and beyond them to the palinodes. Whatever of this, it is hard to imagine after a close reading of the sonnet cycles that Guittone's development in the transitional period was not influenced by his positive rejection of *fin' amors* ideals well before the poetic statements of 1265–6. The sonnets tell only a part, if an important part, of the individual process of Guittone's early development. I have read them as a kind of backdrop to Guittone's courtly period. We must now look at the *canzoni*, the star turns performed against the modest backcloth of the sonnets.

CHAPTER 6

The courtly *canzoni*

The thematic coupling of Guittone's courtly *canzoni* to the first three sonnet cycles, outlined by Pellizzari and reproduced by Margueron, poses several problems which I noted at the beginning of the second chapter. If narrative depends solely on thematic likeness and if the sonnet cycles are simply variations on common themes, the *canzoni* can be linked with the sonnets whose theme they share. Thus Pellizzari's description of each group is simple enough to cover both sonnets and *canzoni*.[1] Margueron's expanded descriptions apply only to the sonnets and bring out the self-contained narrative line of the first three families; he shuffles the order of *canzoni* to match somehow the narrative order of the sonnets.[2]

I have tried to show that narrative in the sonnet cycles relies only partly on thematic variation and that, far from falling into conveniently rounded groups, the sonnets trace Guittone's continuing experiments with received literary ideals. To link the *canzoni* with the sonnets distorts the cyclic and progressive nature of the sonnet families. It adds nothing to the effect of particular shifts of tone, stance and motif which take place within each cycle; and it blurs what the sonnets show to be a steady movement from sentimental idealism to sentimental realism. The sonnets, as distinct from the *canzoni*, are the primary and consistent expression of Guittone's early poetic development. They provide the essential and continuing background to the technically more ambitious but sporadic statements of traditional 'materia amorosa' in the *canzoni*. In this sense Pellizari's thematic subordination of *canzoni* to sonnets is witness to the narrative primacy of the sonnets.

While Guittone frames his sonnets to bring biographical cohesion to the isolated motifs of troubadour lyric, he reverts in the *canzoni* to its characteristically fragmented and fictive discourse. The lack of manuscript evidence for any organic grouping of the *canzoni*, which Margueron sees as an objection to the thematic classification of Guittone's courtly poetry as a whole,[3] supports my contention that the *canzoni* are unconnected, occasional lyrics which we must read and see against the sonnets to assess their place in Guittone's early poetic development. My concern is not so much to place them in the ideal chronology offered by the sonnets (though I shall attempt to do so), as to show where the tensions between the poet's inherited literary formulae and his personal adaptations of those formulae are most in evidence, and in this way to shed light on the continuing process of disenchantment with *fin' amors* which we have already seen at work in the sonnets. Clearly, it would be useful to find out at the start whether the *canzoni* reflect the changes of stance and tone which Guittone makes in the sonnet cycles.

The first two narrative sonnet cycles show no obvious or progressive change of style. They are by and large 'provenzaleggianti' in their verbal patina and in their simple repetitions and periphrases, which reflect the poet's uniformly sober presentation of courtly sentiment. However, in the third cycle there is a noticeable increase of verbal and structural complexity — genre poems worked in as narrative changes, and the *trobar clus* range of internal and end rhymes. I argued that the absence of such features in the first two cycles complemented Guittone's serious effort to identify himself with the persona, and that, whether it was a case of conscious suppression or lack of skill, his direct presentation of the persona's 'fatti d'amore' was not to be marred by authorial intrusions. The presence of these devices in the third cycle compensates for the poet's growing detachment from ideal *fin' amors* sentiments. Where the sonnets had been directed to portray a biographical experience, they now showed the poet's manipulative skill with the traditional materials. A more complex picture of male–female relations overlayed the tremulous, one-sided affair portrayed in the early poems and brought lover and lady onto the same level.

Over-simplified though it is, this summary suggests a number of broad parallels in the *canzoni*. Straightforward expressions of the basic sentimental variants of sorrow, hope and joy, such as cc. iii, v, vi, xxiv, in which the shadow-lady holds sway over her adoring lover, show little sign of that authorial self-consciousness which Guittone translates into formal virtuosity. The *congedo* is remarkable by its absence from these poems.[4] They exhibit that unsophisticated acceptance of *fin' amors* attitudes common to the first two narrative cycles, and several of them coincide with Pellizzari's grouping.[5]

Most of the other *canzoni*[6] are closer in spirit to the phase represented by the third cycle, though not uniformly so. They may incline to a practical and unsentimental 'fare amistade' reminiscent of the *ars amandi*, as in the case of cc. i and iv; or they may develop genre motifs with the high emotional and low situational content of certain sonnets in the third cycle, as in cc. vii, ix, x, and xxiii. Some *canzoni* make heavy weather of standard themes by their terse and obscure syntax (e.g. cc. ix, xiv, xvi); others do so by bravura display of end rhymes and verbal texture (e.g. cc. x, xi, xii, xiii). In these *canzoni* Guittone seems to stiffen the banal content with teasing complexities of form and sound, much as he did towards the end of the third cycle when the story-line lost its way in genre and virtuoso meanderings. One could say that two-thirds of the *canzoni* show all the signs of authorial self-awareness which built up from the end of the second cycle and effectively broke Guittone's commitment to untarnished *fin' amors*. The third sonnet cycle can be regarded as a middle phase between the naivety of *amor purus* (cycles 1 and 2) and the anti-idealism of the 'tenzone con la donna villana' and the *ars amandi*. I shall try to indicate and interpret the signs of Guittone's authorial self-awareness by looking at his use of the tell-tale authorial closing statement, the *congedo*, in the *canzoni* that correspond to this middle phase.

The high-water mark of Guittone's entry as author was the mention of his name in the sonnet exchange, first at the end of the second cycle, ss. 28–30, and then in the lady's reply halfway through the third cycle, s. 59. I noted that these were, paradoxically, moments of climax (complete identity between author and persona) and anti-climax (a mechanical last resort to suggest that identity which the narrative on its own was unable to create). The *canzone* equivalent is the *congedo*, which is common to all the *canzoni* of the middle phase characterized by the developments in the third cycle.[7] Guittone invariably models his *congedo* on the *sirima*,[8] and in the true *congedo*, where he addresses his handiwork or its intended recipient, he stands away from the body of the poem to sign and seal it and send it on its way.[9] One can distinguish the true *congedo* from a closing *sirima* which merely condenses the message of the poem without breaking out of its fictions or showing that the poem is 'merely' a work of art, separable from its creator. The 'lontananza' poem, c. ix, ends with a clear example of an address to the poem:

> Va a le parte d'Arezzo,
> canzon, e a lei dí quale
> spera m'aiuta e vale.
> Remembranza mi sconforta e menaccia;
> ma dí ch'a sua merzede
> di tornar pur ho fede, — e voglio faccia
> di me ciò che li piaccia — e ragion crede.   c. ix, 66–72

[Song, go to the district of Arezzo and tell her of the hope that sustains and strengthens me. Memories disturb and threaten me, but say that I still hope to find myself once more the object of her compassion. And then I shall want her to do with me what she wills and thinks fit.]

The *congedo* of c. iv is a typical signing-off in the context of a real correspondence:

> Ubertin, dolze amico,
> or agio eo ben provato
> ch'amar troppo celato
> ten l'om de gioi d'amor sempre mendico.   c. iv, 61–4

[Ubertino, dear friend, now I have shown that loving too discreetly never brings a man the full joy of love.]

The second *congedo* of c. xiv, like the first, simply sums up the message of the poem without sealing it in an envelope, as it were:

Amore, Amor, piú che veneno amaro,
non giá ben vede chiaro
chi se mette in poder tuo volontero:
che 'l primo e 'l mezzo n'è gravoso e fero
e la fine di ben tutto 'l contraro,
o' prende laude e blasmo onne mistero.   c. xiv, 77–82

[Love, Love, more galling than poison, the man who submits to you willingly
can never see clearly what lies ahead: for from the start, and as it grows, the
affair is brutal and oppressive, and the end of it is the antithesis of all good,
no matter whether any affair wins blame or praise.]

Occasionally the *congedo* will combine an address to the poem with an address
to the recipient and audience, as in cc. xii, xx, and xxi. This suggests two degrees
of withdrawal from the action of the poem, one of the persona (in his capacity
as poet), the other of the author as craftsman. But the *congedo* has the general
effect of drawing a line between the events, sentiments and message of the
poem, and the shaping hand of the persona-poet or author.

A distinction between persona-poet and author is necessary because the
dividing line between the body of the poem and the signature lines is different
in the lines just quoted from cc. ix and iv. In the first case there is a change of
intensity and direction of voice, but it is the same voice, the persona's, as in the
body of the poem. In the second case the body of the poem is merely a sample of
Guittone's work to be perused by the dedicatee, Ubertino. On this basis the
canzoni fall into two groups. Either the persona's voice carries over into the
congedo, as in cc. ii, vii, viii, ix, xiv, xv, xvi, xx, xxii, xxiii; or the voice in the
congedo is clearly that of Guittone himself, as in cc. i, iv, x, xi, xii, xvii, xviii,
xix, xxi.

Several of these *canzoni* can be left out of the immediate discussion. *Canzoni*
viii, ix, xv, xx and xxiii fall in the category of 'lontananza' poems, where the
congedo is the obligatory and sometimes sole means of spelling out the distance
between the lovers. In each case except c. xxiii the proper name of Arezzo gives a
sharpened sense of real separation at the end of the poem.[10] I shall look at the
'lontananza' poems after commenting on several other *canzoni* and will try to
show the importance of c. xv as a fusion of amorous and political motifs.
Canzone xx, which is an example of a poem that qualifies for the 'lontananza'
genre solely on account of its third and last *congedo*, is more important in
another context and will be left to the end of the chapter. *Canzoni* xvii, xviii and
xix are not love poems but they are noteworthy because their political and
ethical 'materia' shows off Guittone in his didactic role, and they build up to
congedi in which he directs the message of each poem to real people.[11] They
suggest that the distinction between the poet and his poetry is most marked
when he abandons the fictions of a lover-persona and the sacred formulae of
fin' amors.

This leaves cc. ii, vii, xiv, xvi and xxii, in which the persona is poet; and cc. i, iv, x, xi, xii and xxi, in which the poet is Guittone. The first five of these remaining *canzoni* end in a *congedo* that extends or summarizes the content of the poem rather than signing it off.[12] Two or three of them show enough formal complexity[13] to recall the virtuoso skill of the middle sonnet phase, yet all of them ring with that archaic reverence for the lady and fear of the cruelty of love typical of the serious stance in the early sonnets.[14] The opening 'gioia' *replicatio* in cc. xvi and xvii brings to mind the bubbling outburst at the beginning of the third cycle (s. 31).[15] If the style and stance of the *canzoni* are at all related to those of the sonnets, all these features together would point to composition somewhere between the early and middle sonnet stages. These *canzoni* retain the fiction of a persona who is poet, still wedded to the ideal of a paragon-lady and the fateful power of love.[16] The *congedo's* assumption that the persona wrote these five *canzoni* can be qualified by lines and ideas from within the body of each of these poems, which give a clearer picture of their place in Guittone's early poetry.

Canzone ii is a deceptively simple poem. The ten-line stanza is short by Guittone's standards, is composed entirely of seven-syllable lines, and each stanza opens with an incantatory cry to the vaguely personified deity:

> Amor, or mira s'hone
> ragion che doler dia,
> ch'a la tua segnoria
> caper quasi om non pone,
> e manti contra voglia
> ne fai amar con doglia   c. ii, 11–16

[Love, now see whether I have reason to complain. No-one can surrender to your power unscathed, and you force many into a bitter experience of love.]

We seem to hear once again the luckless 'fedel' pleading to be accepted into Love's service. But the rhyme scheme is complex[17] and the heart of the lover's complaint is not bared until the fourth stanza:

> Amor, piú ch'altr'om dia
> te piacer, per ragione
> che sí 'n piacere sone
> de la madonna mia,
> che pregar che m'acoglia
> né che 'l servir meo toglia
> non m'è mestier, ciò sai;
> ma non me parrá mai
> forte de lei gaudere,
> né d'alcun suo piacere.   c. ii, 31–40

[Love, I should gratify you more than anyone else because, as you know, I am already so acceptable to my lady that I have no need to beg her to welcome me and receive my devotion. In fact, it will never seem difficult for me to enjoy her and all her beauty.]

The trouble is not that love is unattainable but that love has been too easy.[18]
There was no purifying experience of thwarted desire, not enough prior service
for this suitor of the old school who seems to have landed up with an easy
creature from the world of the *ars amandi*.[19] He turns back to 'Amore', deity
of the code he thought he professed, to salvage the affair and make it satisfyingly
arduous:

> ché, se 'l mal me no sfoglia,
> non mi rende 'l ben foglia   c. ii, 45–6

[for unless I am first consumed by suffering, the good will bring me no
benefit.]

He may be the naive devotee of the early sonnets but she is no cruel paragon
of virtue, and c. ii is one of Guittone's more sophisticated efforts to protect his
ideal closed world from vulgar encroachments.

In c. vii the vigour and continuity[20] of the attack on Love foreshadows the
highly rhetorical onslaught Guittone will deliver in c. xxviii, and the pungently
applied gambling metaphor in the last stanza releases some of the moral indigna-
tion which enables the lover to throw off Love's yoke in the *congedo*:[21]

> como che venta pei' che perta a gioco
> è, segondo ciò pare.
> Per ch'io biasmare te deggio e laudare:
> biasmar di ciò, che miso al gioco m'hai
> ov'ho perduto assai;
> e laudar che non mai vincer m'hai dato;
> perch' averia locato
> lo core in te giocando, e or lo sloco.
>
> Amor, non me blasmar s'io t'ho blasmato,
> ma la tua fellonesca operazione:
> ché non ha già ladrone
> de che biasmi signor c'ha lui dannato,
> ma da sentirli grato
> se merta morte e per un membro è varco;
> com'io te de l[o] marco
> de lo mal tuo non ho grano un pesato.   c. vii, 89–104

[just as at dice a win is worse than a loss, in my opinion. Hence I should
praise as well as blame you: blame you because you made me gamble and
lose heavily; praise you because if you had ever let me win I would have ven-
tured to fix my heart on you, whereas now I can shift it.

Love, if I have criticized you, don't blame me, blame your own misdoing.
A thief has no ground to revile the lord who has condemned him. Rather,
he should feel obliged to him if he deserves the death penalty and gets off
minus only a limb. In the same way your evil burden has not weighed on me
one jot.]

Canzone xiv is a less impetuous *planctus* than c. vii, heavier in stanza structure,
more ponderously archaic in language, and riddled with the Boethian pathos of
present sorrow seen against past joy. As a tissue of high-style lament figures it is

punctuated regularly with rhetorical questions, exclamations and *sententiae*. It combines assorted 'tragic' motifs such as the apostrophe to death (lines 39–40), the threat of suicide (lines 41–2), public ridicule (lines 54–6),[22] and 'lontananza' (lines 57–60). But it develops none of these threads to make a convincing context for such high-powered grief. 'Lontananza', apparently on her initiative (lines 58–9),[23] is not brought out in the *congedo*, as is normally the case when the lament rises from physical separation. Instead, the first *congedo* echoes the idea of mutual suffering in the last stanza (lines 61–6, 73–4);[24] while the second *congedo* foreshadows a later moral complaint against 'Amore', bad from beginning to end.[25] Guittone seems to read his own moral awareness back into his persona's stylized grief, and the *canzone* has a dark colour not evident in the sonnets, which makes it difficult to place with any confidence.[26]

A feature of c. xiv which contributes to its detached and swollen sentiment, is the discreet use Guittone makes of *sententiae*.[27] In the sonnet cycles Guittone adopted the didactic stance to hold his narrative on course. Teaching was not doled out in spoonfuls but came in concentrated doses at well-defined points in the cycles. Its major function was to heighten the effect of identity between persona and poet, now magisterially dispensing the fruits of his knowledge and experience. In the sonnets the didactic stance signals a conscious change of intensity which distinguishes the lover's two roles as devotee and high priest of the religion of love. In the *canzoni*, however, didactic passages, mainly in the form of *sententiae*, are worked into the tissue of many stanzas. They support occasional variations of stock courtly themes with proof that the *fin' amors* system has been absorbed and is reliable:

> Ché gioioso — e novello
> gaio ed adorno bene
> lo viso esser convene, — unde vaghezza
> de fino amore cria.   c. iv, 30–3

[for the face should be joyful, young and beautiful, and when it is it creates the desire for perfect love.]

> Nostro amor, ch'ebbe bon cominciamento,
> mezzo e fine meglior, donna, ne chere;
> ché bona incomincianza in dispiacere
> torna, se è malvagio el fenimento   c. viii, 15–18

[Since our love began so well, its progress and completion must needs be better, my lady; for a bad ending ruins a good beginning.]

> Ché, prima del piacer, poco po noia,
> ma poi, po forte troppo om dar tristore:
> maggio conven che povertá si porga
> a lo ritornador, ch'a l'entradore.
> Adonqua eo, lasso, in povertá tornato ...   c. xiv, 5–9

[Until you experience beauty, suffering means little to you. But when you have it can weigh you down grievously. Poverty is more humiliating when

you fall back into it than if you have been poor from the start. That is why I,
who have fallen back into poverty . . .]

They may be of the same impersonal cast as didactic statements in the sonnets,[28]
yet they appear as insertions only cursorily linked to first-person discourse,
which often pales into comparative insignificance. Compared with the neat
divisions and brevity of the sonnets, the extended structures of the *canzone* and
the more elaborate and varied patterns in the stanza invite changes of stance
within the stanza and from stanza to stanza which the sonnets kept separate.
The persona assumes with equal facility his roles of devotee and priest; yet he
tends to lack conviction because his sentiments rarely spring from a 'felt' event.

Canzone xvi illustrates Guittone's uncertain mixture of the two roles and also
sheds light on the ideal distance between the lover and his lady. It reads more
like an act of contrition than a celebration of the lady's 'pietá',[29] and like its
companion piece, c. ii, explores the lover's predicament when, against all odds,
the lady gives her favour completely:

> Gentil mia donna, gioi sempre gioiosa,
> vostro sovrapiacente orrato affare
> compiuto di ben tutto, oltra pensare
> di mortal cor magn'e mirabel cosa,
> sorprese l'alma mia de tutto amore   c. xvi, 1–5

[My dear lady, joy forever source of joy, your wonderfully noble deeds,
replete with all perfection, a marvel beyond mortal conceiving, have
completely taken possession of my soul.]

By fulsome praise of her 'cortesia' and self-reproach for his own baseness,[30] he
condones her capitulation. Then, in search of a way to remain faithful when
there is no reason for loyalty, he tries to restore her honour:

> Donqua men danno fora
> de la morte d'un om, sí com'io, basso,
> ch'un sol punto d'onor foste fallita;
> ch'onor val piú che vita,
> per che pria morto esser vorria, lasso!   c. xvi, 44–8

[Hence the death of one lowly person, such as I am, would have been less
of an evil than if one small point of honour were transgressed; for honour
is worth more than life, and for that reason I would rather be dead, alas!]

The *sententiae* which open and close the third stanza (lines 25–7, 34–6) show
the blind lover clinging desperately to ideals so as to stave off the reality of 'esta
fallanza' (line 29). And when he contemplates death to silence public scandal
(lines 41–6) he seems to face the consequences of his maxim with some mis-
giving (lines 46–8), for the 'lasso' exclamation comically deflates his noble defence
of 'onor'. In this example Guittone resorts to *sententiae* when the sentiments are
at their most banal and hypothetical. The lover's underlying concern to rehabili-
tate her *in his own eyes* comes to a climax in the last stanza:

che giá fu me, gentil mia donna, noia
vostr'amorosa gioia,
ver ch'ora mi serea destruggimento
d'onne crudel tormento,
potendo vo tornare in vostro stato:
ché dirittura vol che no schifare
deggi'om pena portare,
unde possa mendar ciò ch'ha peccato.   c. xvi, 53–60[31]

[for the joy of love which you gave me, my noble lady, was a burden compared with the blotting out of remorse that I would experience if I could restore you to your former state of honour: because justice demands that no suffering be shirked to make amends for wrongdoing.]

The source of his 'crudel tormento' is the knowledge that she has turned her nobility to baseness (lines 10–11); has turned her honour to shame (lines 21–2). The balancing transitive verbs 'tornare', in lines 11, 22, and 57, emphasize the two-fold movement of descent from and return to that pinnacle from which alone she can inspire the most noble virtues in her lover. It is this knowledge of her proper, distant place which gives a hollow ring to the legal *sententia* in lines 58–60, which barely conceals the lover's dismay at her 'moral' diminution in his eyes.[32] The closing *sirima*, which is not a *congedo* in the strict sense, breaks away from hypothetical gestures of honour and guilt and accepts the *status quo* as if it were a new, down-to-earth beginning not unlike the fresh start in ss. 19–20:

vo serverò de quant'eo so valere,
remosso onne villano intendimento;
e per simil convento
piacciavi, amor, mia fedeltá tenere.   c. xvi, 65–8

[I shall serve you to the limit of my power, with no trace of dishonourable intention, and I want you, love, to accept my devotion with a matching response.]

Canzone xvi, like c. ii, portrays a stage in the persona's knowledge and experience beyond the hopeless suffering of the early sonnets,[33] yet the 'gentil mia donna' anaphora and the archaic tone[34] highlight a will in the poem to recapture a romantic era of the courtly relationship — a pure, lost phase.

This seemingly conscious movement in c. xvi to stave off male cynicism, which recalls the closing sonnets of the *ars amandi*, is not evident in c. xxii. In this last *canzone* of the group where Guittone leaves the *congedo* unsigned, he makes a discreet use of simile and metaphor like that in certain less contorted closing sonnets of the third cycle.[35] This, along with the *sententiae*, the 'gioia gioiosa' incipit and the modest but significant use of *rimalmezzo*,[36] encourages me to read c. xxii as a middle-phase treatment of the ideal lover under the normal stress of unrequited love. The poem displays a thin line of sentiment, archaic in tone and tricked out with a serrated metre and with literary echoes:

> Amor, non mi dispero,
> ca non fora valenza:
> bona soffrenza — fa bon compimento;
> e lo grecesco empero,
> l'ora che Troia assise,
> non se devise — per soffrir tormento,
> né perché sí fort'era,
> che di nulla manera
> vedea che se potesse concherere;
> e pur misel a morte:
> e chi lo suo piú forte
> conquide, dobla laude vol avere. c. xxii, 37–48

[Love, I shall not despair, for that would not be manly: it is steady perseverance that wins out in the end. The Greek nation, when it beseiged Troy, did not flinch from enduring the struggle in spite of its losses, even though because of the enemy's strength it could see no way of emerging the victor; and yet it vanquished the enemy. Thus when the weaker party wins it deserves double praise.]

I had suggested, on the grounds of the 'gioia' opening and the non-authorial *congedo*,[37] that c. xxii might reflect a transitional stage between the second and third cycles, and have now been led to place it later, which only shows that placing of this kind must remain a tentative reflection of features within the poems. At most it is only a loose guide to the emergence of a directly articulate author who translates his control into the very fabric of individual *canzoni*. But using the range of evidence provided by the sonnets and taking stock of the progressively detached stance vis-à-vis primitive *fin' amors* which they outline, one can say that the five *canzoni* with a *congedo* in embryo (c. ii, vii, xiv, xvi, xxii)[38] evince more obvious authorial control than the four *canzoni* with no *congedo* at all (c. iii, v, vi, xxiv). Compared with the naive spirit of those four *canzoni*, all five mark various stages of retreat from a persona who speaks for and embodies (if only fictionally) the author himself. This retreat is even more obvious in the *canzoni* with a *congedo* clearly distinct from the body of the poem, a *congedo* which introduces the poet *in persona propria*. Excluding cc. xvii, xviii and xix these poems are six in number, cc. i, iv, x, xi, xii and xxi, to which we can add c. xiii though it has no *congedo* at all.

At a first reading it seems that four of these poems, cc. x, xi, xii and xiii, are as contorted in their rhyme play as anything in the sonnets; and in the *congedo* of four of them, c. i, iv, xii, xxi, there is a named dedicatee or recipient. These two observations are not unconnected and help to marshall the points relevant to my argument.

The four bravura poems are authorial vaunts in the difficult manner of ss. 77 and 79, and, like those sonnets, juggle the commonplace and old-fashioned courtly catchwords in bewildering patterns of composite, identical and equivocal rhymes. In all of them Guittone distracts the reader's eye and mind from banal content by virtuoso verbal feats. In the most stupefying of them, c. xiii,[39] there is no need or room for Guittone's signature in the shape of a *congedo*. The rhyme scheme of c. x is less tortuous, but the terse, short-line syntax amply reflects the 'schermo' theme and puts up a splendid smokescreen against would-be detractors:[40]

> Ma 'n altra parte fo
> d'amor sembranza e modo,
> ove non sento pro;
> e se ciascuno tro
> ch'altr'a stagion mi modo,
> non so ch'eo faccia o fo;
> or mi piace ch'om creda
> ch'eo pur ad arte parli:
> ch'eo non dico per farli
> lasciar né tener fermo
> ciò che pensa; ché sermo
> non mende tolle 'n preda.   c. x, 37–48

[However, what I do is pretend that I love someone else who in fact doesn't interest me. And if people believe that I am changing tack regularly and don't know what I am doing, I'd like to give the impression that what I say is only sham. I don't speak to dissuade or persuade my audience: gossip can deprive me of nothing that I own.]

The *canzone* ends with a spirited *congedo* which gives a nicely equivocal twist to the signing-off statement:

> Prenda la mia parola
> ciascun sí como vole;
> ché, di ciò ch'esser sole,
> eo per lor non mi stanco,
> che non mi posson manco
> far d'una cosa sola.   c. x, 61–6

[I don't care what construction people put on my words. I have no intention of being other than true to myself, in spite of them. There is not one thing that they can deprive me of.]

Is this the persona smug at the success of his ruse, or the poet in cocky, throw-away mood leaving the slow reader to his own devices? It can only be the latter sense in the first *congedo* of c. xi, where Guittone excludes non-litterati and makes his celebrated claim to the title of virtuoso:

> Scuro saccio che par lo
> mio detto, ma' che parlo
> a chi s'entend' ed ame:
> ché lo 'ngegno mio dàme
> ch'i' me pur provi d'onne
> mainera, e talento ònne.   c. xi, 61–6

[I know that my poetry seems obscure, but I address myself to those who are in love. It is my imagination that spurs me to try out every kind of verse; and I want to do so.]

The poem's cryptic and sententious treatment of the 'worth-in-waiting' theme[41] is so patently an exercise in the obscure style that the 'lontananza' *congedo*, with its place-name fixing a physical distance, comes as a surprise:

> Move, canzone, adessa,
> vanne 'n Arezzo ad essa
> da cui tegno ed ò,
> se 'n alcun ben mi do;
> e di' che presto so'
> di tornar, se vol, so.　　　　　　　　　　　c. xi, 67–72

[Song, make speed at once and go to her in Arezzo to whom I owe whatever good I possess; and tell her that I am ready to be hers once more if she wishes.]

It is almost an apology for the brashness of the first *congedo*, as if Guittone were saying, 'But seriously, the separation I spoke of is the real thing'. I would read this *congedo* as a witty climax to the poem's verbal exploitation of the pasteboard sentiments derived from the 'lontananza' genre.[42] The second *congedo* does not turn c. xi into an anguished lament for the distant beloved. It simply underlines the difference in sound between the voice of the persona (in the second *congedo*) and that of the author (in the first *congedo*). It shows that at a point in his early development, a point to which the latter part of the third cycle corresponds, Guittone was sufficiently detached from the former voice and confident of the latter to mix them at will and experiment with their sound effects.[43]

In the *congedi* of cc. x and xi Guittone flaunts his skill before a general audience without bothering to ease the familiar ideas into familiar, formulaic shapes. In cc. xii and xxi however, he addresses poems on equally commonplace themes to fellow poets, which perhaps explains why these two *canzoni* are more measured and 'poetic', and why the *congedo* of each poem draws no attention to the poet's craftsmanship:[44]

> Va, canzon, s'el te piace, da mia parte
> al bon messer Meglior, che dona e parte
> tutto ciò che l'omo ha 'n esta parte.　　　　　c. xii, 46–8

[Song, please go on my behalf to good Messer Megliore, who bestows and distributes all that one possesses in this life.]

Canzone xii makes a fine show of equivocal and derived rhymes, and the rhymes are a series of *replicationes* on the root word chosen for each stanza:

> Prego fo lei che tuttor sia ben saggia,
> sí non m'auzida alcuna stagion, s'aggia
> temenza ch'eo l'afenda, se non saggia
> che vero sia per affermata saggia;
> ch'eo son sí d'amar lei coverto e saggio　　　c. xii, 37–41

[I beg her to be always prudent lest at any time she kill me through mere suspicion that I might offend her — unless she has clear proof from a reliable witness that any accusation against her is true. I have been so careful and discreet in loving her.]

Yet the lines are all of eleven syllables, straightforward in sense except at the end rhyme as the quotation shows, and painfully archaic in concept and language. These idealistic sentiments are trite and tired, fit for little else but a virtuoso barrage. Left as they are, or were, they show best what he can do with them; and the trick at the end of each line points, line by line, to the facile syllables that precede it.

Canzone xxi is less pretentious[45] and more serious in its restatement of the theme of service, which is perhaps why Pellizzari joined it to the sonnets of the first cycle. The archaic language and the persona's apparently unself-conscious 'sincerity' in the body of the poem certainly recall the early phase of simple *fin' amors* experience:

> Tant'alto segnoraggio
> ho disiato avere,
> non credo aver ned aggio
> al mondo par, secondo mia valenza;
> e ciò considerando
> quanto e dolze e piacere
> su me distese amando,
> vecino foi che morto di temenza.   c. xxi, 33–40

[I longed to be under such an exalted command; I doubt if I shall ever find its equal anywhere, given my qualities. When I realized what sweet beauty surrounded me with her love, I nearly died of fear.]

Yet the second *congedo* reveals Guittone in his role as arbiter of sentimental orthodoxy[46] as he recalls a fellow-poet to the purest sources of their inspiration. In c. xxi Guittone hands out a lesson on a well-tried (perhaps forgotten) subject; terse enough to make Mazzeo read it closely, and sufficiently well-balanced between pseudo-narrative and courtly *sententiae*[47] to prove the case for patience. The first *congedo*[48] gratuitously adds the 'lontananza' motif to express the ideal perfectly. He will 'starle servente/tacitore e soffrente' (lines 85–6). The notion of physical separation is absent from the rest of the poem;[49] so the motif is brought in to seal the *canzone*, as a reminder of a past age of chivalry. It resembles those self-consciously 'provenzaleggianti' sonnets late in the third cycle where the 'lontananza' motif was used for the first time.

The two remaining *canzoni* in this group, cc. i and iv, are also addressed to real people but to patrons rather than poets,[50] and their *congedi* draw the clearest line of all between the body of the poem and the author's signature.[51] These two *canzoni* exploit *fin' amors* idealism and even recall the callous teaching of the *ars amandi* sonnets. The *congedo* of c. iv breaks the 'suffering-servant' rule sacred to the true *fin' amors* lover. It counsels more aggression than he would have dreamed of, and equates 'gioia d'amor' with a euphemistic but hardly sentimental phrase, 'ardimento compiuto':

> ch'ardimento compiuto
> sta bene a donna de vostra valenza.

> Ubertin, dolze amico,
> or agio eo ben provato
> ch'amar troppo celato
> ten l'om de gioi d'amor sempre mendico.   c. iv, 59–64

[for complete and fearless giving befits a lady of your worth. Ubertino, dear friend, now I have shown that loving too discreetly never brings a man the full joy of love.]

Could one suspect that Guittone had ever felt for the trembling, lily-white 'fedel' dedicated to the high ideal of perpetual frustration? The poem is a clever[52] and tongue-in-cheek example of how to twist courtly formulae to suit anti-idealistic ends. In so far as it presents an experience[53] it demonstrates the poet's advice in s. 99 — how to approach 'lei ched è par'. The opening stanza lodges a formal, high-style complaint, 'Ahi lasso', against her scorn, but by the third stanza he has begun to use the best authorities (in this case, on the origins and nature of love) to prove why he should have his 'gioia' with her (lines 25–36).[54] 'Umilmente laudando', he proceeds to argue on religious grounds that she reciprocate:

> Amar chi v'ama tanto,
> amor, giá non fallate,
> ma se voi non lo amate:
> ché Deo chi l'ama merta in cento tanto.   c. iv, 45–8[55]

[Love, you can never do wrong by loving the man who loves you so; rather, you do wrong not to love him. Our example is God, who rewards a hundredfold the one who loves Him.]

And, protesting to the bitter end (lines 53–5),[56] he makes out that his reward, 'ardimento compiuto', will suit a fine girl like her. The *congedo* argues that the best (i.e. most realistic) service is no longer the silent, suffering variety since it gets a man nowhere. Perhaps Ubertino should brush up his ideas. However, Guittone is less jaunty with his cultivated, would-be patron Currado da Sterleto:[57]

> Currado da Sterleto, mea canzone
> vo mando e vo presento,
> ché vostro pregio vento
> m'ha voi fedele e om de ciò ch'eo vaglio   c. i, 106–9

[Currado of Sterleto, I present my song to you, for your noble qualities have won me to your service, however little I may have to offer you.]

The poem he sends him is a longer and more rambling collection of commonplaces than c. iv; yet, like the *canzone* sent to the ex-*podestà* of Arezzo, it combines the multiple formulae of *fin' amors* devotion with didactic asides[58] and comes to a head in a clear demand for action (lines 93–105). As in the *ars amandi* sonnets love loses its mysterious quality of self-generation (lines 1–6), to become a commodity that can be 'used' and 'made':

> vorrea che l'amistá nostra de fatto
> ormai, donna, s'usasse . . .
> Ché de fare amistate
> certo lo tardare pareme matto   c. i, 96–7, 100–1[59]

[lady, now I'd like our love to express itself in deed . . . for any delay in practising our love seems quite absurd to me.]

Although the confident teaching of the *ars amandi* sonnets[60] takes on in this *canzone* the spaciousness and literary depth of a wide range of images,[61] it remains a set piece, 'mea canzone' (line 106),[62] submitted by the author for his patron's delight and approval.

I have dwelt at some length on the *canzoni* with an authorial *congedo* because all of them illustrate various degrees of withdrawal from simple commitment to *fin' amors*. It may not be possible to mark out these steps in number and order, but it seems that when Guittone is most inclined to exercise his ingenuity on the rhyme schemes and syntax the ideas are trite in content and narrow in range, whereas the more spacious and flowing stanza patterns lend themselves to a sophisticated and often ambiguous treatment of the familiar courtly commonplaces. Either way he leaves little room for the illusion of a first-person 'experience' of love, and it is significant that only two of the *canzoni* we have looked at, cc. xi and xxi,[63] hint at a real event as motor force of the poem's sentiments. In each case it is the physical separation evoked by the 'lontananza' genre; and in neither case does it carry the conviction of a genuine experience. There is a contradiction in terms between a lover's closing address to his distant lady and a poet's address to a real-life correspondent, if the two are combined in the poem as they are in cc. xi and xxi.

There are, however, several remaining *canzoni* which develop the 'lontananza' motif in a more thorough-going fashion, and since they pinpoint the two roles of author and persona in an unmistakable way, they provide a fitting close to this discussion of Guittone's extended courtly poems. The four *canzoni* in question are cc. viii, ix, xxiii and xv. The first three are conventional expressions of fear and hope generated by separation. The last, a mixture of courtly and non-courtly themes, is remarkable when read in the context of all the poems[64] where Guittone seeks to recapture a situational impetus for stylized and vapid sentiments.

We have seen that Guittone can use the *congedo* to underline the fictional nature of the persona's words. In a 'lontananza' poem the *congedo* has the opposite effect because that genre turns the conventional distance of mind, heart and body on which the lyric 'closed circle' depends, into a concrete reality. When the lover turns to his poem and sends it to the distant beloved, the *congedo* performs the special function of identifying the persona as lover and poet, particularly when the place *ad quem* remains vague[65] and the *congedo* summarises the poem's message. If the place is named and has some historical connexion with the author, we can presume that he wants us to see *him* as the persona. The place name 'Arezzo' will be to the *canzoni* what the proper name 'Guittone' is to the sonnets. It suggests a certain poignancy when we recall that by 1263 he would be exiled from the city, and that the great post-conversion laments for the decline of civic virtue, in particular 'O dolce terra aretina' (c. xxxiii), are born of bitter experience of the town to which many of the love poems had been addressed. It could well be that the courtly 'lontananza' poems, written before his exile, reflect his foreboding in a suitable literary genre.

In the three conventional 'lontananza' poems Guittone uses both kinds of dissimulation, c. xxiii being less explicit than the other two and proportionately lower-pitched in tone:

> Va, mia canzon, lá ov'io non posso gire,
> e raccomanda mene
> a lei, che m' ha per suo leal servente;
> e dí che sia piagente
> di dareme matera e 'nsegnamento
> di dir lo mio talento,
> com'io potesse lei . . .   c. xxiii, 52–8

[Go, my song, where it is out of bounds for me, and commend me to her whose loyal servant I am. Tell her to please teach me how I can express to her my longing.]

The *congedo*, neutral and periphrastic in the old style, hardly alters the situationally nondescript character of the rest of the poem:

> Fallenza forse pare
> a lei ch'io son partuto
> di lá ove stava, e stogli or piú lontano.   c. xxiii, 35–7

[Perhaps she thinks that I did wrong to leave the place where she was, and from which I am now even more remote.]

The 'io' rests in his self-imposed torment confident that it proves his worth (lines 33–4, 45–7), while the three stanzas sketch a calm and facile world of commonplaces.[66] It looks a slight and early piece untroubled by the biographical needs which complicate cc. viii and ix.

'Lasso, pensando quanto' (c. ix) has the mark of a later poem. The terse, short-line syntax, accentuated by regular *rimalmezzo*, sustains a dense litany of high-style lament; yet the very rhetoric of that lament undermines the sense of physical separation which might have made it convincing:

> (pensando) . . . che sollazzo e canto
> e ben tutto ch'avia
> m'è or, per mia follia, — corrotto e noia;
> e ch'entra gente croia
> ed en selvaggia terra
> mi trovo; ciò m'è guerra, — onde morria
> de mie man, s'altri osasse
> a ragion darsi morte.   c. ix, 4–11

[and when, in my brooding, I see that joy and song and every good that I once possessed has now, through my folly, become a grievance and a burden, and that I am now thrust into loathsome company in a foreign land — all this torments me so much that, if one could rationally defend suicide, I would kill myself.]

The Boethian memory of past happiness is not caused by the present reality of 'gente croia' and 'selvaggia terra' (lines 7, 8) but is complementary to it; and the topography of exile etched in those commonplace phrases[67] is at once submerged under a flood of sentimental hyperbole.[68] The sense of place and physical distance is extraneous to the purgative note of contrition, and not *prior* to it, as cause to effect. The desert wilderness evoked in the closing lines, instead of setting the lover in a barren and menacing 'selvaggia terra', is merely a simile for transferred religious sentiment:

> e no mi fa soffrire
> talento d'acquistare
> a lei tosto tornare, — ov'a ben vegna;
> ma, perché 'n parte soe,
> u' po, come 'n deserto,
> prender de fallo om merto, — e' qua steroe
> en mal, mentre seroe — del mendo certo.　　　c. ix, 59–65

[what makes me suffer is not the longing to win a speedy return to her, and so regain a lost good; but, rather, it's the fact that I am now in a place where sin can be expiated, as in a desert, and that I shall suffer here until I know that the debt is paid.]

Exile becomes a punishment for sin rather than a source of grief — a purgatory in the religion of love.[69] The contrast between these obscure, halting lines and the matter-of-fact *congedo* shows how easily Guittone can drop the artifice of stereotyped self-encouragement:

> Va a le parte d'Arezzo,
> canzon, e a lei dí quale
> spera m'aiuta e vale.　　　c. ix, 66–8

[Song, go to the district of Arezzo and tell her of the hope that sustains and strengthens me.]

The persona's anguish is apparently Guittone's; the protagonist of the poem is obviously the Aretino himself. If the author is the protagonist in the *congedo* he must also be the 'io' in the rest of the poem, and so the *congedo* signature becomes the key and proof of genuine 'lontananza' which the body of the poem on its own fails to establish.

Like the sonnets late in the third cycle, which attempt to vary and prolong the narrative with fresh events, c. ix loses itself in the elaborate emotional responses long since derived from the event. The biographical *congedo* is a device to rescue those disembodied sentiments, as mechanically applied as is the poet's name in ss. 29 and 59.[70] It will hardly carry weight unless 'lontananza' is shown to be a physical separation, because the phrases for grief, hope and self-denial carry their own topic charge and can be varied in intensity and sequence to create a pathos independent of the genre's situational core. If the supposed separation of lover and lady is merely emotional, the disproportion between the event and its emotive effects within the poem may be even greater, as is the case in c. viii, 'A renformare amore e fede e spera'.

Despite the *congedo* c. viii is not strictly a 'lontananza' lament. Whatever the the nature of the lover's recent 'folle partita' (line 9), it has already been healed by her 'dolze saluto' (line 12)[71] when the poem begins (lines 6–14). From the second stanza onwards the tone encourages positive, mutual enjoyment, as if they were present to one another:

> Nostro amor, ch'ebbe bon cominciamento,
> mezzo e fine meglior, donna, ne chere . . .
>
> Adonque, dolze amor, viso m'è bene
> che bon conforto de' porger fra noi
> ciò, ch'eo posso onne ben sperar de voi,
> e voi, secondo el parer meo, de mene   c. viii, 15–16, 43–6

[Since our love began so well, its progress and completion must needs be better, my lady . . . therefore, sweet love, it is clear to me that we must draw comfort from the fact that I can count on all good from you and that, from my side, you can count on the same from me.]

The lover coaxes his lady at close range (lines 15–16, 29–30, 57–60), with an assurance glibly based on impeccable *sententiae*:[72]

> Noia e corrotto intralassar dovemo,
> pensando quanto dolze e amorosa
> será nostra amistá, poi che 'n gioiosa
> parte dolze d'amor rassembreremo;
> ch'usando l'om pur de portar piacere,
> non conosce che vale;
> ma, sostenendo male,
> a bene tornando, dolzore
> piò che non sa gli ha savore   c. viii, 57–65

[We shall forget all grief and worry when we consider how sweet and gentle our love will be once we harvest the sweet fruits of love in a state of joy. If a man is accustomed to nothing but pleasure he does not value it; but if he regains a good after an experience of suffering it will taste sweeter than he could have imagined.]

Since he shows the resourcefulness advocated in the *ars amandi* rather than the long face of a 'fedel lontano', the mention of Arezzo in the *congedo* opens up a distance which had been closed in the first stanza. Yet the poet addresses himself directly to the lady, not to bridge the gap between them but simply to praise her:

En le parti d'Arezzo, o nel distretto,
che voi, dolze amor, siate,
mando che vi deggiate
per ciò ch'ho detto allegrare,
e perché sete for pare
fra le forzose al mondo donne Artine;
ché, sí com'è piú fine
or d'ogn'altro metallo,
son elle, amor, for fallo
piú fine ch'altre a ciascun bene aletto.　　　　c. viii, 71–80

[In Arezzo or nearby, wherever you may be, sweet love, my message is that
what I've said should bring you joy, and that you are peerless among the
splendid women of Arezzo, themselves more splendid than any other. For
just as gold is superior to all other metals, so they, my love, are without
doubt more perfect than other women in the eyes of every chosen lover.]

The emphatic biographical note, 'le parti d'Arezzo, o nel distretto', 'le forzose
Artine', is muted by his vision of a mounting pyramid of praise, as if Guittone
could not choose between the faint echoes of 'lontananza' in the poem (lines
6–10, 19) and its bolder plea for mutual love.

In the 'lontananza' poems Guittone comes face to face with the problem
that besets all his courtly poetry. In an effort to restore some sense of reality to
the residue of ideal emotions clustering round the genre motif, he tries to
imprint on them the seal of his own experience. The sonnets (ss. 72–5, 80) were
worked into a biographical narrative; the *canzoni* present the poet-lover as
absent from his native city. Neither way is convincing, and the failure of the
'lontananza' *canzoni* to resolve the traditional formulae into biographical terms
typifies the noble failure of all Guittone's *fin' amors* poetry. But we cannot judge
the intensity of his effort to revitalize the 'lontananza' motif unless we look in
some detail at c. xv, 'Gente noiosa e villana', one of the most remarkable poems
in his *canzoniere* and the most telling witness to that authorial process I have
tried to describe.

Margueron assigns c. xv to the year 1262 or 1263,[73] a poem written during
Guittone's voluntary exile after the Guelph defeat at Montaperti. In it the poet
attacks corruption in Arezzo, justifies his departure from his native city, and
ends with two stanzas on the theme of amorous 'lontananza'. This closing
section suffers by comparison with the bitter, personal tone of the first seven
stanzas and has been summarily dealt with by various scholars more intent on
the political and biographical clues in the rest of the poem.[74] Yet the 'lontananza'
stanzas cannot be dismissed as a 'canonical addition' because, for the first and
only time in Guittone's courtly poetry,[75] the lament of a distant lover can
spring from a *real* separation. Political exile offers the ready-made and indis-
putable biographical proof which Guittone had tried to fabricate in the *congedi*
of his earlier 'lontananza' poems, and we must see how he grafts the ritual
phrases of love-longing on to the fact of political exile.

In a traditional 'lontananza' poem the place *a quo* is sacred to her memory. By contrast, the place to which the lover goes is 'strana', 'selvaggia', and 'crudele'; and 'la gente', 'croia' and 'villana'. Whatever the reasons hinted at for his departure[76] he takes no satisfaction in the departure itself, while his fear and hope take on a certain credibility when they grow out of nostalgia for the place he has left behind. *Canzone* xv reverses this order in every detail:

> Gente noiosa e villana
> e malvagia e vil signoria
> e giùdici pien' di falsia
> e guerra perigliosa e strana
>   fanno me, lasso, la mia terra odiare
> e l'altrui forte amare:
> però me departut'ho
> d'essa e qua venuto   c. xv, 1–8[77]

[Loathsome and coarse inhabitants, an evil and corrupt government, deceitful pillars of law, a dangerous and ominous war; all this, alas, makes me hate my native city and cleave to another. This is why I have left it and come here.]

This pessimistic moral stricture which runs right through the first seven stanzas clashes with the traditional optimism of the lover's desire to return. Guittone tries to resolve that clash by making the 'lontananza' stanzas prolong the exile theme as a narrative extension:

> Solo però la partenza
> fumi crudele e noiosa,
> che la mia gioia gioiosa
> vidila in grande spiagenza   c. xv, 99–102

[However, leaving the city did distress me for the one reason that I saw that my joyful joy would remain there very unhappy.]

He alters the direction of grief to make the *lady* express in direct speech that regret which is normally expressed by the lover, thus creating in poetic terms a lively sense[78] of the effect of his departure within the city:

> ché disseme piangendo: — Amore meo,
> mal vidi el giorno ch'eo
> foi de te pria vogliosa,
> poi ch'en sì dolorosa
> parte deggio de ciò, lasso, finire   c. xv, 103–7

[for she said to me through her tears, 'My love, I rue the day when I was first smitten with love for you, since because of it I must end up, alas, so wretched.]

The literary reminiscence of grief at parting, adapted to suit his voluntary exile, salvages some worth and honour for the otherwise unredeemable city[79] as she makes a typically male *fin' amors* profession of total self-dedication to her absent lover:

> ch'eo verrò forsennata,
> tanto son ben mertata
> s'eo non fior guardat'aggio
> desnore ni danaggio
> a met[t]erme del tutto in tuo piacere.   c. xv, 108–12[80]

[that I shall go mad. This is what I deserve for disregarding all shame and taint to put myself completely in your hands.]

The second stanza, which sustains the liveliness of reported speech (line 113), shows that in this, as in the previous stanza, Guittone isolated from the traditional theme just those elements compatible with the exile motif. The most stoic and elevated reaction to 'lontananza' was to accept it as a test of sure worth and to wish for no change.[81] The lover's voluntary acceptance of separation is only a small step from his choice of it; and Guittone now fastens on the ideal of acquiring merit by distant service because it dovetails with his positive choice of exile:

> ma la ragion che detto aggio di sovra
> e lo talento e l'ovra
> ch'eo metto in agrandire
> me per lei più servire,
> me fa ciò fare, e dia portar perdono   c. xv, 117–21

[But the reason that I gave above, and the longing and the effort that I expend on perfecting myself to serve her more faithfully, all this obliges me to go away and should win me forgiveness.]

The poem's two streams of thought meet in these lines. He would like to show them as intertwined and undivided. The earlier 'ragion' (on the corruption which forced him to leave Arezzo, lines 15–42, and his resolve not to return until peace and reason were restored, lines 75–9, 90–8) is part of the same continuing discourse, line 117. This, and the desire to perfect his love service, are joined by a simple conjunction which gives them parity, lines 117–18. And the unity of the two voluntary choices (of exile for political reasons and separation for *fin' amors* reasons) is hammered home by an *exemplum* from the most altruistic literature on the subject:[82]

> ché già soleva stare,
> per gran bene aquistare,
> lontan om lungiamente
> da sua donna piacente,
> savendo lui, ed a · llei, forte bono.   c. xv, 122–6

[for in times past one was content to remain for a long time remote from one's lovely lady, in the hope of great reward — a virtue that sorely tried both parties.]

Guittone consciously evokes a past literary ideal, 'già soleva stare', to balance the acrimony of the earlier stanzas. The ascetic terminology of *fin' amors* purification covers both the civic virtue he alludes to in line 117, and the courtly self-perfection in lines 118–19. The two together have made him 'de lei longiar'; the two together become a single reason for 'perdono'. The soft, conventional optimism of 'per gran bene acquistare' salves the hurt feelings which Guittone's strident self-justification in the early stanzas barely concealed. It turns an otherwise necessary and fatefully imposed wrench of separation into the virtue of a chosen course of action.

Guittone's will to balance the logic of exile with an idealized emotional reaction is borne out by the presence and order of the double *congedo*. The first echoes the 'lontananza' stanzas; the second, the exile stanzas. The whole poem takes on a chiastic structure[83] in which the sentiment of parting and the experience of exile, given equal treatment in the matching *congedi*, are meant to assume equal importance in the body of the poem:

> Va', mia canzone, ad Arezzo, in Toscana,
> a lei ch'aucide e sana
> lo meo core sovente,
> e di' ch'ora parvente
> serà como val ben nostra amistate:
>   ché castel ben fornito
> e non guaire assallito
> no è tener pregiato,
> ma quel ch'è asseggiato
> e ha de ciò che vol gran necestate.
>
>   E anco me di' lei e a ciascuno
> meo caro amico e bono
> che non dia sofferire
> pena del meo partire;
> ma de sua rimembranza aggio dolere:
>   ch'a dannaggio ed a noia
> è remesso e a croia
> gente e fello paiese;
> m'eo son certo 'n cortese,
> pregi' aquistando e solazzo ed avere.   c. xv, 127–46

[Go, my song, to Arezzo in Tuscany, to the lady who keeps on wounding and healing my heart, and tell her that it must now be clear that our love is worthwhile. It is not the well-stocked castle under no attack that wins respect, but the one that is beseiged and lacks the provisions that it needs.

More than that, tell her and each of my dear, good friends that my departure must not cause them suffering. I am the one to suffer when I think of them, for they have been left behind, to their harm and affliction, in the midst of objectionable people in a degenerate town, whereas I am in civilized company gaining esteem, comfort and wealth.]

The inconsistency of tone that breaks through the juxtaposition of the 'lontananza' stanzas with the exile stanzas is heightened in the close pairing of the two *congedi*. Discords are inevitable. There is an archaic periphrase for the tantalizing shadow-lady, lines 128–9, and a plain line for Guittone's friends, line 138; a courtly 'pregio' won by bearing with separation, lines 132–4, and an ethical 'pregio' that comes with gladly staying away, lines 145–6; the hint of nostalgia for 'Arezzo, in Toscana' as his goal once the siege is over, lines 127, 132–6, and a ruthless application of the 'foreign land' epithets to his own native city, lines 142–4; a *sententia*[84] to build up *her* morale, lines 132–6, and complacency in his own good fortune, lines 145–6. Yet Guittone holds together fearlessly the two clusters of ideas by joining the second *congedo* to the first with a bland conjunction, lines 136–7, and by addressing the second *congedo* to *her* as well as to his friends, lines 137–8.

Just as in the final stanza, where the 'ragion' for his exile and the dictates of *fin' amors* perfection were pinned together by a simple conjunction to become a single reason for his going away, so now 'Arezzo, in Toscana' is the lover's *terminus ad quem* and the exile's *terminus a quo* — the lady is lifted down from her pinnacle to be thrust among the exile's friends. The second *congedo* stands the stock farewell on its head. Those left behind are the ones to be pitied; it is they and not the exile who find themselves 'entra croia gente e fello paiese'.[85] Yet the poem's audacity lies in its assumption that, if an individual's civic honour can serve a *fin' amors* ideal (lines 117–21), the lady should not be spared the exile's comfortless words to his real friends. In the context of exile-language she takes on a concrete quality she never had in the conventional 'lontananza' poems.

Canzone xv may not stand comparison with Dante's 'Amor, da che convien pur ch'io mi doglia'[86] but the linking of real exile to literary 'lontananza', common to both, shows how promising Guittone's experiment was. In the other 'lontananza' poems he had tried to freshen the stale formulae with a personal signature, 'va ad Arezzo'. Political exile at once restored a core of reality to the motif. The only problem was how to bring the two into fruitful conjunction because, as the first stanza of c. xv shows, the exile's raw disgust contradicts the elegiac yearning which was the only emotional response allowed in the 'lontananza' motif. *Canzone* xv is not a polished synthesis but it is a striking advance on the biographical experiments in the rest of his courtly poetry. It is a transitional poem in the thematic as well as the chronological sense. It is not simply a foretaste of later laments on civic themes, such as c. xxxiii, but a confident return to the pervasive courtly theme of 'lontananza'. Guittone can return triumphantly to the most esoteric concept of *fin' amors* purification because his exile restores to 'lontananza' its long-lost colour of real event. In this sense c. xv looks back over the range of poems on the theme of separation. It is a recapitulation at a point of change and leads us to the one remaining courtly *canzone* which gathers together a series of earlier statements, and which will bring this study of Guittone's early poetry to a close.

'Ahi lasso, che li boni e li malvagi' (c. xx) is Guittone's pre-conversion defence of womankind, and older sister to the long *canzone*, 'Altra fiata aggio giá, donne, parlato' (c. xlix), which recalls it in its opening line. *Canzone* xx attracts little notice to itself. The stanza scheme is unremarkable apart from a short third *congedo*. The poet's feminist stand is based on common scholastic arguments which end with praise of a lady who is a paragon of feminine virtues and the glory of her sex. Margueron assigns the poem to the transitional phase just prior to Guittone's entry into religious life.[87] Since it is the major statement of his attitude to women at the end of the courtly period, it will be useful to recall again the changes in that attitude as they were registered in the sonnets, which give an extended picture of Guittone's absorption of the troubadour tradition.

In the first three cycles the lady is 'saggia' or 'orgogliosa' depending on the emotional tide; she is a constant, unseen spur to a pure form of male courtly idealism. Yet at various points in the *fin' amors* sonnets Guittone refused to toe the traditional line; and one sensed that even then he saw the lady as something more than a cypher. In s. 5, 5–6, Guittone supposed, by way of contrast, that an ugly woman could have all the other courtly attributes. In s. 19, 1–8, the lover admitted that he, like others, had used the code to deceive women. The lady, in ss. 37–49, undercut her serious suitor by pointing out the nonsense in his *fin' amors* hyperbole. What I described in the narrative cycles as a gradual process of authorial disenchantment with the archaic stance and attitudes, is marked by an intermittent but progressive levelling of the male and female roles until, in the 'tenzone con la donna villana', they are reversed. The *ars amandi* presumed that the courtly code was useful only for seduction, and that all along the lady knew and played the game.

Her plunge on the barometer of esteem corresponds to the drop in first-person *fin' amors* idealism. The genre conventions that govern the last two families of sonnets leave no room for the language of male devotion, but it is significant that, having tried the serious stance, Guittone turned to genres closer in spirit to everyday reality.[88] His question in s. 106, 9–11, which sought to reconcile the *ars amandi* teaching with its practical effects, argues that Guittone had a lively awareness of courtly and anti-courtly literature as mirrors and models of social conduct.

Canzone xx takes up the unanswered question of s. 106.[89] In practice men do exploit the sentimental residue of the courtly code, and women are despised when they succumb.[90] Only someone who knew the exalted position they once held in literature could seek to salvage some of that lost respect; and this is what the opening lines of the poem make clear will be his aim. When, in the sonnets, Guittone expressed his innate personal sympathy for women, they were real people with a moral dimension, rather than literary protagonists subject to the tyranny of a code of manners in full decline. A suffering lover could not have defended his lady. There was nothing to defend because her exalted place was not in danger. But in the perspective of Guittone's hind-sighted vision of courtly literature and his probing of its 'real' content, his present defence of women against courtly exploitation presumes that they are no longer at the top of some feudal ladder. Anti-idealistic poetry reflects real-life *mores* in amatory affairs. The poet will make good her descent in esteem not by recalling the altruism of the first poetic but by a fresh, non-literary statement of her place in creation. His earlier sympathetic insights into the lady of literature, as if she had moral and emotional susceptibilities, are in c. xx translated into a thorough-going statement on behalf of real women, identified with those ladies of the past who once ennobled their faithful servants. There are several passages in the first two stanzas for which these general observations are poor substitutes:

> Ahi lasso, che li boni e li malvagi
> omini tutti hano preso acordanza
> di mettere le donne in despregianza;
> e ciò più ch'altro far par che lor agi.
> > Per che mal aggia el ben tutto e l'onore
> che fatto han lor, poi n'han merto sì bello   c. xx, 1–6

[Alas, good and evil men alike have all conspired to bring womankind into disrepute, and this seems to give them more satisfaction than anything else. For this reason, cursed be all the good and honour that ladies have conferred on men, now that they have received such a fine reward.]

These lines recapitulate the history of courtly experiments which Guittone unfolded in the sonnets. The 'boni e malvagi', Guittone's real contemporaries, have their literary counterparts in the 'tenzone con la donna villana' and certain of the *ars amandi* sonnets. But once upon a time in the lyrics on which the narrative cycles were based, those same ladies were the source of their lovers' worth and honour. Guittone's sarcastic *exclamatio*, lines 5–6, imposes a continuity of experience on past literary idealism and present behaviour:[91]

> Non per ragion, ma per malvagia usanza,
> sovra le donne ha preso om signoria,
> ponendole 'n dispregio e 'n villania
> ciò ch'a sé cortesia pon' e orranza.
> Ahi, che villan giudicio e che fallace!   c. xx, 13–17

[Men have lorded it over ladies not on rational grounds but through depraved habit, despising in ladies what, in themselves, they hold to be refined and honourable. What a crass and false judgement that is!]

Again, keeping in mind the decline of *fin' amors* as traced in the sonnets, these lines objectify that dethronement of earlier veneration implied in the *ars amandi*. There, women were seen as bound by the courtly system, predictable in their textbook manoeuvres. Male 'segnoria' was to be won by a deceit which ignored the standards of conduct set by *fin' amors*, yet appealed to *fin' amors* to justify sexual exploits as amorous, and therefore courteous. This double standard is the 'malvagia usanza' which had already crept into the narrative sonnets.

Guittone now applies it from the personae in his poems to men in real life, all of whom have abandoned the old ideals.

The poet then launches into a chain of arguments[92] to prove the superiority of women. The climax to this demonstration is a 'proof' drawn from Scripture in the sixth stanza[93] — Genesis and the Incarnation. This is the ultimate vindication of female worth. It is a theological fact unaltered by the way women may act under the pressure of male advances. But if this is incontrovertible it is too remote from the contingencies which prompted Guittone's defence. He now adds a final, 'derived' argument which draws the practical and moral considerations of the previous four stanzas back into the context of *fin' amors*:

> Vale per sé: nent'ho detto a sembrante;
> apresso val ché fa l'omo valere:
> ché 'ngegno, forzo, ardimento, podere
> e cor de tutto ben mettere avante
>   donali donna en su' amorosa spera;
> for che el non saveria quasi altro fare
> che dormire e mangiare.   c. xx, 73–9

[So far I have shown the lady's nobility in her own right; and I have hardly done her justice. But she has this added dignity, that she transmits worth to the man; for the understanding, energy, abandonment, strength and desire to pursue what is perfect, are all bestowed on him by the lady when he places his loving trust in her. Outside of that a man would be able to do nothing but sleep and eat.]

Once more the central planet of the courtly cosmos, 'madonna' radiates to her servant that 'vertú' without which he is no more than a beast.[94] The juxtaposition of arguments is as remarkable as that between the seventh and eighth stanzas of c. xv,[95] and is achieved by an equally bland syntactic transition, 'Vale per sé ... appresso val ...', lines 73–4, except that in c. xx the closing stanza brings the argument full circle. The poet had begun his defence by contrasting the 'good and honour' which women conferred on men in high courtly literature, with the abuse they now suffer in real life. He had confirmed the privileged place given her in literature by a series of non-courtly proofs which set her once more at the pinnacle of creation. For if she had lost respect outside the true, closed courtly circle she could surely win it again by arguments drawn from somewhere else outside that system. Hence the easy passage from her creation in Genesis to the courtly virtues she bestows on her faithful lover.

I have spoken in chiastic terms of the logic with which Guittone sets out his argument: *fin' amors* feminine perfection is debased by immoral conduct; moral argument restores it. Side by side in one poem are a grasp of the idealistic current in courtly literature and a competent array of non-courtly teaching. This is a view which Guittone himself seems to countenance, for in the last five lines of the body of the poem he states his conclusion in *sententiae* which retain the balanced opposition of past *fin' amors* ideal and present practice, and show even the verbal equation of a chiasmus proper:[96]

> Adonque il senno e lo valor c'ha l'omo
> da la donna tener lo dea, sì como
> ten lo scolar dal so maestro l'arte;
> ed ella quanto face a mala parte
> dall'om tener lo pò simel mainera.   c. xx, 80–4

[Hence a man must attribute to the lady any wisdom and nobility that he has, just as the pupil draws his skill from the teacher. By the same token the lady should attribute to the man whatever wrong she does.]

In the first *congedo* Guittone pinpoints as the exact target of his moral broadside men like the male persona in the 'tenzone con la donna villana' and the model womanizer in the *ars amandi*. In the course of his defence Guittone narrows his sights from 'omini tutti', line 2, to those sympathetic to his arguments, and he presumes that his own appeal to a literary ideal of feminine worth will affect their conduct — the others are not worth worrying about:

> Prova altra no 'nde fo di ciò c'ho detto,
> ma miri ben ciascuno se ver dico,
> ché già no me desdico
> de starne a confession d'omo leale;
> e partase d'usar sì villan male
> solo cui villania par e menzogna:
> ché 'l remanente trar de sua vergogna
> non sirà tal ch'io già n'aggia deletto.   c. xx, 85–92

[I shall add no further proof to my argument, but let everyone consider whether I am speaking the truth for I shall never refuse to accept the verdict of an honourable man. Only the man who considers it base and untruthful should desist from the malpractice of abusing ladies. Dragging the rest out of their depravity is not a task that would ever give me any pleasure.]

At the end of the first stanza Guittone had brought forward his ideal lady, 'gioia gioiosa', into the company of 'le donne in despregianza'.[97] Since his defence has salvaged an ultimate, moral value for the first poetic of chivalry, he can now resume the archaic, sentimental style of address to his 'gentil donna'. With her perfection now vindicated, she compensates as literary paragon for the present defects in her sex:

> Gentil mia donna, fosse in voi tesoro
> quanto v'è senno en cor, la più valente
> fora ver' voi neente;
> e sed eo pur per reina vi tegno,
> e' vi corona onor com'altra regno:
> ché tanto è 'n voi di ben tutt' abondanza,
> che viso m'è, Amor, che la mancanza
> d'ogni altra prenda in voi assai restoro.   c. xx, 93–100

[My noble lady, if you were as rich as you are wise of heart, the most aristocratic lady would be nothing compared to you. And yet, if I look upon you
as a queen it is because honour is your crown, where a mere diadem crowns a
regent. There is such a surfeit of perfection in you, my love, that I believe that
the imperfection of every other woman is more than made good in you.]

We saw the effect in 'lontananza' poems of a place name in the *congedo*. In the
short *congedo* which brings c. xx to an end[98] it continues the line of return to a
re-vitalized veneration of the *fin' amors* lady. Emotional idealism, already
restored by abstract argument, takes on the colour of a real situation and an
authorial experience. The 'gentil donna' is no figment of his imagination but a
lady in the poet's home town:

> Ad Arezzo la mia vera canzone
> mando, Amore, a voi, per cui campione
> e servo de tutt'altre esser prometto.   c. xx, 101–3

[To Arezzo I send my true song, to you, my love, on whose behalf I vow to
be the champion and servant of all ladies.]

At first sight the admixture of 'profane and sacred' in c. xx[99] is an obvious
sign of Guittone's transition from courtly to moral themes, indicating an
unresolved tension between the weight of past literature and a growing trust in
his didactic vocation. Yet c. xx is a recapitulation of the entire history of
Guittone's pre-conversion poetry because it imposes a moral dimension on his
earlier experiments with idealistic and anti-idealistic writing. The woman's
position is a touchstone by which literary attitudes become real-life attitudes.
And if we read c. xx back into the rise and fall of *fin' amors* as traced in the
sonnets, Guittone seems to argue that the devotion to 'madonna' in the earliest
phase was the right homage, but for the wrong reasons, because its godless and
illogical sentimentality led inexorably to the selfish eroticism displayed in the
tenzone and the *ars amandi*.

In his last and most self-aware defence of *fin' amors* Guittone reinforces the
base of 'madonna's' pedestal with logic and theology, then lifts her back on to
it with the ancient festal chants of the first poetic. As a retrospective poem c. xx
helps to explain why the lady in ss. 37–49 should have questioned the sincerity
of her lover's suit. She is the mouthpiece of Guittone's sympathy for a real
person, read into the literary persona of the courtly lady. On his behalf she
questions the emotional depth of the lover's traditional formulae; and she
anticipates the criticism Guittone levels in c. xx at debased *fin' amors*, just as
c. xx is a near forerunner of the conversion manifestoes in their attack on his
love poems. By the time he wrote c. xx the movement which I traced in the
sonnets was probably complete. The difference in Guittone's criticism between
ss. 37–49 and c. xx is the difference between the author as persona consciously
adjusting the levels of discourse to make each narrative pass for biography,

and the author as moralist judging his own written work as a barometer of social attitudes.

Guittone's blanket rejection in middle life of his secular love poetry as writing, teaching and experience is not a sudden *volte-face*. It is the last in a series of re-appraisals which he made throughout the early years of his poetic development. It is a final and public step where the others had been partial and hidden. Yet Guittone had already passed judgement on his *rime d'amore* before he entered the Gaudenti. 'Ahi lasso, che li boni e li malvagi' is addressed not only to readers of courtly lyric but to 'omini tutti'. By the time the poet in exile sent this 'vera canzone' to his beloved Arezzo he had already discovered his true voice.

Summary of the ideal development in
Guittone's early poetry

In this study I have traced the growth of Guittone's poetry from its *fin' amors* beginnings (the three narrative sonnet cycles and many of the *canzoni*), through anti-idealistic genres (the *tenzone* and the *ars amandi*), to the *sirventesi* (cc. xvii, xviii and xix) and the combined *sirventese-fin' amors* poems (cc. xv and xx). The chronological order for the poetry of Guittone's 'prima maniera' did not enter into my considerations, but Margueron's table shows that the ideal order is not at variance with the chronological order. The *sirventesi* were probably written between the mid-1250s and 1262, while cc. xv and xx are assigned to the years 1262–5. The only date one has for the vast majority of the courtly poems, is the *terminus ad quem*, 1263. The following table summarises the development of Guittone's early poetry as described in the preceding chapters.

Serious presentation of classic *fin' amors*; faithful 'fedel' and remote paragon lady. The lover's sentiments are polarized into joy and anguish. The language is 'provenzaleggiante', with little technical virtuosity. Guittone betrays a stirring uneasiness with *fin' amors* as a life-style, yet identifies himself wholeheartedly with the lover at the end of the second cycle. Text, pp. 38–55	ss. 1–18	cc. iii, v, vi, xxiv.
	ss. 19–30	The lover records his sentimental experience directly and with relative simplicity. No self-consciousness in the form of a *congedo*; these *canzoni* largely free of virtuoso display. Text. pp. 92, 100.
	Suggested re-ordering of closing sonnets in second cycle: 23, 26, 27, 24, 25, 28, 29, 30. Text pp. 51–3	
	s. 115. Text, p. 137, n. 25	Overlapping the end of the second sonnet cycle and the beginning of the third, cc. ii, vii, xiv, xvi. *Fin' amors*, serious, 'provenzaleggianti'. The *congedo* is not an authorial signature but a summary by the persona-poet of his
Guittone's uneasiness with the archaic literary ideal breaks out in the *tenzone*, ss. 37–49. Text, pp. 60–68. This break in the proper relationship between	ss. 31–80 can be divided into: ss. 31–59, narrative sequence based on the polarity of 'noia' and 'gioia'	

lover and lady is partly healed by a return to courtly cliché, ss. 50–9, and then, by a series of genre sonnets in which Guittone tries to enliven the emotional content with events. Text, pp. 68–79	ss. 60–80, genre variations, in which 'lontananza' is prominent, ss. 72–5, 80. Virtuoso feats, ss. 77–9	'own' experience in each poem. Text, pp. 95–100.
		c. xxii; no *congedo* signature, but contains 'literary' figures like those in several sonnets in the closing sequence. Text, pp. 99–100.
		cc. viii, ix, xxiii, match the 'lontananza' sonnets. The *congedo* identifies Guittone with the persona, 'va ad Arezzo'. Text, pp. 105–9.
	Suggested re-ordering of closing sonnets in third cycle: 72, 73, 74, 80, 75, 76, 77, 78, 79. Text, pp. 76–7	cc. x, xi, xii, xiii; bravura poems like ss. 77–9. The *congedo*, a signing-off device, reveals Guittone in his role as author. Text, pp. 100–3.
	ss. 113, 114, 117 are of a piece with the closing sequence in the third cycle. Text, p. 137, n. 25	c. xxi contains features from the entire early sonnet range — *fin' amors* idealism, facile use of 'lontananza' motif, a named dedicatee in the second *congedo*, technically resourceful. Text, p. 103.
Non-narrative exploration of anti-idealistic currents in the lyric tradition. The *tenzone* is a verbal exercise with little bite or vivacity. Text, pp.	'Tenzone con la donna villana', ss. 81–6 *ars amandi*, ss. 87–110	cc. i, iv. As teacher, with a well-defined specialist audience, Guittone handles the courtly formulae with skill and exploits the sentiment

80–82. The *ars amandi*
is managed with some
verve but Guittone
questions the cynical
exploitation of *fin' amors;*   ss. 112, 116.
author not identifiable   Text, p. 137, n. 25.
with the teacher. Text,
pp. 82–9

with 'male'
callousness.
Technically assured.
The *congedo*,
addressed to a real
correspondent,
shows a distinction
between the author's
creative function and
his literary sentiments.
Text, pp. 103–5.

cc. xvii, xviii, xix

Sirventesi;
didactic, hortatory
genre, as traditional
as 'materia amorosa';
an intimation of
Guittone's 'moral'
manner. All three
poems are written to
real people; the poet
signs his work in the
congedo. Text, p. 94.

cc. xv, xx

Transitional poems
written just before
the palinodes: c. xv,
a confident return to
courtly 'lontananza';
a core of reality
restored to the
sentiment by docu-
mented political
exile. Text, pp.
109–13. C. xx, a
moral defence of
fin' amors; a last
attempt to salvage
the sentimental ideal
from debasement in
real life. Text,
pp. 113–19.

The palinodes
Text, pp. 4–5, 14–33.

Chronological table

(taken from Margueron, *Recherches*, pp. 115–16, and reproduced by
permission of Presses Universitaires de France)

1254–60	c. xvii
September 1260–May 1261	c. xix
Late 1261	c. xviii
1262–3	l. xiv
	c. xv
Before 1263	cc. i-xiv, xvi, xxi-xxiv
	ss. 1–28, 30–117, 121, 123, 130, 131
1262–5	c. xx
	s. 221
Before 1265 or even 1260(?)	s. 212
	l. xi
Before 1265(?)	ss. 217, 230
	l. xxxvii
Shortly before 1265	c. xliii
	l. v
1265–94	cc. xxxv-xxxix, xliv, xlv, xlviii-l
	ss. 139–53a and 153b, 155–6, 158–62, 166–73, 175–203, 207, 213, 215, 219, 222–5, 227–9, 231–3, 236, 239.
	ll. i, iv, ix, xv, xvii, xxii, xxiii, xxiv, xxv, xxvi, xxxi, xxxii, xl
1265–6	cc. xxv-xxx
	ss. 163–5, 174, 205, 210, 211, 218, 220, 234, 237
1266	c. xxxii
Late 1266	c. xli
Late 1266–early 1267	c. xl
1265–9	s. 209
1266–8	l. xxviii
Soon after 1266	ll. xix, xvi and xxi
About 1270	l. xiii
1272–8 (or –1283)	l. vii
1273 at the earliest	c. xxxiv
1273–91	l. xxvii

Before May 1276	ll. iii and vi
1277 or 1279	c. xlvi
1278	c. xlii
After 1278	l. xxxvi
1279–85	s. 226
	l. ii
1281	s. 157
1282–94(?)	s. 216
Before April 1284	s. 154
1285–8(?)	c. xxxiii
1285–93 and probably 1290–3	ll. viii and xxix
1285–94	ss. 240–51
	l. xx
Before 1286	l. xviii
Before 1288	s. 214
February–March 1288	c. xlvii
1289	letter (lost) to the Florentines
1290–1	l. xii
1290–3	c. xxxi

Notes

Notes to Chapter 1

1. For a survey of Guittone criticism up to 1961 see M. Marti, 'Ritratto e fortuna di Guittone d'Arezzo', *Realismo dantesco e altri studi* (Milan–Naples, 1961), pp. 145–55. Cl. Margueron, now completing an edition of the letters and preparing an edition of the poetry, is the acknowledged specialist, and his *Recherches sur Guittone d'Arezzo: sa vie, son époque, sa culture* (Paris, 1966) is an indispensable guide for any study of Guittone's poetry. For sound general studies, each with its own emphasis, see: M. T. Cattaneo, 'Note sulla poesia di Guittone', *GSLI*, 137 (1960), 165–203, 325–67; M. Marti, 'Ritratto', pp. 126–55; A. Tartaro, 'Guittone e i rimatori siculo-toscani', *Storia della letteratura italiana* (Milan, 1965), pp. 351–428; A. E. Quaglio, 'I poeti siculo-toscani', E. Pasquini and A. E. Quaglio, *Le origini e la scuola siciliana* (Bari, 1971), pp. 243–335; Contini, *PD*, ɪ, 189–91. For Dante's attitude to Guittone see M. Marti, 'Guittone d'Arezzo e i guittoniani', *Enciclopedia dantesca*, ɪɪɪ (Rome, 1971), 334–6.
2. See Margueron, *Recherches*, p. 22, note 30. The Gaudenti were founded in 1261 by two Bolognese nobles, the Guelph Catalano di Guido di madonna Oria, and the Ghibelline Loderingo degli Andalò. Dante's scant regard for their work as *podestà* in Florence (*Inferno*, xxɪɪɪ, 100–8) passes through the founders to the Order as a whole.
3. For Guittone's influence on Dante's *Rime*, see Foster-Boyde, ɪɪ, 1–3, 192, 212–13, 228. See also E. Fenzi, 'Le rime per la donna Pietra', *Miscellanea di studi danteschi* (Genoa, 1966), pp. 229–309.
4. There are twenty-four pre-conversion *canzoni*; xvii, xviii and xix are not love poems; xv and xx are courtly only in part.
5. See B. Panvini, *Le rime della Scuola siciliana* (Florence, 1962), ɪ, li.
6. See Margueron, *Recherches*, pp. 41–7.
7. Scc Margueron, *Recherches,* pp. 89-91
8. 'No è 'l mal più che 'l bene a far leggero', c. xxv, 81; cf. c. xxx, 5–8, 73.
9. This is the precise poem whose metre Cavalcanti emulates in 'Donna me prega' (Contini, *PD*, ɪɪ, 522–29).
10. See Margueron, *Recherches*, pp. 121–42, 'La notion d'amitié chez Guittone'.
11. Until Margueron's text of the letters appears, the complete text is *Le lettere di Fra Guittone d'Arezzo*, ed. F. Meriano (Bologna, 1923). Marti presents an improved text of sixteen of them, with an introduction, in *La prosa del Duecento*, ed. C. Segre and M. Marti (Milan–Naples, 1959), pp. 25–93. For dates see Margueron, *Recherches*, pp. 95–113. See also Margueron's advances on the new edition in *Studi e problemi di critica testuale*, 2 (1971), 72–98; and *Studi e problemi di critica testuale*, 7 (1973), 5–16; 9 (1974), 5–12. For a general treatment see C. Segre, *Lingua, stile e società* (Milan, 1963), pp. 95–175; A. E. Quaglio, *La poesia realistica e la prosa del Duecento* (Bari, 1971), pp. 105–18, essential bibliography pp. 235–6.
12. See Margueron, *Recherches*, pp. 143–263; and for a list see Marti, 'Ritratto', p. 131.
13. Charity, s. 195, is an odd lady out among the virtues, with no parallel vice. The list of virtues numbers eleven, as against ten vices.
14. See F. Egidi, 'Un *Trattato d'Amore* inedito di Fra Guittone d'Arezzo', *GSLI*, 97 (1931), 49–70.
15. The second poem, unnumbered, is a strophe of eleven heptasyllables.
16. I use the expression loosely here to cover all sonnets longer than fourteen lines.
17. Compare Foster-Boyde, ɪɪ, 36–7, who speak only of the 20-line variety used by Dante. There is only one 20-line poem among Guittone's double sonnets (s. 248). It has no heptasyllables but adds four hendecasyllables to the second *pes* and one hendecasyllable to each *volta*.
18. Guittone's double sonnet matches in variety the post-conversion *canzone* stanza and adds to the number of stanza patterns he created.
19. Four 16-line sonnets, ss. 161, 162, 163, 247; one 18-line-sonnet, s. 160, with a *frons* of eight hendecasyllables, and two heptasyllables added to each *volta*; one 20-line sonnet, s. 248, with no heptasyllable but four hendecasyllables added to the second *pes* and

one hendecasyllable added to each *volta*; twenty-two 22-line sonnets, ss. 139–56 (153a and b), 158, 159, 239. Since Guittone uses *rima alternata* the scheme for the *pedes* is AaB AaB, AaB AaB. The *volte* have the scheme CcDdC, DdCcD, except for ss. 145 and 156 on three rhymes, CcDdE, CcDdE. The 27-line *stravagante*, s. 157, has the scheme AaB AaB, AaB AaB; CcDdC, DdCcD, EeFfE.

20. 'Ahi, che villano e che folle follore', s. 163, makes a pair with s. 164, 'Ahi, come matto è ben senza questione'. If s. 164 was written soon after conversion, as I shall suggest it was, then s. 163 could well have preceded it and be one of his first palinodes.

21. The other post-conversion sonnet with internal rhyme, s. 240, is the first poem in the *Trattato d'Amore*.

22. Margueron has suggested 1281 for s. 157; see *Recherches*, p. 93.

23. Cattaneo, *Note*, pp. 349–58 ends with the *ballate sacre*; and see esp. p. 353, note 1. Quaglio *LIL 1*, pp. 296–8 reproduces 'Meraviglioso beato', c. xxxvii, as his last poem.

24. See A. Roncaglia, 'Nella preistoria della lauda: Ballata e strofa zagialesca', *Il movimento dei Disciplinati nel settimo centenario dal suo inizio (Perugia — 1260)*, ('Deputazione di storia patria per l'Umbria, Appendici al Bolletino', n. 9) (Perugia, 1962), pp. 460–75.

25. See Panvini, *Rime*, p. l.

26. See *Laude Dugentesche*, ed. G. Varanini (Padua, 1972), pp. ix–xxxii; and L. Banfi, 'A proposito di una antologia di laude dugentesche', *GSLI*, 151 (1974), 261–77.

27. The *ballate* numbered xxxv–xxxix are only in MS. Laur. Rediano 9; l is only in MS. Banco Rari 217 (Palatino 418), where, with a page missing, only the first eight lines survive.

28. See for example c. xxxv, 93–103 and c. xxxvi, 49–57.

29. For s. 153b see G. Contini, 'Guittone in quarantena', *Studi in onore di A. De Stefano* (Palermo, 1956), pp. 561–7.

30. See c. xlix, 159–70. See also c. xlvi, 17–28, in which he praises the stylistic and thematic range of his late friend Jacopo da Leona; see Contini, *PD*, I, 232–4.

Notes to Chapter 2

1. For an exhaustive bibliography see Margueron, *Recherches*, pp. 448–94. For essential works see Quaglio, *LIL 1*, pp. 333–4.

2. *Rivista di cultura classica e medioevale*, 7 (1965), 1057–67.

3. For the importance of this MS. see Contini, *PD*, II, 822, and Gianfranco Folena, 'Cultura poetica dei primi fiorentini', *GSLI*, 147 (1970), 8–11.

4. See Tartaro, *Conversione*, p. 1058.

5. See Quaglio, *LIL* 1, pp. 259–300.

6. Two of the *sirventesi*, cc. xv and xix, are among the *rime d'amore*, while two others, cc. xxxiii and xlvii, are among the *rime morali*. Quaglio, p. 276, speaks of a natural progression from amorous to political themes, and from moral to religious, which points to an ideal order for the whole *canzoniere*. Margueron's chronological table reproduced on pp. 123–4 'agrees' with the MS. bipartition.

7. For the traditional nature of the palinode see Olive Sayce, 'Chaucer's "Retractions": the conclusion of the *Canterbury Tales* and its place in literary tradition', *Medium Aevum*, 40 (1971), 230–48.

8. See for example s. 211, 12–13, 'E tu vietal, bel conte, in cortesia/li traiti miei e perigliosi motti'.

9. Tartaro, p. 1057, describes this standard sentimental extremism as 'momenti antitetici di un dramma che non conosce scioglimento'.

10. My argument will support the view that there was a development within the 'prima maniera'. I do not share the view that Guittone's 'onne mainera', c. xi, 65–6, and the re-appearance of the wider Provençal range (political and moral *sirventesi* as well as love poems) happened 'all at once' or that it can be assumed to exist diffused through all Guittone's courtly poetry.

11. See M. Marti, 'Dante e i poeti del suo tempo', *Cultura e scuola*, 4 (1965), 36–45.

12. See Contini's review of Egidi's edition in *GSLI*, 117 (1941), 55–82, '. . . . non molto gli giova il sonetto . . .' (p. 82). It could be argued that the brevity of the sonnet precludes the occasionally complex expression of ideas that I shall claim for them. But we shall see that the sonnet is particularly well-suited to express individual facets of complex authorial attitudes, and may in some cases antedate related *cauzoni* as trial runs, so to speak.

Notes to Chapter 2, continued

13. See Margueron, pp. 85–94, 115, for the chronology and table summary. Of the other poems which he assigns to 1265–6 see especially s. 163 and the spirited s. 174, two confessions that mention neither love nor writing.
14. A step-by-step argument in the *quartine* is condensed in a rhetorical question: lines 1–3, objective moral consequences; lines 4–6, objective emotional consequences; lines 7–8, practical *post-eventum* consequences. Shorn of its literary pretensions, love becomes simply a culpable action, 'amare', lines 2, 10. Each third-person pronoun in the last *terzina* is ambiguous, as if the poet were not sure what, in terms of lines 1–11, he experienced; but line 14 should read 'merzé de Lui', see s. 210, 14. Among many corrections, Contini has proposed for s. 164, 7, 'e tutte gioi, che cria amore o pone'.
15. For a typical courtly self-dedication to Love, with a religious aura of salvation within the *fin' amors* credo, see s. 35, 5–8.
16. 'Fu' 1, 'partio' 2, 'departi" 3, 'tornò' 5, 'presi' 7, 'obbrio' 8, (imperfect, like 'partio'). 'Allora', lines 3, 5, 7, in the strong position at the head of the line, hammers home the expanding, repetitive description of 'lo giorno' in the *quartine*.
17. A fateful day in the good sense when she showed 'merzé', in the bad sense when their meeting began his history of woe.
18. See ss. 10, 11, 12, 13, 14 for the reverence with which he describes his return to favour.
19. It is not enough to say that verbal echoes of earlier poetry are merely a dramatic device to heighten the change. By lifting the love poetry on to a 'real' plane he does of course contrast two systems and underlines his choice; but to do this he must presume a continuity between present and past which is not assumed for this particular sonnet — it will be seen to be at the centre of his vision of the 'prima maniera'. Did Margueron have this in mind when he put s. 210 first in his list of sonnets that follow Guittone's return to faith, p. 90?
20. In the absence of Gualtieri's sonnet this is only conjecture, but Guittone repeats the question at the end of the *captatio*, lines 7–8, to preface his answer.
21. Triple *replicationes*, 'conto', 'conte', 'conta', 1–2; 'gradir', 'agrada', 'gradire', 2–4; close rhyme sounds in the *quartine*, '-eri'/'-ire'; a *coblas capfinidas*-type device to join *terzine* to *quartine*, 'servire', 8, 'servir', 9.
22. This might explain the repeated recantations of his love poetry in the poems written at the time of conversion (to make sure that at least one clear renunciation reached the various circles of readers), and why, in the *canzoni*, those attacks are followed by thorough-going moral treatises. The earlier poems would go unchallenged until eclipsed by more potent (and obviously sincere) statements to the contrary.
23. The last line points to a danger in both content ('vertude strussi') and style ('vizi ornai').
24. The paratactic 'e tu' in line 12 (as bland as the conjunction 'ed io' in s. 164, 12), and the repetition of 'vietar', 'vieto', 'vietal', in lines 10, 12, give the colour of a 'dunque' conclusion to the last *terzina*. Compare line 10 with c. xxvii, 38.
25. See Margueron, pp. 91, 240–2.
26. At Professor Margueron's suggestion I have followed the reading in Vaticano lat. 3793 for line 14, which lacks a syllable in Egidi's edition, '. . . che 'n vita siate eternali'.
27. For the poison metaphor in its courtly context see s. 24, 3–4; for the sweet nothings of the *captatio*, see s. 116, 1–4.
28. Margueron, p. 242, reads 'triaca', 12, as 'l'image par laquelle il désigne la nouvelle orientation, morale et religieuse, de sa poésie . . .' But if 'pomi' are poems, and if the 'venenosi' are the love poems collectively, then 'quelli', which are the true antidote for 'essi', 13, must be the moral/religious poems seen as a collection of individual poems already written or in writing. The balanced *terzine* suggest to me that Guittone imagined a whole corpus split down the middle, one side compensating for the other because, like the other, it already exists.
29. The core of the argument is that since Montuccio and the others have a choice of poems they should now choose the other kind. There is no excuse to dwell on the 'venenosi' any longer because Guittone has long since discarded them.
30. For example, there would be no room for self-reproach or diffidence in the cut and dried homiletic formulae in s. 164, 1–11.
31. The ideal order of the four sonnets in relation to the moment of conversion would be: ss. 210, 211, 164, 237.
32. 'Se lo pensare — a lo parlare — sembra', 9. The hypothesis is central to Guittone's argument because it presumes that courtly writing can reflect a commitment to the courtly ethos that words can translate the poet's inner convictions.

33. Similar neat and programmatic balance of past and present; in both, love is the formidable deity; in both, prominent first-person words of rejection, with diction modelled on the binomial and repetitive style of traditional love lyrics ('varrò-valer', 2; 'fuggo e disvoglio', 3; and see s. 210, 3–4); in both, a straightforward syntax of consecutive clauses that link challenging statement (c. xxv, 1–2; s. 210, 1–2) to an act in time, 'poiché', c. xxv, 3; 'ch'allora', s. 210, 3.

34. Not by the past-tense antitheses of s. 210 but with binomial present-tense verbs 'fuggo', 'disvoglio', 'mi spare', lines 3–4 — as if he were still rejecting it, and as if the ruthless, axiomatic logic of his argument in the body of the poem were the expression of a revulsion he still feels. The parenthetic discussion, lines 5–11, with its verbs in the present tense, tends to underline the fact that, as a credo, the traditional literary opinion continues to be valid for others.

35. These confident and programmatic incipits (see also cc. xxv, 1–2; xxvi, 1–3; xxviii, 1–4) reveal not only Guittone's certainty of a change of direction but a new vigour in his voice, vibrant because at last it can speak directly through the subject matter. They can be matched in the pre-conversion *canzoni* only by the incipits of cc. xix and xx on political and moral themes.

36. The problem of rhetorical exaggeration in the congeries, as in the binomials and paradoxes of this poem, is relevant in the strictly biographical sense; see the discussion in Margueron, pp. 36–40. It is precisely the excessive, slavishly matched and repetitive nature of Guittone's statements about the past in relation to the present which shows he will leave the reader in no doubt that the past 'I' must be seen as an earlier version of the present 'I'. Verbal play in such passages does not lessen their seriousness. Likewise, the biblical patina of line 6, which Dante uses to open the *Commedia*, exaggerates the period of time by leaving it indistinct, but affirms an identity of person from birth to the present — it covers the whole past.

37. *Canzone* xxvii, 20–38 can be compared with s. 211, 9–14. In both passages culpable past action in general (c. xxvii, 20–5; s. 211, 9–11) hardens into the activity of writing in particular (c. xxvii, 26–31; s. 211, 12–14). Several lines are strikingly similar — c. xxvii, 25, and s. 211, 11; c. xxvii, 38, s. 211, 10. In s. 211 the facile mixture of compliment and verbal repetition, neatly balanced by a crisp message, suits the narrowly public context of a reply sonnet to a particular individual. *Canzone* xxvii expresses private sorrow and private joy in the grand manner, rich with inflated rhetoric and echoes of the courtly style.

38. One might argue that the 'io' of 'ch'amai', 27, and 'in fare me', 30, is the author as author — the 'ch' as referring to 'trovai' and not 'disamor', the 'me' of 30 being the writing self — and say that he could lose God, 31, quite satisfactorily simply as a writer, without assimilating the persona to himself. Such a reading does not follow the more natural sense order in 27 — the relative to the nearest noun — and would obscure the paradoxical play of 'disamor ch'amai'. In the second case, 30, the first-person references ('amai', 'in fare me', 'guai a me') tend, in a line of mounting tension and 'logical' progression, to equate the depravity of the deceived (in their 'real' morally responsible persons) and the deceiver (in his 'real' person).

39. In the double 'guai', 32, 33, he ties together self-reproach ('guai a me' refers back to the first-person verbs of 26–31) and general exhortation to the unspecified 'chi'. The 'chi' of that warning is strictly speaking the 'altrui' of 30, but the preaching tone projects the voice out and away from the speaker. The neatness of this change of tone from convert to poet to moralist makes s. 164 sound particularly clumsy.

40. 'Folle', 36, matches 'muto', 31; 'nemico', 37, echoes 'nemico', 33; but 'meo dire', 36, accords less well with 'd'omo ch'è senza legge', 35 — the conclusion does not sustain the volume of declamation in lines 33–5.

41. Cavalcanti mocked Guittone's logic in 'Da più a uno face un sollegismo', Contini, *PD*, II, 557. Segre, *Lingua*, pp. 107, 156, notes a lack of strict logic in Guittone's apparently logical use of co-ordinating conjunctions. I would argue that beyond the immediate context of the conjunction itself there is a more spacious and less rigid structure in which a 'però' clause can function as a logical conclusion, and where the logic need not be confined to the matter of the argument. Here it lies in the way he makes the hortatory voice 'grow' out of a first-person confession.

42. For example, 'masnada', 78, 'zambra', 80, 'carizia', 83; 'tragran devizia', 84; nominal constructions, 83–4, 85; cryptic play of short and long lines makes difficult sense of the simple message in 88–95.

43. 'E voi, Amor', 77, may apostrophize the daughter, mother and bride of God in 58. Normally it is 'Amor' who has a troop of devotees, not 'madonna', 78; yet 'Amor' could hardly have a 'figlio onorato', 80. The confusion of roles in the literary relationship seems to have excaped Guittone in his haste to apply the archaic terminology to his new love.

44. There is a rhetorical question in the third stanza of c. xxxii, 60–5, which recalls the sensual *otium* evoked in this passage. It comes as a climax to the universal social and moral disorder which Guittone outlines in the second and third stanzas of that *canzone*. He distills the world of ephemeral longings into the language of 'fatti d'amore', with its myth of perfect, sustained pleasure. Margueron, p. 90, sees the alternation of mood between contrition and enthusiasm as psychological support for dating the poems that follow conversion.

45. I noted in s. 210 how he celebrated his conversion in the language of the lover's return to 'madonna's' favour. In c. xxvii it is as if, having made a clean breast of the past in the opening stanzas, he is free to recall the courtly language in a new context. We shall see that this is a central notion in cc. xv and xx.

46. See the *Trattato d'Amore*, ss. 240–51, published by Egidi in 1931.

47. 'Lecciaria', line 5, a highly-coloured word, defines the polarity between the cool, supremely human faculty of 'ragion' and the bestiality of lust. The fifth line links the sense and syntax of *frons* and *sirima*. It strips away the sentiment from the actions of 'chi tec' (Amor) ha contratto'; and it opens the way to a confession of his own 'lecciaria' in a kind of cause and effect process.

48. See c. vii, 33–48, and the ideals of 'ver', 'onor', and 'saver' in c. xxviii, 7–9. In the courtly laments the poet exaggerates 'his own' misery and the power of love by describing the effects of his sentimental disarray in terms of the human faculties and virtues; 'saver mi tolle', vii, 34; 'sì son disonorato/e tenuto noioso', vii, 39–40 — he invokes a 'moral' perspective for rhetorical effect. In the *rime ascetiche* that moral perspective is the simple and serious norm against which past actions are to be judged. In a passage such as c. xxviii, 7–9, the moral language he had used as special pleading and which had lifted the tone of his *fin' amors* lament is now used to deflate just those pretensions.

49. See Quaglio, p. 265, 'si è ripetuto fino alla noia . . . che Guittone si rinchiude in un esercizio formalistico, di mero diletto retorico . . .'.

Notes to Chapter 3

1. See Margueron, p. 404, where he sets out folio numbers for the sonnet groups up to s. 110 in both MSS.

2. See A. Pellizzari, *La vita e le opere di G. d'Arezzo* (Pisa, 1906), pp. 37–59, summary on pp. 58–9. His cycles, with short titles, are as follows: (i) 'Amore corrisposto', ss. 1–18, 112; cc. i, iii, iv, xxi. (ii) 'Lealtà in amore', ss. 19–30; cc. ii, v. (iii) 'Poesia di gioia — amore del poeta; ripulse della donna, lamenti del p.; pietà della donna, ringraziamenti del p.; donna-schermo, lontananza', ss. 31–80, 118; cc. vi, vii, viii, ix, x, xi, xii, xiii, xiv, xv, xvi, xx, xxii, xxiii, xxiv. (iv) 'Tenzone', ss. 81–6. (v) 'Ars amandi', ss. 87–110. (vi) 'Varie', ss. 111, 113, 114, 115, 116, 117. He omits cc. xvii, xviii, xix.

3. See the review of the Pelligrini edition by M. Pelaez, *GSLI*, 41 (1903), 351–64. His analysis of the sonnet themes is as follows: ss. 1–27 treat variously of love, 28–30 short correspondence, 31–6 variations on the theme of love, joys and sorrows of the lover, 37–49 a *tenzone*, 50–8 a change in the lover's attitude, 59 she changes tack, 60–79 he expresses all his joy in two episodes, 65–6, 72–6; 80–6 a sharp *tenzone* with his lady; 87–110 *ars amandi*; 111–18 various. Pelaez does not align the *canzoni* and the sonnet groups.

4. See Margueron, p. 403:
   (i) s. 1–18 et c. iii, iv, i et xxi: histoire d'un amour malheureux d'abord, ensuite partagé, et comportant l'exposé de quelques règles concernant l'attitude de l'amant et de la dame.
   (ii) s. 19–20 et c. ii et v: histoire d'un amour sincère de la part de la femme, alors que l'homme feint des sentiments qu'il n'éprouve pas. Pellizzari, p. 44, donnerait volontiers comme titre à cette série: 'De la loyauté en amour'.
   (iii) s. 31–80 et c. xxiii, xxiv, xxii, vii, xii, xiii, x, vi, xvi, viii, ix, xi, xx et xiv: long cycle

130

de la 'gioia', 'senhal' de la dame, comprenant six épisodes: exposé de la situation; — sentiments de l'homme; — déclaration d'amour; — refus de la dame et 'contrasto'; — reproches de l'amant, qui change momentanément le 'senhal' en celui de 'noia'; — capitulation de la femme, joie de l'amant, bientôt traversée de jalousie, d'où recours à une 'donna schermo', et aussi de tristesse due à l'éloignement de l'homme ou de la femme.
(iv)   s. 81–6: 'contrasto' réaliste et grossier entre l'amant et sa dame.
(v)   s. 87–110: 'art d'amour.'
(vi)   s. 111–17 aux sujets d'amour variés, mais indépendants, selon toute probabilité, des séries précédentes.
Margueron keeps s. 112 in the sixth group and leaves aside cc. xv, xvii, xviii and xix.

5.   See Tartaro, p. 1058.
6.   Unlike Pellizzari, Margueron rearranges the *canzoni* out of printed numerical order, presumably to show a correspondence between the themes of individual *canzoni* and the narrative moments in the sonnet cycles, especially the third.
7.   I understand the *ars amandi* to be anti-courtly, that is, not idealistic, in its cynicism. The handful of sonnets 111–17 exist only in MS. Vat. lat. 3793.
8.   See Quaglio, p. 265, who seems to take the *a priori* view.
9.   See Quaglio, pp. 267–8, 287.
10.   See pp. 123–4 for Margueron's table. See his discussion, *Recherches*, pp. 85–94.
11.   See Margueron, p. 87.
12.   By 'early' I mean the printed (i.e. manuscript) order not the chronological order, but I shall show that it also refers to a stage in his poetic development.
13.   See the descriptive studies by R. Baehr in *ZRP*, 73 (1957), 193–258 and 357–413, and 74 (1958), 163–211. Also Franca Ageno, *La retorica nelle poesie di Guittone* (Parma, 1969 — 'dispense').
14.   See for example ss. 1, 1–3; 2, 7–8; 12, 7–8; 18, 1.
15.   See for example ss. 1, 2, 'fa posanza'; 3, 10, 'in guerigion mi pone'; 7, 9, 'usando cortesia'; 8, 1, 'Pietá di me . . . vi prenda'.
16.   See Corti, pp. 334–5; and see the discussion in Boyde, pp. 62–5.
17.   Note such lines as ss. 3, 12–14; 7, 5–8; 16, 5–8.
18.   There is rarely syntactic linkage between *quartine* and/or *terzine*, and hardly any structural inversion. The sense/syntax line is horizontal.
19.   See Quaglio, p. 267, where the point is well made; also pp. 261 and 281.
20.   In a fine discussion of the *sententia* in courtly lyric, Boyde, pp. 308–11, argues convincingly that the courtly poet speaks as both devotee and celebrant of the rite, that *sententiae* come naturally to his lips, and that there is no clean division between 'materia amorosa' and moral or didactic themes. I would say that, quite apart from incidental *sententiae* which may work their way into single sonnets taken individually, Guittone assumes a full-blown didactic manner at certain points in the 'narrative' development (or stagnation) to lift the narrative line out of unself-conscious persona discourse on to a more self-aware authorial plane.
21.   'Omo valente — lo malvagio', 1–3; 'donna laida — quella ch' ha bieltá', 6–7.
22.   Paired observations, both dependent on 'con mi dol vedere', line 1, both contrasts between ideal and reality, both apparently equal objects of lament.
23.   Inner quality ('valente'), material reward ('povero'), 1, 2; inner quality ('vile'), material reward ('manente') 3–4; courtly manners ('cortese'), physical appearance ('laida') 5–6; physical appearance ('piacente'), manners ('orgogliosa'), 7–8.
24.   After which the last *terzina*, as often in Guittone's sonnets, is a banal make-weight, especially in this case when the formula for a more severe criticism had been laid down in lines 5–8.
25.   Lines 2, 3, 3–4 (triple), 5, 7, 8, 10–11 (contrast), 14. See also the Provençalisms in lines 2, 3, 4, 8, 13, 14.
26.   Guittone's concern for the woman who has all the courtly virtues (complete in their triple synonym) but is unloved because unattractive, is remarkably modern and anticipates the clear-eyed, non-courtly assessment in c. xx and s. 151 of the female position vis-à-vis the male attitude in courtly literature. See s. 14, 3–4, for the conventional association of 'laidezza' and 'viltà'.
27.   The suppressed terms argue that the persona is the 'omo valente' unrewarded. The particular application in lines 9–11 takes only one alternative in each *quartina*. But the comprehensive balance in the *quartine* introducing (for mere sake of balance?) so much that is of no use in his 'particular case', is a sign that the reasoning process does not

      spring out of the courtly situation. Guittone probes it and grapples with it, holding himself off from the persona in the process.

28. See cc. xxvi, 1; xxvii, 1; ss. 163, 1–2; 164, 1; 172, 1.
29. Marti, *Poeti*, p. 20, speaks of the female image, 'borghese e comunale', projected by the *stilnovisti*. Those ladies are the descendants of the 'donne Aretine' to whom Guittone addresses some of his courtly poems.
30. It is hard not to see parallels between ss. 9–13 and the passages in the conversion poems which I have already discussed. The analogies and terms of ss. 9–11 give a religious or ascetical aura to his change of attitude. The lover exemplifies a spiritual truth, s. 11, 1–8, in his own experience, s. 11, 9. He reproaches himself for his earlier 'lies', s. 12, 7–8 and excess, s. 12, 3–4. He encourages his audience to emulate his virtues, s. 13. The lover's return to mental and 'moral' sanity, s. 12, 5–6, anticipates what Guittone will say to describe his conversion, s. 210, 5–8, c. xxviii, 10–11; as does the sharp contrast between past and present, s. 12, 5; cf. s. 210, 5. The change of narrative direction in the first cycle suggests that a combination of religious myth-making, self-reproach and didacticism, by which he adopts several different stances to the event, is not peculiar to the conversion proper but has a counterpart, and even a *model*, in his courtly 'experience'.
31. He refers to the harsh words in ss. 3, 1–5; 4, 2; 5, 12–14; 6, 3–4; 7, 5–7.
32. The transition from general 'follor' to the particular 'follor' of writing, s. 211, 11–13, c. xxvii, 26–7, is matched in s. 12, 3–4 by a general 'dismisura' which is then specified as 'sparlare' — the particular complaint symptomatic of the entire malaise.
33. The strong position of the two infinitives, rounding off each *quartina*, underlines the change from lover immersed in an event, ss. 10, 11, to lover as poet, tying together the narrative threads of the previous sonnets and 'realizing' them as written experience.
34. The boldness of his claim is almost deflated by the prosaic terms of the analogy.
35. Compare this claim with that in c. i, 10–15, a 'Sicilian' simile that avoids any direct and facile analogy between 'madonna' and nature, and helps to explain Guittone's objection to Guinizzelli in s. 111, 5–8.
36. See Boyde, p. 312. The 'complacent, portentous manner . . . normal in the 1270s and 1280s' can be pushed back two decades and still be normal.
37. The range of alternatives, on his and her side, will increase as the pure idealism diminishes in later cycles. Emphasis will shift from the *emotion*, caught and unravelled, re-phrased this way and that, to the *event* which gives rise to it.
38. Enough has been said about Guittone's endemic didacticism to show that the pulpit stance and the sententious current in courtly literature will have been congenial to him. A conscious change to teaching at this point is a shift into a higher, more authorial gear.
39. See ss. 13, 7–8; 14, 1–2; 16, 9–10; 18, 1–4, 9. Sonnets 13 and 16 show how the technique of balancing general principles against a particular experience pulls Guittone away from 'experience' as a first-person re-living of the event.
40. See s. 16, 9–11, in 18, 1–4. These retrospective links, a typical device in the sonnet cycles, justify the closing didactic burst and keep a thread of continuity between poet-teacher and poet-lover, but there is no further 'event' in the narrative.
41. See ss. 13, 1–3; 15, 1–11; 16, 1–8; 17; 18, 9–11.
42. In its consistently archaic diction, easy syntax, unforced rhymes, and in the solid core of 'argument' in each sonnet.
43. For male smugness see ss. 14, 1–2; 16, 5–11; and the over-protesting of s. 16, 12–13.
44. In a sense narrative progress and the lover's self-reproach/self-encouragement are mutually exclusive since the lover can only long for and serve 'madonna' (and thus show his worth) if the situation remains static.
45. For example *sententiae*, ss. 16, 3–5; 18, 14; rhetorical questions, 13, 9–11, 13–14; 16, 7–8.
46. See ss. 19, 5; 27, 5; 33, 1; 39, 1, where 'merzé' is a synonym for 'prego' and 'clamore'. In the list of male virtues, s. 13, 9–11, it is his cry for mercy, as in s. 10, 11, and not the 'mercy' shown by the lady. The teaching in s. 13, 9–14 conflates that in ss. 10, 5–8 and 11, 3–6, where the axioms are stated as hopes or fresh realizations rather than assured *post eventum* rhetorical questions, as in s. 13.
47. That is, if s. 13, 1–4 were more than a mechanical device to make 'teaching' look as though it flowed from experience.
48. I doubt if 'laida o vil', s. 14, 4, is really an alternative here, otherwise Guittone might imply that a woman could be 'laida ma saggia', or 'vil ma bella'. Lines 5–7 suggest that 'laida o vil' are complementary and synonymous, like 'bella e cara e saggia'.

49. There is no suggestion that s. 5 was written after s. 14, the more 'modern' after the more 'archaic'. The narrative links, verbal echoes, etc., within each cycle show that the printed order is a reliable guide to the original sequence, even if chronology is unknown. I have tried to show that if Guittone reverts to the pure heart of *fin' amors* idealism he does so first because the didactic manner fastens on the rules of conduct implied in those ideals, and second because though he supplants the narrative 'io' he saves face with the tradition by fixing on its axiomatic principles.

50. Pellizzari and others have shown that Guittone drew on Provençal sources; Cattaneo and others have shown that his borrowing is not always slavish.

51. See Boyde, pp. 308–13.

52. Compare s. 19, 1–8 with s. 12, 5–8 for 'sincerity' of repentance and the objective grasp of courtly literature each confession implies.

53. Lines 5–8 of s. 19 cover the story in ss. 1–12 — the plea for mercy ss. 1–10, and her acceptance, which gives rise to the praise in ss. 11–12. The particular sonnets referred to in lines 5–6 would be ss. 7, 8, 9, 10.

54. Is 'enfingitore', s. 19, 1, just the make-believe of false sentiments compared with sincere love? Or is it Guittone's reflection on make-believe literary romances, woven out of fictive sentiment and postures? See Pellegrini's gloss on 'ora' as 'ai nostri giorni', p. 31, which places the first cycle in a temporal perspective. He notes a 'certa elevatezza e sincerità di sentimento' in the sonnet, which explains his reading of 'ora'. He sees Guittone as making a moral judgement of modern abuse of the courtly code.

55. According to the last six lines of s. 20 the repentant lover has won his lady, and narrative can only begin again by showing him once more 'disioso di voler amare', s. 21, 2.

56. Sonnet 20 repeats s. 19 as indirect speech to the lady; an 'event' in two sonnets, which begins with the lover's inner, uncommunicated recognition, s. 19, and ends with a complete confession to the lady, s. 20.

57. There is a suggestion in s. 23, 12–13 that his inability to respond (s. 20, 12–14) is punishment for his previous deceits, but this is not developed as it might have been.

58. The vaunt begins, s. 21, 12–14, with a simple variation of the seal image which Guittone uses polemically in c. xx, 49–52 to prove that once love does take hold of a woman she will sacrifice everything for it.

59. Is 'poi ch'' in line 3 causal or consecutive? — 'my poetry is worthless because it does not bring me her favour' (the 'loco' periphrase is common for 'madonna', or 'gioia' or her favour); or, 'because I can't win her favour my poetry is worthless' — Pellegrini's 'poiché' does not make it clear. The repetitive 'provenzaleggiante' language suggests the latter sense.

60. For the moment I shall read ss. 26, 27 in the printed order, though there is a case to put them before s. 25.

61. Is the 'l'om' of s. 22, 9 the 'ciascum omo' of s. 19, 1?

62. Pellegrini's understanding of s. 19, 2 as Guittone's latter-day evaluation of 'fatti d'amore' suggests that in the second cycle Guittone meant to recapture perfect *fin' amors* ideals in spite of contrary pressures such as the scoffers in s. 22, 9.

63. Though s. 23, 9, 'che m'è dolor mortal vedere amare', is not unlike s. 5, 9, 'ma lo dolor di voi, donna, m'amorta', and shows that a verbal echo can persist in a different context.

64. Synonymic repetition, s. 25, 2, 4, 10–11, 12, 13; periphrases, lines 3–4, 8.

65. For line 10, see s. 164, 3. In the latter sonnet the line is a criticism of love *in general*, which pushes aside 'real' obligations. In s. 28 it is a periphrase for an adverb like 'intensely' or 'whole-heartedly' and expresses the author's amazement at unrelenting love for unresponsive women, which is the persona's state in ss. 26, 27. See Margueron, *Recherches*, pp. 154–7 for Guittone's contact with Bandino, and see s. 221, where Bandino is given advice.

66. Sonnets 28, 1–2; 30, 1; and see the longer formalities in ss. 204–5 (Guinizzelli to fra Guittone) and ss. 208–9 (Ubertino to fra Guittone). Bandino's more expansive *captatio* and preamble which covers both *quartine*, s. 29, 1–8, is closer to the typical division of the correspondence sonnet into *captatio* (*quartine*) and message (*terzine*). Does Guittone's less flowery address in s. 28 rise from the urgency of the problem in the narrative, which he has taken on; and in s. 30 does he need the whole sonnet to end the cycle on an adequate note of praise with the lover's goal 'achieved'?

Notes to Chapter 4

1. Any change could only be for the worse, which in turn would need to be reversed.
2. I suggested earlier that ss. 26, 27 would make more sense in the narrative if read before s. 25. This would make the last *terzina* of s. 25 a logical introduction to the correspondence.

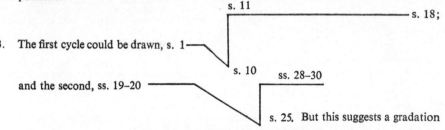

3. The first cycle could be drawn, s. 1

and the second, ss. 19–20

between ss. 1–10, and 20–25, which the poems hardly show.

4. Margueron, p. 403. As already noted the episodes apply to the sonnets (ss. 31–80) and not to the *canzoni*, although he alters the numerical order of the *canzoni* to suggest thematic likeness between certain *canzoni* and the various episodes in the sonnet cycle.
5. This would be covered by Margueron's first two headings, 'exposé de la situation' (ss. 31–2), and 'sentiments de l'homme' (ss. 33–6). He does not define the limits of his episodes with sonnet numbers, possibly because it is not always clear where one episode ends and the next begins. For example, is s. 49 the end of the *tenzone* or the start of his attack on the lady?
6. From inner monologue to teaching in the first cycle; and to the public airing of a private problem in the second.
7. The tone changes abruptly from s. 31 to s. 32. There is a similar unexplained downward movement in s. 21, which, after the optimistic preface of ss. 19, 20, sets the second cycle in motion along pessimistic lines.
8. See also ss. 33, 3–4, 12–14; 34, 9–10; 37, 2.
9. See ss. 28, 12–14; 75, 12–14; and ss. 115–16 and 204–5. The effect of the formula in s. 38, 12–14 is the same as that in real-life sonnet correspondence.
10. See ss. 32, 9–11; 36, 1–4.
11. Pellegrini's reading of s. 38, 10–11 is preferable to Egidi's: 'or mira como cresce signoraggio/tale fedel qual tu voli me dare'. See Pellegrini's gloss, p. 60. She questions the *fin' amors* reversal of the male-female order of command.
12. Her use of the word 'consiglio' for his blandishment, s. 38, 12–14, is surely tongue-in-cheek.
13. See s. 40, 1–8. The *sententiae*, metaphors and scriptural echo (lines 7–8, cf. Matthew, vii, 15), are her way of poking literary fun at his serious, copy-book efforts.
14. Pellegrini's gloss, p. 63, brings out this sense.
15. The verb 'partire' grows insistent from this point on, cf. ss. 44, 1, 9; 46, 10; 48, 9.
16. She is also, in a sense, the 'donna pro cortese e canoscente/ch'è laida sí, che vive in dispiacere', envisaged by Guittone in s. 5, 5–6, except that there he comments on the shallowness of courtly male *mores*, while in s. 44 she encourages the lover to spurn her 'laidezza' in true courtly style.
17. The broken, argumentative language of s. 44 is enhanced by a colloquial tone in lines 7 and 13 — 'you are wasting your time . . . don't take it to heart'.
18. For language close to s. 47, 1–8 see ss. 4 and 26.
19. The general effect of the stylistic contrast which I have noted between his and her discourse can be illustrated by ss. 47 and 48. Sonnet 47: the opening *planctus — exclamatio*, 1–2, strengthened by triple synonymic repetition, 1, sets up two alternatives for discussion — 'partire', 3–6, and 'stare', 7–8. *Conversio*, 4, binomial, 5, hyperbole 6. 'Stare non posso', 7, matches 'partire non poss'eo', 3. *Replicatio* of 'noia', 8 and 9; rhetorical question and antitheses, 12–13, obvious archaisms, 'no osa', 7, and 'mille fiate anti', 10. The closing *terzina* is a question and answer *subiectio*. The rush of repetitive figures, as a parenthetic discussion following the opening *exclamatio*, is neatly resolved by question and answer. The traditional procedure corresponds to a fictional and topic discussion. Her reply, s. 48, which contains only one binomial and the makeweight 'avacci' . . .

Notes to Chapter 4, continued

volenteri', 3–4, rests on a taut balance of obligations — 'If I were . . . I would, but I'm not, so I won't', 1–6. These two alternatives (of *action*, not sentiment) are two premisses which find their conclusion in 9–11: 'Donque' — an affirmative in the form of a rhetorical question. His question, s. 47, 12–13, had no more to it than otiose, chiastic word-play, 'spiaccio . . . servire/deservir . . . piacente'. In her question, the repetition of 'mutar', s. 48, 10–11, drives home the logic. The rider, 12–14, prosaic like the rest of the poem, underlines a message clear *in sententiis et in verbis*.

20. His repetitive, periphrastic diction, s. 49, 1–4, 5–6, 9, confirms her constant accusation of empty posturing on his part.
21. See Pellegrini, p. 89. 'Dopo una quasi parentesi, composta dai sonetti xlix-lviii, nei quali il poeta esprime con varie forme di finta rassegnazione, di sdegno, di dolore disperato il suo cordoglio per l'ultima risposta (son. xlvii) avuta dalla Donna, qui il dialogo ripiglia.' (son. xlvii) should read (son. xlviii).
22. See Egidi, p. 349, note to s. 59.
23. The 'rechesta' in s. 49, 5–8 is echoed in s. 50, 5–6. And note the echo of s. 47, 12–14 in s. 50, 11–14, and that of s. 32, 1–2 in s. 50, 1.
24. Her base rejection calls for a stiff verbal reaction which comes in s. 52.
25. See ss. 51, 4; 52, 6, 9; 53, 2; 54, 6; 55, 1; 57, 9–11, 14.
26. The alternating sentiments of resolve (ss. 50–2), indecision (s. 53), self-reproach (s. 54), dilemma (s. 55), fresh resolve and a threat (s. 56), renewed conflict and hope (s. 57) create a tension of despair which is highest in s. 58. In what sense are these changes of sentiment 'finte' (cf. Pellegrini, p. 89, note 21 above)? The 'rassegnazione' would only be 'finta' to the lady in the *tenzone*. To the lover it is serious and genuine because it is part of his sentimental range in the adversative situation.
27. Sonnet 60, 1–4 makes this clear in its reference to *his* 'villan' behaviour, in ss. 50–8, and *her* earlier harshness in the *tenzone*. The 'humbling of her desire', 60, 4, recalls s. 10, 9–14, where the lover had broken her pride with his humility.
28. For line 1 see s. 58, 9–14; line 2 see s. 53, 1–2; for line 5 see s. 48, 9–11; for lines 7 and 8 see s. 41, 9–11 and the earlier requests in s. 32, 9–11, etc.
29. See Egidi, p. 349, note to s. 59. I would see s. 59 as a reply not to s. 49 but to the lover's extended statement, ss. 49–58, which follows s. 48.
30. Though it fits more neatly into the sequence of events than a letter 'from abroad' as it were. The *quartine* contain an expression of sympathy, 1, like a *captatio benevolentiae* and a recapitulation, 2–8. The *terzine* contain the message of encouragement, sharply set off from the *quartine* and imperative in mood, 9–11.
31. Helped by the binomials, 1–2, 9, 13 and the adverb 'ben dobbramente', 12. Compare her advice, 9–12, with Bandino's in s. 29, 9–11. The problem is the same in both cases, s. 28, 3–4 and s. 58, 3–6.
32. The play on 'ragion', 5, as her every justification, and 'ragion', 7, as his copy-book language, recalls the *tenzone* debate between integrity and correctness, as does the third 'ragione', 11, what is his by rights.
33. Her guarded invitation, s. 59, 9–14, is hardly the green light but it looks a piece of coy euphemism compared with s. 42.
34. See ss. 12, 19, 50.
35. See s. 60, 2–3, cf. ss. 52, 53, 54, and all the pejorative phrases in ss. 50–8; s. 60, 3–4, cf. s. 59, 9–12 (and see s. 10, 12–14); s. 60, 9–11, cf. s. 59, 9–11; s. 60, 12–14, cf. s. 59, 12–14; s. 61, 12–14, cf. s. 59, 9–12 (and see s. 41, 9–11). Compare s. 60 with s. 12 for two different reactions to earlier complaint against the lady.
36. See s. 62, 1–2, cf. s. 54, 1–8; s. 62, 3–8, cf. s. 54, 9–10. This is the last of the narrative interlacing threads as such. S. 64, 12–14 echoes s. 45, 12–14 as a stock 'feudal' sentiment — the same notions account for a chance likeness between s. 70, 3–8 and s. 54, 1–8. The 'fallo' referred to in s. 76, 2–11 may be the vituperation of ss. 50–8, but is probably sparked off by the neighbouring self-pity in ss. 72–5.
37. Though the *tenzone* itself was a genre interlude the absence of direct speech in the genre poems that now follow makes them look like a retreat into merely literary adventures.
38. See esp. ss. 60, 65, 68, 77–9.
39. The '-ato' rhyme in the *quartine* is repeated in the *terzine*; the '-ento' rhyme in the *quartine* is matched by an assonance '-ente' in the *terzine*. But for this one slight change, the rhyme scheme would be AB throughout the sonnet. Compare s. 9 for an experiment with *rimalmezzo* (but with a normal rhyme scheme) at a turning point in the narrative movement.

40. See lines 3, 4, 9, 11, 12, where the caesura violates the natural sense pause. Foster-Boyde, II, 228, note that the internal rhyme is a 'very Guittonian feature'. In the pre-conversion poems Guittone uses it in four *canzoni* (iv, ix, xxi, xxii) but in only two sonnets, 9 and 60. In s. 114 the line is broken, but not by a *rimalmezzo*. It would seem that in the two love sonnets it is an authorial sign of heightened emotional intensity.

41. Sonnet 65, 5–8. 'Ed emmi greve ciò; ma pur campare/vòi dai noiosi e da lor nòi me paro,/ad onore de lei, che'n beltá pare/no li fo Elena che amao Paro.' Compare s. 68 and the *rime identiche*; 'gioia', lines 2, 4, 6, 8; and 'sia', lines 9–11.

42. See s. 78, 11–14; 'ch'al mio voler non faccia e festa e vilia./Merzé di lei ch'ogni on nemico ontra,/ver cui bastarda fu Sarna Subilia,/per che tutto ben meo d'essa m'acontra.' Note the rare '-ardi' rhyme in s. 66, 1–8.

43. Pellegrini, p. 116, embarks on his gloss with a dry smile. In s. 77 the *replicatio* on 'porta' occurs twice in each line and brings a rash of *rime ricche* and *derivative*.

44. Though they are more elaborate than Pellegrini allows, p. 121. 'Altro sonetto, questo, che riscontra al lxxvii quanto a "replicacio" di una stessa parola: punto...'. The *replicatio* on 'punto' and 'gente' springs from alternate end rhymes (the AB rhyme) in the *quartine*; with a similar triple *replicatio* in the *terzine*. The rhymes in the *quartine* are a mixture of identical, lines 1 and 3, 2 and 6; equivocal 1 and 5; derivative 1 and 7; and in the *terzine*, identical, 10 and 13, and equivocal, 9 and 12, 11 and 14.

45. See Foster-Boyde, ss. 10, 1–2, and 60, 1–2, for a similar opening by Dante.

46. The poem warns the curious to mind their business and curb the gossip of others. It envisages a public situation in which the lover, showing his inner state in true *consequens pro autecedente* style, is exposed to the gaze of the vulgar mob.

47. The line anticipates ss. 71, 117, and c. xxvii, 9–11. Is this the loss of 'segnoraggio' which the lady had questioned in s. 38, 10? I had suggested it was male 'segnoraggio' in the more normal, real-life terms; but, either way, the fact that she questions his foolish excess places her outside the courtly context.

48. Parallel, binomial lines, 5, 9, 11. ('ennudo e de lo senno fore', 5, seem virtual synonyms; 'ennudo' is glossed further on in the sonnet, but not 'de lo senno fore'). The analogy, 5–11, and conclusion, 12–14, are examples of Guittone's logical turn of phrase.

49. See Boyde, p. 308 on the *sententia*. He quotes Matthew of Vendôme, 'Et illud quod datur per generalem sententiam, "docetur", "probatur", "perhibetur" per aliud speciale, quod subjungitur', *Documentum*, II, i, 5. This is relevant to Guittone's technique of applying a general statement to a particular case.

50. See s. 68, 1–4. 'De tutte cose è cagione e momento,/che omo vole, o dice, o face, gioia:/ch'ha onore a prode e piacere'n talento/l'om solamente per venire a gioia.'

51. The 'io' of 'Ben meraviglio...' is an onlooker and not the protagonist. Given the three parties in the situation, guardian, lady and lover, the confusion that arises over the third-person pronoun (lines 3, 4, 5–6, 7, 11, 14) enhances the poem's air of *exemplum* — as if Guittone were saying, 'Now take, for example, the case where...' The logical 'donque' in line 9 suggests that a textbook problem has found a textbook answer.

52. See sonnets 64, 67, 68, 70, 76, 77, 78; all show varying degrees of hyperbole and verbal display, and make steady recourse to the notion of feudal service.

53. This is not quite true of ss. 62 and 63. Sonnet 62 begins as a praise poem, lines 1–8, and ends with a description of her harshness. The *terzine* are a negative proof of the miracle of mercy that has been worked in his favour, but admit the chance of a painfully humiliating experience in love, and lead downwards from s. 62, 1 to s. 63, 7–8.

54. The *quartine* hold some word-play: identical rhyme, 1–7; *replicatio*, 'guardo, guardi, guardato', 6, 7, 9; a rare word in rhyme, 'embardi', 3.

55. See s. 117 and c. xxvii, 9–11, also ss. 49, 5–10 and 63, 5.

56. Lines 5–14. Presumably the jealous lover wishes to stifle the sources of his jealousy. His eyes and ears are an obvious target for mutilation (self-inflicted out of fear), though the 'dark thoughts' of line 6 don't necessarily imply the presence of a rival. The 'scuro loco' seems to anticipate the 'scuritate' and 'mezzo scuro' in 'Donna me prega'. The 'om muto', 7, seems an unnecessary complication, akin to other passages where Guittone's argument is so exhaustive that it defeats itself. 'Alcun om muto', line 7, may be concessive — Pellegrini, p. 108, glosses the line 'quando sento alcuno sia pur muto' — though 'temendo ch'altro sia', 9, points to the contrary (not 'temendo per forza di gelosia che trattisi di ben altra cosa', Pellegrini, but 'afraid lest he be vocal'). If the rival is 'muto', the lover hardly needs to be 'sordo', except to quell the hyperbolic anguish of lines 9–10. Note how '*sento* lá stando', 8, suggests that sight (lines 5–6) has already

been lost, and that the senses are going out one by one as he speaks of them. This dramatises the hypothetical 'tal fiada'/'tal'/'tal', 2–3, which proposes a selective loss of sense in rotation, only one lost at a time. The lover's tongue, 12–14, is a source of praise not jealousy, and the last sense is not part of the fear context to which the other two belong. The lover's sight seems to have been restored by line 13 (*consequens pro antecedente*) and the notions of 'figura' and 'intenzone' give a philosophical twist to his argument, underlining its theoretical quality. The 'wisdom of restraint' in the last line will recall Iacopone da Todi, lxxii, 23–4 'lo cor deventa savio,/celar so convenente'. These mutilations are a normal part of the damage done by Love, cf. s. 117. Changed here to positive desires in s. 71 they express the lover's satisfaction at his possession of 'madonna' *without* the help of his key senses.

57. See s. 80, 12–14. She would restore his 'coraggio en allegraggio' automatically if this separation were ended. Here, separation is not the *source* of grief, as it should be in a true 'lontananza' poem, but lies in that vague region of 'lontananza' sentiment disembodied from 'lontananza' event (as do several of the so-called 'lontananza' *canzoni*). In ss. 72–4 he seems to have left her. In s. 80, 5, she seems to have left him, especially if 'sete lungiata' is transitive, as it often is.

58. See Margueron, p. 294; he notes that in s. 72 Guittone departs from his Provençal 'lontananza' models and, like the Sicilians, substitutes for their bitter memory of past pleasure an evocation of the lady's presence. The *quartine* of s. 72 describe not a comforting illusion but a nightmarish hallucination in which her face appears, 1–2, disappears, 7, and appears again, 8, and where the very sense of her presence is both cause and effect of madness, 4–6. In the *terzine* the nightmare subsides into a calm dream, but unlike the straightforward use of the polar star as a metaphor for 'madonna's' face in Guittone's supposed models (cf. Margueron, p. 287), he makes her the guide *and the goal* of his journey; Christ-Child to his Magi, the word made flesh, '. . . e incarnat'ella', 11. 'Madonna's' two-fold presence in the *quartine*, as a disembodied image of her face, 2, and as sign of his physical proximity to her, 6, is fused in the first *terzina* with the result that her luminous face, 10, now leads him to her bodily presence, 11. A separate and detailed study of the 'lontananza' motif in Guittone's poetry and in relation to the Sicilians and *stilnovisti* would show that he paved the way for later use of 'lontananza' sentiment in the context of political exile. See, for example, Lapo Gianni's imitation of s. 72, 'Sì come i Magi a guida de la stella', Contini, *PD*, ii, 602.

59. See ss. 63 and 71, 65, 66, and 79.

60. Cured because he returns to 'merzé'/'gioia' praise in ss. 76–8.

Notes to Chapter 5

1. See Pellegrini, p. 125. He notes the affinities with ss. 51–5, 'ma in questi il tono è ben altrimenti sprezzante che in quelli'. And see Pelaez, p. 360.

2. See ss. 52, 5–8; 53, 1–4.

3. The *tenzone* ends abruptly when he cries off, s. 85, leaving her the last say. The echo of s. 81, 1–2 in s. 82, 1–2 is a *tenzone* link rather than a narrative link.

4. See sonnets 50, 1; 51, 3, 5; 52, 1; 53, 1, 5, 7; 55, 5.

5. The clumsiness of s. 82, 9, 'i.e. . . .', underlines her euphemistic reading of s. 81, 5–8. She rejects him not because of his bestial desires but because he is 'tutto dispiacente', s. 82, 10.

6. See ss. 82, 1–4; 83, 1–4; 84, 1–4; 85, 1–5; 86, 1–8 — in each case the sonnet opens with a reaction to the *language* in the previous sonnet.

7. Sonnet 83, 5–6 could be a jibe at her courtly pretensions, as if she were a fallen member of a chorus of noble ladies, but the reading of line 6 is uncertain. Egidi prefers the Vatican version which would give the sense I have suggested. Pellegrini has 'dann'e disnor a me con tuo sermone'; see his note, p. 129.

8. Repetitive, especially in the language of abuse, for example ss. 81, 9–14; 83, 3–4, 11–12; 85, 12–14. Archaic lexical tone, for example ss. 81, 3 'talento dire', 10, 'tutta stagione'; 82, 12 'coralmente'; 84, 2 'ad isciente'; 86, 4 'ciascuna dia', 7–8 'niente pare/inverso'. Simple periphrases of the *conversio* type, for example ss. 81, 5, 7, 14; 83, 7; 84, 5–6, 7, 9–10; 85, 6, 13–14.

9. *Rima composta*, lines 4/6, 'par te'/'parte'; *replicationes*, 4/5 'par te'/'parto', 5/6 'vinciuto'/ 'vincente'; *rima identica*, 10/14, 'danno'/'danno'.

10. In their introductory note to Dante's *tenzone* with Forese, Foster-Boyde, pp. 242–4, speak of 'the other genre' and the broad division between idealism and anti-idealism in early Italian secular literature. They note that both traditions were 'literary' and part of the recognized theory of the day; that the *DVE* classification is based on that theory; that the *tenzone* was for Dante an enjoyable experiment in a new sphere. The last remark also applies to Guittone in ss. 81–6, but a brief comparison between the two groups of six sonnets would show how far Guittone was from a brilliant comic style; brilliant, in Dante's case, partly because it is a real exchange, full of pointed, personal and topical allusions. For Dante's political crisis and the *tenzone* with Forese Donati see M. Marti, 'Sulla genesi del realismo dantesco', *GSLI*, 137 (1960), 497–532, now in *Realismo dantesco e altri studi* (Milan–Naples, 1961), pp. 1–32.

11. Pellizzari, pp. 61–121, notes dozens of Provençal 'sources' for Guittone's love poetry. See Margueron, pp. 297–300, for his debt to Capellanus and his original changes to the *De amore libri tres*; pp. 301–6 for the Ovidian echoes.

12. See ss. 87, 1–3; 89, 11–14; 91, 9–14; 103, 13–14; 106, 1–8; 110, 1–6, 9–11.

13. Those definitions, to which he makes a respectful bow so as to give his treatise a look of completeness, conflict with the practical certainty of success which the 'insegnamenti' promise.

14. See s. 91, 1–8.

15. See s. 48, 8, 14. Her phrases, 'esto misteri', 'esto fatto', deflate her suitor's pretence.

16. See Margueron, pp. 299–301, for Guittone's adaptation of the social categories.

17. See ss. 101, 12–14; 102, 5–8; 104, 9–12; 105, 9–11. Ambiguous use of object pronouns and the subjunctive emphasize the tightly-knit interaction of male and female, ruse and counter-ruse in these situation sonnets. Note similar 'confusions' in the secrecy/'schermo' sonnets, ss. 63, 101–14; 79.

18. See ss. 101, 12–14; 105, 9–11. Sonnet 102, 5–8 refers to s. 94, 5–8. Read s. 104 with s. 69 — two very different treatments of the 'malmaritata' theme.

19. *Sermocinatio* in ss. 100, 9; 102, 9; 104, 5–12; and indirect speech in ss. 101, 9–11; 102, 5–8.

20. See for example ss. 102, 9–14; 103, 9–11.

21. Pellegrini, pp. 174–5, speaks of 'insormontabili difficoltà ... quanto a senso', especially in the second *quartina*, a difficult MSS. reading. Egidi, p. 335, seems satisfied with Pellizzari's gloss on the *quartine*. Neither comments on the *terzine*. 'Quello afare', line 14, may have the blunt connotations of 'tal mercato', s. 94, 8, and 'esto fatto', s. 48, 14, but in this softer moment is probably a simple periphrase for 'their love'.

22. See s. 12, 2 for 'coralmente' in its proper context; also c. xvii, 5–8.

23. See s. 11, 12–14, where he was grateful to be her vassal.

24. The sharply etched 'malmaritata' detail in s. 108, 12–14 may have been drawn in to enliven a picture suddenly flat after s. 106. It seems a throw-back to the lively 'malmaritata' scene in s. 104 and stands out against the loosely 'provenzaleggianti' counsels of all three sonnets. Note the three nouns in s. 109, 5–8, with '-tor'/'-dor' suffixes, and see Corti, p. 321.

25. The last group which can be attributed with confidence to Guittone comprises ss. 111–17 (only in the Vatican MS.), an assortment of odds and ends which one would be tempted on thematic grounds to fit into the other families. Pellizzari put s. 112 in the first cycle, 'amore corrisposto'. However, they do span the range of commitment to, and detachment from, courtly idealism covered by the previous sonnets, and can be assigned to various stages in Guittone's early development in so far as they are marked by the sonnet families. Sonnet 117 is a neat *explicatio* of the tyrannical power of love to which the persona was subject in the first narrative cycle. The theme of mutilation invites self-analysis in front of an audience whenever it occurs: compare s. 117, 3 and s. 71, 4. Of the two reply sonnets (cf. Margueron, p. 144, 'problèmes ... plus imaginaires que réels'), s. 115 is closer to the idealising phase, 'e torna l'amor odio e l'odio amore', 13, to which Guittone returns in s. 107. The more elaborate proem in s. 116, 1–8 hardly softens the spirit of male complacency in the *terzine*, which, though more callous than ss. 100–5, show no trace of the poet's dilemma in s. 106, 9–11. The two otiose displays of sheer virtuosity, ss. 113 and 114, recall Guittone's technical mastery of the difficult style late in the third cycle. Sonnet 112 echoes the tension in the *ars amandi* between male superiority and the call to a more genteel, old-fashioned respect, lines 3–4, 9–10. The opening threat, 1–2, repressed until the last four lines, would be right in practice even if wrong in principle — it is the only way men ('ciascun') can bring women to heel.

Notes to Chapter 5, continued

The authorial detachment which I see as the end product of Guittone's sonnet experiments finds clearest expression in s. 111. The simple metaphors from nature which he objects to in Guinizzelli's verse would signify a sentimental veneration of the lady which is no longer valid in Guittone's eyes, nor valid for his contemporaries. In the opening *captatio benevolentiae*, 1–2, he admits that his own early efforts in that direction were misguided. 'Ragione', 10, sounds the death knell of literary idealization. Does the last line mean that men are 'in fact' superior to women? See the reversal of this claim in c. xx, 61–72, where women seem to be made of organically superior stuff. Although the last *terzina* may echo the male superiority complex of the *ars amandi*, s. 111 could well be a post-conversion poem, in view of Guittone's reflection on his own idealizing efforts, 1–2, and the 'a ragion' criterion, 10. See Margueron, pp. 213–14, who fixes 1265 as the *terminus ante quem* for Guinizzelli's sonnets by taking s. 111 as a post-conversion poem. Margueron, pp. 115, 157, assigns s. 221, 'Mastro Bandin, se mal dett' ho d'amore', to the period just before conversion, 1262–5. He reads the opening line as referring to poems like s. 54, but the abusive interlude (ss. 50–6) which follows the *tenzone* in the third cycle, is directed at the lady who had just rejected her suitor. Margueron corrects the 'amore' in Egidi's text to 'Amore', but is disinclined to see the rational argument in the poem as 'un désaveu formel, prononcé au nom d'un idéal religieux'. The sonnet has parallels in c. xxviii, 76–86, and s. 237. In the *canzone* the poet makes a massive rational assault on the personified figure of 'Amore', and in the first *congedo*, lines 76–86, as if to prove his impartiality or lack of personal spleen, he admits that Love has treated him kindly. It is a kind of *captatio benevolentiae* to both Love and the reader, and is matched by s. 221, 1–6. And just as Montuccio and the others, in s. 237, are encouraged by rational and 'poetic' arguments to change their diet, so Bandino in s. 221 should see that Love has deceived him and no longer deserves his fidelity. Margueron's suggested date, 1262–5, *Recherches*, p. 87, seems convincing to me.

26. See Contini's review in *GSLI*, 117 (1941), 79–80. He notes certain Guittonian features in ss. 121, 123, 130 and 131 but on stylistic grounds rejects the whole series as spurious.

Notes to Chapter 6

1. 1. 'Amore corrisposto'. 2. 'Lealtà in amore'. 3. 'Poesia di gioia'.
2. For example first cycle, ss. 1–18, c. iii, iv, i and xxi. See Margueron *Recherches*, p. 402.
3. See Margueron, *Recherches*, pp. 402–3.
4. The rhyme scheme in c. xiii precludes a *congedo* modelled on the *sirima*.
5. Pellizzari joins cc. i, ii, iii, iv, v and xxi to the first two cycles.
6. *Canzoni* xvii, xviii and xix are excluded on thematic grounds. *Canzoni* xv and xx are special cases as will be seen. My grouping coincides roughly with Pellizzari's; see pp. 120–2.
7. All except c. xiii. But even in c. xiii, 33–40, the last stanza in the poem, the poet reflects on his ingenuity.
8. *Canzone* xii has a three-line *congedo* with a rhyme scheme the same as the last three lines of the stanza. Presumably the stanza is built from a four-line *frons* and a five-line *sirima*, but the *sirima* may be only of three lines. *Canzone* xx has a third *congedo* of three lines in a scheme following the last three lines of the stanza.
9. There are several borderline cases. *Canzone* ii ends in a *sirima*, lines 51–6, addressed to 'Amor', with the persona as poet, but is a signing-off within the context of the poem. *Canzone* xiv ends with two pseudo-*sirime*, lines 71–82, addressed to 'Amor' by the persona, which sum up the poem's anguish. Both *canzoni* are typical of the early idealistic phase. By using the *congedo* as a correspondence formula Guittone seems to go beyond Dante's later definition in *Convivio*, ii, xi, 1–2. In his reliance on the *sirima* scheme he is less original than Dante, who also uses the stanza scheme or an independent scheme. See nos. 13, 25, 33, 47, and 61 in the Foster-Boyde edition.
10. *Canzone* xi also ends with a *congedo* to 'essa . . . in Arezzo', lines 67–72, and Pellizzari put it among the 'lontananza' poems. The virtue of suffering displayed by all fine lovers in the vale of tears is not confined to separated lovers. Physical separation is not spelt out anywhere in the poem except the second *congedo*. The first *congedo* seems more relevant to the essential meaning of the poem. See also c. xiv which has no 'lontananza' *congedo*, but which Pellizzari labels 'lontananza' presumably on the basis of lines 58–9.

11. In line with the elevated lament of c. xix the *congedo*, lines 91–7, is an ornate and dissimulating address rather than a signature.
12. *Canzone* ii, 51–6, a mixture of conclusion topos and signature, which underlines the lover's complaint with a threat. *Canzone* vii, 97–112, two *congedi*, one to 'Amor', the other to 'madonna'. The first is a *retractatio* which anticipates the first *congedo* of its post-conversion sister, c. xxviii. The second is a final appeal to 'valente donna' to show mercy, more a climax to the argument than a formal closing of the poem. *Canzone* xiv 71–82, two *congedi*, the first to his lady, 'amor', the second to the deity, 'Amore amaro' — both are *sirime* with little signature content. *Canzone* xvi, 61–8, begins with an anaphora common to the stanza incipits, and is distinguished from them only by its length. *Canzone* xxii, 61–6 sums up the persona's hope.
13. See c. vii, elaborate stanza scheme, evenly balanced between long and short lines; relatively difficult syntax. *Canzone* xiv, 14-line stanza, all lines hendecasyllables except the tenth; difficult syntax, Provençal patina. *Canzone* xvi, anaphora incipit throughout. *Canzone* xxii, two internal rhymes in each stanza; archaic '-anza', '-enza' endings prominent in all four poems.
14. For example cc. vii, 1–4, 41–2, 105–10; xiv, 15–18; xvi, 1–4; xxii, 19–24.
15. Note the 'noia'-'gioia' rhyme in c. vii, 85–8, the special mark of ss. 31–6; also 'noia'-'gioia' in c. xiv, 1–5, 57.
16. See ss. 12, 1–8; 25, 1–4; 37, 1–4.
17. See Pellegrini, p. 211. Five rhyme sounds, '-ere, -ai, -ìa, -ìa, -one'; five stanzas. All the permutations, with each stanza picking up the final rhyme and working backwards through the rhymes of the previous stanza. *Canzone* xviii has the same ten-line, seven-syllable stanza, and the same opening rhyme scheme, a b b a, c c d d, e e, but does not run through the permutations.
18. Egidi's subtitle tends to confirm a first impression that the lover is out of love, but his note to lines 38–40, p. 292, makes the true sense clear.
19. Compare with s. 106, 9–11 where similar success raises another problem for a less naive lover.
20. A line of attack drawn up in line 14, 'lo nome e l'effetto', is pursued in stanza 1, 'nome', and stanza 2, 'effetto'. The balance of seven- and eleven-syllable lines gives occasional lively effects; see lines 69–72, 85–8, 96.
21. A second *congedo*, lines 105–12, addressed to 'valente donna' is excluded as spurious from Segre's text in Contini, *PD*, I, 192–6. In it the lover coaxes his lady to show her favour freely, with no obligation to Love.
22. Line 56, '. . . a mal grado del mondo e di Dio'. Is it because the lament motifs are jumbled that the notion of divine displeasure should exaggerate his courtly grief? Is line 27 an echo of Lam. Jeremiah i, 12, 'attendite et videte si est dolor sicut meus'? See Dante's 'O voi che per la via d'Amor passate', Foster-Boyde, no. 10.
23. See s. 80, 5 where *she* seems to have gone away. It is not verbally clear because it is here 'felt' as an event.
24. Which in turn matches and possibly 'expiates' the guilt he feels when he recalls being captivated by her beauty and conquering her, lines 15–21. But see c. xvi, 8–12 where the 'debonaire core' is hers as she responds to his devotion. Is the 'dibonaire core' of c. xiv, 19 his or hers?
25. See c. xxiii, 35–45. As I understand c. xiv, 81–2 the lines mean, 'and the end is the absolute opposite of good, whether the deed wins praise or blame'. The etymological play, 'Amore-amaro', line 77, applied to the deity, is also applied to the lady in line 15.
26. See Quaglio's remarks, p. 266, about the 'acre sapore di certa tradizione cristiana medievale', which he illustrates with s. 78.
27. See lines 5–8, 23–5, 67–8.
28. See for example c. xxiv, 37–42.
29. Egidi's subtitle reads, 'Celebra la pietá della sua donna'. Margueron, p. 27, note 49, sees c. xvi as 'une variante du lieu commun . . . de la supériorité de la femme'.
30. See c. xvi, 6–12, 13–21, 25–36.
31. Pellegrini, p. 305, glosses, c. xvi, 53–7 'ché in addietro io piansi e soffersi (*mi fu noia*) per consequire l'amore vostro (*vostra amorosa gioia*), mentre adesso recherebbe fine ai miei tormenti il potervi ritornare come eravate una volta, (indifferente alle mie preghiere)'.
32. If the 'pena' of line 59 is his 'crudel tormento', line 56, he must put up with it since what is done is done — and hope that the suffering of disillusionment will make amends for his part in the affair.

33. See for example s. 10, 9–14, where the growing distance between them can still be pegged back by his 'umiltá'.
34. See for example lines 12–14, 22–4, 29–31.
35. There are 'literary' similes and metaphors in the sonnets, which match those in c. xxii. For the sower/seed parable in the simile, lines 25–7, see s. 78, 1–4 (abundance), and also the ecclesiastical echoes in ss. 70, 12–14 and 72, 9–11. For the heroic, martial metaphor, lines 37–46 (esp. 40–2) see the memories of past literature in s. 62, 9–11 (Lancelot), s. 65, 8 (Helen and Paris), and s. 78, 12–14 (the Sybil). The *sententiae* in lines 4–12, 39, 47–8, 58–60 all appeal to an ideal feudal/courtly order of conduct, a hope guaranteed by such maxims as ss. 68, 1–8 and 69, 7–8.
36. *Rimalmezzo* in the third and sixth line of each stanza in c. xxii accentuates the facile rhymes and jerkiness of the poem. This, along with the awkward and often elliptical syntax, for example lines 14–18, 31–2, 52–4, seems to mirror the poem's undigested mixture of 'old' sentiment and 'new' devices.
37. The 'Amor' of lines 37 and 61 is the lady and not Love. The *congedo* is not a signature but a dutch-courage turn to tried and trusty weapons — note the cast-iron opposition of vices and virtues, lines 64–6. It is hardly the theme of the poem in spite of Egidi's subtitle.
38. The *congedo* is present in form (the *sirima* scheme), but barely present in substance (authorial signature).
39. *Coblas unissonans*, see Pellegrini, p. 277.
40. See ss. 65, 79, 101, in which difficult syntax and virtuoso rhymes illustrate the motif of secrecy.
41. See c. xi, 25–36, 37–9, 45–8, 55–60. The obscurity of which he boasts in lines 61–2 is compounded by the dense interplay of *rime equivoche, composte* and *tronche* throughout.
42. The 'sincerity' of the 'lontananza' *congedo* disappears in the blatant trickery of *rime composte* which give two pairs of *rime ricche* ('adessa' — 'ad essa', 67–8; 'ed ho' — 'me do', 69–70), and a taut closing *rima equivoca* ('so' — 'so', 71–2). 'So', 72, may be 'su' or 'suo' (cf. Egidi, p. 299), but it is not 'sono'.
43. In c. xxi, also with a double *congedo*, the persona's farewell to his poem, 81–8, precedes the author's, 89–96, which suggest a more natural movement towards authorial control than is the case in c. xi.
44. The first stanza of c. xii is the only one with an enjambment between the fourth and fifth lines, so the *frons* is probably of four lines only. See Margueron, p. 234, Egidi, p. 301, and Pellegrini, pp. 272–3 for the sense; and Margueron, p. 234, note 194 for the textual alternatives. He restores the Rediano 9 reading to line 47, 'ch'e donn'e parte'.
45. A 16-line predominantly 7-syllable stanza, with *rimalmezzo* in 3 of the 4 hendecasyllables, in lines 4, 12 and 16. The *coblas capfinidas* link is not strict.
46. See Margueron, pp. 230–2 for Guittone's contact with the Messinese poet Mazzeo di Ricco.
47. See lines 9–16, 41–6, 65–8 for the consecutive relationship of conduct to maxim, a relationship now 'seen' by the poet and passed on for Mazzeo's benefit. The 'Percival' simile, 75–6, is in line with the echoes of romance literature in ss. 62, 9–11 and 65, 8.
48. Lines 81–8. As already noted, authorial prominence in the second *congedo* makes it a true finale to the contrived temper of the whole poem.
49. It also lacks the convincing detail of a place name, and purposely so, because the only proper name in Guittone's mind is Mazzeo di Ricco. It would obscure the *real* sending of the poem in the second *congedo* if he gave the impression in the first *congedo* that he were also sending it to a 'real' lady.
50. See Margueron, pp. 259–60 for Ubertino's activity as poet.
51. In both poems Guittone looks back at a finished piece of work: a *canzone* in c. i, 106, and a 'proof' in c. iv, 62.
52. There is a tricky alternation of *rimalmezzo* after the third and seventh syllables in lines 2, 4, 6 and 8 of each stanza.
53. It is couched as an argument addressed directly to a lady, lines 1–4.
54. Guittone's witty use of the Capellanus definition is rich in suitably archaic binomials, lines 25, 27, 30, 31, 35.
55. See Pellegrini's gloss to lines 45–8, p. 220.
56. The hiatus in line 54 brings in 'piacere' as an afterthought — an unlikely stable-mate for 'onore' but closer to the persona's preoccupations.
57. See Margueron, pp. 178–80.
58. For example lines 30–42, 64–70.

141

59. Pellegrini, p. 206, reads 's'usasse' as the lover's wish for 'amicizia . . . in atto più che in parole ovvero in sentimenti'. The phrase is similar to 'l'amoroso usaggio' in c. iii, 11, which looks innocent enough in that context. It looks less innocent in the last stanza of c. i, where a mercenary and selfish attitude betrays itself in every other line.
60. See especially ss. 99–102.
61. Greek painting, 10–15; medicine, 37–9; Ciceronian *amicitia*, 72–5; divine service, 79–84.
62. The long stanza, balanced evenly between seven- and eleven-syllable lines, leaves no doubt that Guittone wanted to show Currado polished and substantial wares.
63. The first *congedo* of c. xxi and the second *congedo* of c. xi. *Canzone* xiv, 57–60, brings in the 'lontananza' motif to pile on the agony rather than explain it, and the double *congedo* gives no hint of distance.
64. Not only the *canzoni*, viii, ix and xxiii but the sonnets 72–5, 80.
65. Margueron, p. 30, n. 57, seems to put c. xxiii, 52 on the same level as cc. xv, 127, xx, 101–2 and the other *congedi* which name Arezzo.
66. The stanzas are strictly *coblas capfinidas* with a slight 'composed' trick in lines 17–18, 'è 'n grato/En grato'. An outline of the sentimental changes will show how the commonplaces can be strung together. Between the opening and closing grief of separation, 1–4 and 60–2, praise, 5–15, leads to repentance, 16–17. Her good disposition, 23–8, bridging *frons* and *sirima*, turn his doubt and dumbness, 18–21, into the honour of holding his peace, 33–4. Fear of her censure, 35–7, leads through the secrecy motif, 41–7, to a certainty of his honour, 44–51. Lines 22–8 echo the Sicilian 'image' motif, so favoured in their 'lontananza' poems and expressed with particular force by Guittone himself in s. 72.
67. Such phrases are common in Sicilian 'lontananza' poems; see for example Panvini, I, p. 491, 38–9. See also Egidi, s. 74, 9–11; and for c. ix, 9–13, see s. 76, 3–8.
68. The suicide wish and Ovidian court, 9–13; the divine paragon 17–20, 46–51.
69. Confusion between physical separation and the inner, literary wanderings of the hapless lover ensures that the nature of his 'sin' remains obscure. But reading c. ii, 41–50 as a gloss on c. ix, 20–5 it would seem that he won her favour too easily.
70. Margueron, p. 30, n. 57, takes the mention of Arezzo as a sign that Guittone travelled in his youth, and quotes this and the other *canzoni* which name the town, including c. xxiii, 52. He seems less convinced about the references to separation in the 'lontananza' sonnets. I would not deny that the mention of Arezzo may be a biographical reference — quite the contrary, because my argument for authorial as against persona prominence at that point depends on its being biographical. But I would see it primarily as a poetic device. If ss. 72, 5 and 74, 9–10 are not biographical, are lines 7–9 of c. ix biographical, in the light of the *congedo*?
71. The phrase 'retornato in tutto stato bono', 14, implies spatial movement only when crossed with the opening of the *congedo*, line 71, 'En le parti d'Arezzo . . .'.
72. Guittone keeps his *sententiae* for the *sirima* of stanzas 2, 4 and 5. Lines 19–28, an *exemplum* of two lovers using distance to prove their fidelity; 47–56, hardship endured as proof of worth; 61–5, pleasure enhanced by prior suffering. The solemnity of these axioms is undercut by the suppressed sensuality of lines 22–3, 44–5 and 58–9.
73. See Margueron, pp. 49–53, 56–7, 89, 115.
74. Margueron, *Recherches*, pp. 49–50, 'pièce curieuse où le thème traditionnel . . . interfère avec des préoccupations de morale civique . . .'. Later, p. 168, he implies, by analogy with c. xxxii, that in its mixture of traditional and autobiographical elements c. xv also witnesses the original vigour of Guittone's poetic personality. Quaglio, p. 270, takes up Cattaneo's observations on the union of love themes and political material, 'tipo provenzale', but in his form-content summary, pp. 275–6, he passes quickly over the last two stanzas and first *congedo*; '. . . il risentimento del cittadino cede alla convenzione del modello provenzale che governa i versi con immagini canoniche'. See G. Folena, 'Pensamento Guittoniano', *LN*, 16 (1955), 100–4. He divides the poem into three sections: politico-moral, stanzas 1–3; personal justification, stanzas 4–7; amorous motif, stanzas 8–9.
75. Cattaneo notes, p. 192, that of the four political *canzoni* in the *canzoniere*, two (xv and xix) are in the courtly section and two (xxxiii and xlvii) are in the religious section, but that all four are transitional poems.
76. A 'fallo' of some sort or a business trip. The reason for the departure is invariably vague. See for example *Vita Nuova*, IX, 1.

Notes to Chapter 6, continued

77. See also lines 75–9, 97–8.
78. *Sermocinatio* also enlivens stock situations in ss. 102 and 104. The political context of this exile poem turns the lady into a city dweller and anticipates that change in her social status brought about by the *stilnovisti*. See Marti, *Poeti*, p. 20.
79. This is not unlike Guittone's apparent reluctance in the *ars amandi* to abandon courtly language altogether. The old civilities counteract some of the modern vulgarity.
80. See for example s. 37, 9–11. In c. xv it anticipates the superior devotion of women once they are in love, in c. xx, 49–60.
81. See cc. viii, 52–6; xxi, 83–8.
82. It could be argued that the *exemplum*, lines 122–6, is simply ballast for the 'lontananza' addition, to give it a seriousness matching the exile tones. And in an obvious sense the two claims which coalesce in lines 117–20 are irreconcilable. In line 117, which summarises the earlier stanzas, he argued that he was better off out of the city; in lines 118–20 his departure is a necessary delay. But this merely repeats what others have said: my interest is to see how Guittone *adapts* the sentimental atmosphere of 'lontananza' to the rest of the poem.
83. Political apologia, lines 1–98; lover's separation idealized, 99–126; lover's separation, 127–36; political apologia, 137–46.
84. See lines 132–6; a *sententia* (which echoes 122–6 and is equally 'literary') in the form of a metaphor that acts as an elliptical negative simile. The *sententia* follows the opening lines of the first *congedo*, 'Tell her it will be all right because "castel ben fornito" . . .'.
85. Lack of logic extends to the last line, 'acquistando e sollazzo ed avere', which Guittone fills out with apparent pleasure in the material well-being he had criticized in the second stanza, lines 15–19, 25–6.
86. See Foster-Boyde, no. 89, a lament for the physically and morally disruptive force of carnal love, which ends in an exile *congedo* sending the poem to Dante's pitiless native city. See Foster-Boyde, II, 330–40 for commentary. In the last stanza of his mountain song Dante draws a vivid picture of his harsh Casentino place of exile, lines 61–8. In the *congedo* he combines a claim for the depth of his passion, lines 82–4, with a rebuke to the city, in such a way that the rebuke dominates the whole *congedo*. Florence, 'nuda de pietate', and a chain of love that shackles him to a wilderness, add up to a total, oppressive harshness. The poem's 'inner' emotive force is encased in the 'outer' reality of political exile.
87. See Margueron, p. 87.
88. I may not have proved that the MSS. sequence for the courtly sonnets reflects the chronological order of composition, but my contention is that both MSS. do reflect an ideal order imposed by the poet on his *canzoniere*, in much the same way as Dante in the first half of the *Vita Nuova* imposes an ideal order on certain of his early *rime*.
89. I noted on pp. 87–8 that s. 106, 12–14 is not an answer but a preface to the closing sonnets, which fall back on the old ideals and language.
90. See c. xx, 44–5, '. . . falla e fa donna fallare:/adonque che diritto ha 'n lei biasmare?'.
91. The *exclamatio* seems to come from the ladies themselves. In line 6 there begins a deliberately obscure use of third-person pronouns. Who is doing/defending/speaking what?
92. See Margueron, p. 87; the arguments are psychological, moral and theological. Lines 18–22, divine and natural law binding on men as well as women; 25–8, crime rate higher among men than women; 29–36, women stand up to male advances better than men would do to female advances; 37–48, since men use their superior power and intelligence to seduce women they have no right to abuse them; 49–60, once a woman has placed her affections she is more generous and devoted than any man; 61–72, she owes these superior qualities to the divine plan — her creation (from the flesh of man, not from clay) and her role in the Redemption.
93. Lines 62–4, 69–72. Compare lines 62–4 with the trite simile for direct creation in s. 12, 13–14.
94. See c. xxv, 61–3 for man's bestiality in exactly the same terms, and the human vocation 'drittura operare'.
95. In both poems the return to a courtly motif comes at roughly the same point.
96. Lines 80–1, 'l'omo'–'donna'; 83–4 'ella'–'l'om'. The chiasmus is more a natural expression of balanced male–female relations than a contrived device; much as the overall form of c. xv illustrates Guittone's effort to integrate literature and experience, and is not a chiasmus in the strict sense.

97.   Lines 7–12. The ladies too are the archetypal chorus, but in temporal perspective they are seen first as the women despised in present-day male *mores*, lines 2–3, 10.

98.   Was it because of this *congedo* alone that Pellizzari numbered c. xx among the 'lontananza' poems? The lack of any other evidence within the poem bears out my earlier distinctions between degrees of intensity in 'lontananza' passages. Although it is only three lines long the last *congedo* is the only true *congedo* of the three. Guittone stands aside from his poem to send it to that city where he had seen courtly ideals in decline.

99.   The phrase is Margueron's, p. 87. Naturally enough he emphasizes the poem's moral values as sign of its transitional nature. Similar remarks conceding the presence of erotica could be made of c. xv, though c. xx announces a number of tell-tale conversion motifs, not present in c. xv, which were soon to be taken up in the palinodes: c. xx, 7–s. 164, 13 (he rebels against lovers before rebelling against Love); c. xx, 13–14 – c. xxv, 79 (the particular 'bad habit' by which men despise women foreshadows that general 'bad habit' which prevents 'ben far'); c. xx, 23 – c. xxviii, 12–15 (reliance on rational argument apparent before the palinodes); c. xx, 89–92 – c. xxv, 76–80; c. xxvii, 87–89 (in the first defence of womankind, as later, he admits that rational argument will win few converts).

Select bibliography

Boyde

P. Boyde, *Dante's Style in his Lyric Poetry*, Cambridge, 1971.

Cattaneo

M. T. Cattaneo, 'Note sulla poesia di Guittone', *GSLI*, 137 (1960), 165–203, 325–67.

Contini

Poeti del Duecento, ed. G. Contini, 2 vols, Milan–Naples, 1960 (*PD*, i, ii).
GSLI, 117 (1941), 55–82 (review of Egidi edition).
Dante Alighieri, *Rime*, Turin, 1965.²
'Esperienze d'un antologista del Duecento poetico italiano', *Studi e problemi di critica testuale*, Bologna, 1961, pp. 241–72.
Letteratura italiana delle origini, Florence, 1970.
Varianti e altra linguistica, Turin, 1970.
'Un nodo della cultura medievale: la serie *Roman de la Rose — Fiore — Divina Commedia*', *Lettere Italiane*, 20 (1973), 162–89.

Corti

M. Corti, 'Studi sulla sintassi della lingua poetica avanti lo stilnovo', *AMAT*, 18, n.s. 4 (1953), 263–365.

De Robertis

D. De Robertis, *Il libro della 'Vita Nuova'*, Florence, 1970.²

Egidi

Le rime di Guittone d'Arezzo, ed. F. Egidi, Bari, 1940.
'Un "Trattato d'Amore" inedito di Fra Guittone d'Arezzo', *GSLI*, 97 (1931), 49–70.

Fenzi

E. Fenzi, 'Le rime per la donna Pietra', *Miscellanea di studi danteschi*, a cura dell'Istituto di letteratura italiana dell'Università di Genova, Genoa, 1966, pp. 229–309.

Foster-Boyde

Dante's Lyric Poetry, ed. K. Foster and P. Boyde, 2 vols, Oxford, 1965.

Laurenziano Rediano 9

Il Canzoniere Laurenziano Rediano 9, ed. T. Casini, Bologna, 1900.

Margueron

Cl. Margueron, *Recherches sur Guittone d'Arezzo: sa vie, son époque, sa culture*, Paris (Presses Universitaires de France), 1966 (*Recherches*).
'La prima delle *Lettere* di Fra Guittone (testo e commento)', *Studi e problemi di critica testuale*, 2 (1971), 72–98.
'Noterelle di critica testuale guittoniana', *Studi e problemi di critica testuale*, 7 (1973), 5–16.
'Immagini, metafore e miti nelle *Rime* e nelle *Lettere* di Guittone d'Arezzo', *Lettere Italiane*, 25 (1973), 461–90.

Marti   M. Marti, 'Ritratto e fortuna di Guittone d'Arezzo', *Realismo dantesco e altri studi*, Milan–Naples, 1961 (*Ritratto*).
Con Dante fra i poeti del suo tempo, Lecce, 1971.[2]
La prosa del Duecento, ed. C. Segre and M. Marti, Milan–Naples, 1959.
Poeti del Dolce stil nuovo, ed. M. Marti, Florence, 1969.
'Guittone d'Arezzo e i guittoniani', *Enciclopedia dantesca*, vol. III, Rome, 1971, pp. 334–6.

Mengaldo   Dante Alighieri, *De Vulgari Eloquentia*, ed. P. V. Mengaldo, Padua, 1968.

Menichetti   Chiaro Davanzati, *Rime*, ed. A. Menichetti, Bologna, 1965.

Panvini   B. Panvini, *Le rime della Scuola siciliana*, Florence, vol. I, 1962, vol. II, 1964 (*Rime*).

Pelaez   M. Pelaez (review of *Le rime di Fra Guittone*, ed. F. Pellegrini), *GSLI*, 41 (1903), 354–64.

Pellegrini   *Le rime di Fra Guittone d'Arezzo*, ed. F. Pellegrini, Bologna, 1901.

Pellizzari   A. Pellizzari, *La vita e le opere di Guittone d'Arezzo*, Pisa, 1906.

Quaglio   E. Pasquini and A. E. Quaglio, *Le origini e la scuola siciliana*, Bari, 1971 (*LIL I*).
A. E. Quaglio, *La poesia realistica e la prosa del Duecento*, Bari, 1971.

Roncaglia   A. Roncaglia, 'Nella preistoria della lauda: Ballata e strofa zagialesca', *Il movimento dei Disciplinati nel settimo centenario dal suo inizio (Perugia — 1260)*, (Deputazione di storia patria per l'Umbria, Appendici al Bollettino, 9), Perugia, 1962, pp. 460–75.

Segre   C. Segre, *Lingua, stile e società*, Milan, 1963 (*Lingua*).
La prosa del Duecento, ed. C. Segre and M. Marti, Milan–Naples, 1959.

Tartaro   A. Tartaro, 'La conversione letteraria di Guittone', *Rivista di cultura classica e medievale*, 7 (1965) (Studi in onore di A. Schiaffini), 1057–67.
'Guittone e i rimatori siculo-toscani', I, II, *Storia della letteratura italiana*, Milan, 1965, pp. 351–428.

Varanini   *Laude dugentesche*, ed. G. Varanini, Padua, 1972.

INDEX